Webster's

Pocket
Business
Dictionary

Second Edition

Staff

Editor, Second Edition: Carol G. Braham
Editor, First Edition: Jay N. Nisberg
Consulting Editor: Margot Havens
Copyeditor: Ann Bradley

Managing Editors: Jennifer L. Dowling, Jan Berman
Database Manager: Constance A. Baboukis
Systems Manager: Paul Hayslett
Director of Production: Patricia W. Ehresmann
Production Associate: Michele Purdue
Senior Production Editor: Joseph Vella

Editorial Director: Sol Steinmetz
Publisher: Charles M. Levine

Random House Webster's

Pocket
Business
Dictionary

Second Edition

Random House

New York

This is a substantially revised and updated edition of the *Random House Dictionary of Business Terms* published in 1988. First edition also published in hardcover as *The Random House Handbook of Business Terms*, both edited by Jay N. Nisberg.

Trademarks
A number of entered words which we have reason to believe constitute trademarks have been designated as such. However, no attempt has been made to designate as trademarks or service marks all terms or words in which proprietary rights might exist. The inclusion, exclusion, or definition of a word or term is not intended to affect, or to express a judgment on, the validity or legal status of the word or term as a trademark, service mark, or other proprietary term.

This book is available for special purchases in bulk by organizations and institutions, not for resale, at special discounts. Please direct your inquiries to the Random House Special Sales Department, toll-free 888-591-1200 or fax 212-572-4961.

Please address inquiries about electronic licensing of this division's products, for use on a network or in software or on CD-ROM, to the Subsidiary Rights Department, Random House Reference & Information Publishing, fax 212-940-7370.

Typeset and printed in the United States of America.
Visit the Random House Reference & Information Publishing Web site at www.randomwords.com
Second Edition
0 9 8 7 6 5 4 3 2
ISBN: 0-375-70059-5 (Vest Pocket)
New York   Toronto   London   Sydney   Auckland

Preface

Random House Webster's Pocket Business Dictionary is an updated and expanded second edition of the *Random House Dictionary of Business Terms*, first published in 1988. In the years since the dictionary's original publication, the vocabulary of business has grown at an astonishing rate. The executive, the student, the investor, the job seeker, the consumer—all are affected by the world of business, and all need to know its specialized terminology.

A common thread runs through the vast world of business: the making, marketing, and management of a product or service. The catchall term "business" encompasses fields as diverse as personal finance, economics, insurance, manufacturing, retailing, marketing, and much more. Some entries in this dictionary are not strictly "business"—several other fields of activity cross over into the business world. The presence of computers in the home and workplace has made it necessary for everyone to be literate in computer terminology. Even the vocabulary of law and government is relevant to business.

Most of the entries in this dictionary are commonly encountered, basic terms covering the general and technical vocabulary of business. In addition to these standard terms, the reader will find a great many slang and informal usages, such as *dead-cat bounce* and *road warrior*. Abbreviations and acronyms, such as *IRA* and *NAFTA*, are conveniently listed in the main A-Z section.

The experienced business professional may wish to investigate terms that are outside his or her particular area of expertise. The novice or layperson will learn the technical vocabulary, the jargon peculiar to business, but will recognize that many of these terms have passed into the general vocabulary. For example, *bottom line* refers to the last line of a financial statement, but also means "the crucial factor" or "the outcome."

The selection of entries and the clear, concise defining style is intended to be useful and informative to a wide range of readers. The editors hope that this dictionary will serve the needs of those who want authoritative information, but prefer an edition that is handy and affordable.

A

AAA 1. See **American Academy of Advertising. 2.** See **American Accounting Association. 3.** See **American Arbitration Association.**

AAAA See **American Association of Advertising Agencies.**

abandonment 1. The relinquishing of real property with no intention of repossessing it. **2.** The withdrawing of a claim or legal action.

abatement Cancellation or reduction of an expenditure, tax, charge, or levy.

abatement clause A section of a lease that releases the tenant from the obligation to pay rent when an event classifiable as an act of God prevents occupancy.

ABC analysis See **ABC inventory management.**

ABC Data Bank Also called **ABC Newspaper Audience Research Data Bank.** A research service that provides demographic data about the readership of all daily and Sunday newspapers belonging to the Audit Bureau of Circulation.

ABC inventory management Also called **ABC analysis.** A system used to track and control inventory selectively by dividing it into three categories of use or value: A (high), B (medium), and C (low).

ABC Newspaper Audience Research Data Bank See **ABC Data Bank.**

abnormal spoilage A deterioration of inventory or raw materials that exceeds the level expected during normal or efficient business operations and sales (generally considered an expense rather than a product cost).

aboriginal cost The price paid for an asset by the first company to use it for public service, calculated by a formula in general use among public utilities and used in the calculation of expenses in order to prevent the increased prices paid in subsequent exchanges from increasing the expenses (and rates) of other utilities.

above-the-line 1. Referring to an expense or source of income that is current or routine. **2.** (*motion pictures*) Referring to the creative costs of a film (e.g., story, stars, director, producer). See also **below-the-line.**

abrogation of agreement The cancellation of a contract or of a section of a contract.

absentee management Ownership of property or of a business by a person who does not reside on the property or hires someone else to manage the business.

absolute frequency The number of data units in a category used for statistical measurement.

absolute liability. See **strict liability.**

absolute sale A nonconditional sale in which neither buyer nor seller imposes obstacles to or delays in the completion of the transaction. See also **conditional sale.**

absolute threshold The lowest level of intensity at which a stimulus can be detected. See also **just noticeable difference.**

absolute title Ownership with no conditions or reservations.

absorbable risk A risk or potential loss that a corporation is confident it can cover either with current capital or with amounts set aside in a self-insurance fund. See also **self-insurance.**

absorption costing Also called **full costing.** The practice of allocating all manufacturing costs (including materials, labor, and overhead) in relation to the number of units produced. See also **direct costing.**

abstract of title A detailed outline of all legal actions that have taken place in regard to a piece of land, including transfers of title, mortgages, and liens.

accelerated depreciation Depreciation of an asset at a higher rate in early years than in later years, for the purpose of reducing tax liability. See also **sum-of-the-years'-digits method; units-of-production method.**

acceleration clause A contractual agreement that specifies that an entire debt becomes due immediately if the debtor fails to pay according to contract.

acceptance needs See **need for acceptance.**

acceptance sampling The use of a sample of

items from an incoming shipment to indicate the acceptability of the shipment as a whole.

acceptance theory of authority A management theory that stresses the placing of much decision making in the hands of subordinates rather than the reserving of all decisions to top management, and that for the theory to succeed in practice, subordinates must resolve their conflicts without recourse to higher authority.

access To gain entry to (data stored in a computer, etc.).

accessing Internal processing of information by means of the pictures, sounds, words, and feelings that make up an individual's memories.

accommodation endorsement An endorsement made by one individual to another in order to add his or her credit to the second individual's commercial paper or negotiable instrument.

accord An agreement between a debtor and a creditor or between persons engaged in a controversy as to the way in which an obligation is to be discharged. See also **satisfaction.**

account 1. A chronological record of debits and credits kept in a ledger to account for transactions involving a class of items (e.g., notes receivable) or a particular person or company. 2. A person, company, or class of items assigned a page in a ledger for the recording of pertinent transactions. 3. A customer or client.

accountability 1. The condition of being liable for the performance of tasks for which one has the necessary authority and for which one accepts responsibility. 2. The procedure for reporting up through the chain of command the results of tasks accomplished within or by a work group or subsystem.

accountancy (*chiefly British*) The practice and profession of accounting.

accountant A person skilled in the practice of accounting. See also **accounting; certified public accountant; chartered accountant; independent accountant.**

Accountant's Index A periodical published by the American Institute of Certified Public Accountants, listing in detail all accounting literature published since the last issue.

accountant's report See **audit report**.

account debtor An individual who is obligated to pay.

account executive Also called **account supervisor; contact person.** A person in an advertising or public relations agency who is responsible for executing agency services for a client, and who may assume as much authority over the creation of a product as is required by the client.

account form A common balance sheet format, with assets on the left and liabilities and owners' equity on the right. See also **report form**.

accounting A system and process of gathering and recording financial information that provides a continuous balance between assets on the one hand and liabilities and equity on the other; also provides a record of property owned, liabilities, investments, etc., and facilitates the preparation of financial reports.

accounting equation Also called **accounting identity.** A transaction expressed in the form of debits and credits in a double-entry bookkeeping system.

accounts payable Liabilities to creditors, carried on open account, usually for purchases of goods and services.

accounts receivable Claims against debtors, carried on open account, usually limited to debts due from the sale of goods or services.

account supervisor See **account executive**.

accrual A debt that has been incurred or an asset that has been generated but that has not been paid, received, or recorded. See also **accrued expense; accrued income; accrued interest**.

accrual accounting The recording of expenses along with the revenues they ultimately generate rather than at the time when they are paid, based on the reasoning that expenses are incurred in order to generate revenues. See also **cash accounting**.

accrued depreciation See **accumulated depreciation**.

accrued expense Also called **accrued liability.** An expense incurred and still owed, such as unpaid wages, salaries, interest, utility bills, insurance premiums, and other expenses normally scheduled to be paid within 30 days.

accrued income Income due to be received, reflected in an accounting system by a debit to an asset and a credit to an income account.

accrued interest Interest payable on a bond that has accrued since the issuer last paid interest (an amount added to the market price of the bond if it is sold before maturity).

accrued liability See **accrued expense.**

accumulated depreciation Also called **accrued depreciation.** The total depreciation taken on an asset from the time of original purchase to the present (a contra asset normally deducted from an asset account to derive net book value).

accumulated earnings tax A federal tax on retained earnings beyond a reasonable amount for anticipated needs, imposed as a means of preventing principal stockholders from avoiding the tax on accumulated business income.

accumulation plan A systematic program to buy an investment at regular intervals and reinvest the dividends and capital gains earned from the amounts previously invested.

ACE See **Active Corps of Executives.**

achievement needs See **need for achievement.**

achievement-oriented leadership A style of leadership in which the leader sets high standards, shows a high degree of confidence, and provides stimulating goals for subordinates to strive for.

acid-test ratio Also called **quick ratio.** Current liabilities divided by total cash, receivables, and marketable securities; a rough and conservative indication of a company's ability to meet its obligations. See also **liquidity ratio.**

ACME (*acronym for a*im, content, *m*ethod, *expecta*tion) A format used by professional sales trainers to evaluate the effectiveness of each sales training program they consider for use within a given context.

acquisition cost Also called **historical cost; original cost.** The net invoice price of an asset.

across-the-board **1.** Embracing all categories or classes. **2.** Appearing (as a television program) at the same time of day every day of the week (the weekend usually excepted). **3.** Uniformly affecting an entire population (e.g., a uniform salary increase granted to all employees regardless of position or seniority).

action-event area Also called **area of choice and chance.** A critical point in a decision tree, representing a proposed course of action and the probable consequences that may be expected to flow from it. See also **decision tree.**

action maze A pattern of simulated actions developed to improve decision-making skills by requiring a trainee to select one alternative response to an incident and follow it through alternative avenues of decision making, each response leading to additional information and new consequences.

action planning The use of surveys and group process activities with the objective of improving motivational levels, internal communications, and general cooperation among employees: a human resource technique.

action research 1. The use of innovative ideas of proactive members of an organization to motivate a research team to investigate new ideas on an ongoing basis. See also **proactive. 2.** See **data-based intervention.**

Active Corps of Executives (*acronym* ACE) An advisory group of business executives who work with the Small Business Administration to provide assistance to small firms. See also **Service Corps of Retired Executives.**

active income 1. Salary or wages. **2.** Income from engaging in a trade or owning or managing a business.

activity ratio Any of four formulas used to measure the efficiency with which assets are being used. See also **average collection period ratio; fixed asset turnover ratio; inventory turnover ratio; total asset turnover ratio.**

act of bankruptcy Any action within the legal definition of bankruptcy that results in an individual's or corporation's qualifying as bankrupt.

act of God (*insurance*) An event of natural origin (e.g., flood, earthquake) that causes property loss and can be neither foreseen nor prevented by reasonable care.

actual authority The authority given to an agent by a principal.

actual damages The damages caused by failure to fulfill the terms of a contract, exclusive of incidental damages.

actuary An expert in pension and life insurance plans, trained to calculate expected liabilities and the income that must be generated to cover them, taking into consideration the costs of premiums, the cost of operations, and earnings on the company's reserve funds.

additional paid-in capital See **capital surplus.**

add-on A purchase added to a charge account in a retail store, which generally follows a standard procedure to determine the amount of such purchases that may be added to a customer's previous balance before the recorded amount has been fully paid.

address A number or other code that identifies the physical location of data stored in a computer's memory.

ad hoc (*Latin*) For this; for the particular purpose at hand.

ad hoc committee A temporary committee created to deal with a specific situation.

adjustable-rate mortgage (*abbr* ARM) Any mortgage whose interest rate may increase or decrease periodically, along with monthly payments: usually offered at a rate lower than that of the fixed-rate mortgage. See also **renegotiable-rate mortgage; variable-rate mortgage.**

adjusted book value The value of inventory adjusted to reflect the current actual worth of the items.

adjusted gross income Actual money received less allowable deductions and exclusions.

adjusting entry Also called **adjustment.** A final journal entry made at the end of an accounting period to reflect a change in assets, liabilities, expenses, or revenues that was not recognized or was not calculable at the time the change occurred (e.g., an adjustment for ending inventory, uncollected accounts receivable, depreciation, accrued amounts).

adjustment 1. A change in an account to correct

an erroneous entry. **2.** See **adjusting entry. 3.** The determination of the amount of indemnity an insured will receive.

administrative assistant A person employed to aid an executive, as by coordinating office services and supervising the flow of work.

administrative expense Generally, the cost of running an administrative office or department (e.g., salaries of office personnel, rent, legal services), in contrast to manufacturing or sales expense: an allowable deduction from income for tax purposes.

administrative intensity The size of an organization's administrative staff in relation to the size of its production staff, a ratio that changes in accordance with changes in the size of the organization. Growth leads to increased need for coordination and for administrators to deal with problems; conversely, when growth leads to an increase in specialization, resulting efficiency in the use of administrative skills leads to a decrease in administrative personnel.

administrative ratio The ratio of managers to subordinates in an organization.

admiralty law The body of law dealing with maritime matters.

admission of partner The legal introduction of an individual into a partnership and thus the creation of a new partnership, which must be reflected in entries recording how the new partner joined and the assets and/or liabilities that that partner contributed.

admitted company A company licensed to do business within a state.

adoption notice A notification that a carrier accepts the obligations of its predecessor.

adoption process The process by which an individual or organization acquires psychological acceptance of a new product or innovation, from first awareness of the product to the final decision to purchase it. See also **AIDA process; AIDCAS process; diffusion process.**

ADP See **automatic data processing.**

ad referundum (*Latin*) To be referred; an indication that although a contract has been signed, certain issues remain to be clarified.

ad valorem tax A tax, such as the typical property tax, based on appreciated value or cost.

advance dating The application of a code to goods shipped by sea that are on their way to but have not yet cleared an inland customs point.

advance from (by) customer Also called **deferred income; deferred revenue.** A liability incurred when a customer pays for goods or services that he or she has not yet received (often recorded under accounts payable).

adverse opinion An opinion rendered by a certified public accountant (usually an external auditor) or by a lawyer that a company's financial statements do not accurately or fairly reflect its financial position or history, the results of its operations, or changes in its financial position, or the opinion that generally accepted accounting principles have been breached or used inconsistently.

adverse possession Acquisition of property to which one does not have a legal right or clear title.

advertisement A public message paid for by a sponsor and appearing in print or in the broadcast media for the purpose of promoting a product, service, or idea. See also **announcement.**

advertising The use of sales messages paid for by a sponsor and communicated through the mass media, as on a television broadcast or in a magazine, usually on a repeated basis to an audience of potential buyers or consumers.

advertising agency A company that specializes in creating and developing advertisements for clients, and whose services include preparation of layouts and copy, media selection, and marketing research.

advertising theme The pivotal concept of an advertisement or ad campaign, often used to specify and amplify the differences between one product and another in the minds of the target audience.

advisory relationship A balanced relationship between a line manager and a general staff involving an exchange of information for the purpose of identifying and solving staff problems, such that specialists, via the manager, provide enough information and assistance to the general staff to enable them to solve their problems without overstepping the boundaries of their responsibilities.

affidavit A written statement that has been signed before a person who is legally authorized to administer oaths and that is usually legally binding.

affiliate 1. A (usually independent) television or radio station that contracts to broadcast programs provided by a major network on a regular basis. **2.** A business that contracts to work with another business.

affinity card A credit card issued in conjunction with an organization, as a university, sports club, or corporation.

affirmative action Active recruitment of members of all social groups without discrimination on the basis of race, religion, sex, age, or national origin, for the purpose of promoting equal employment and educational opportunities.

affirmative action program A program of active recruitment of women and minority employees, mandated by the Civil Rights Act of 1964 for companies that employ more than 50 people and have government contracts.

AFL-CIO See **American Federation of Labor; Congress of Industrial Organizations.**

after cost An expense incurred after the revenue that the expense generated has been received (e.g., the expense of repairing or servicing a machine that was sold under warranty or leased under a service contract).

aftermarket 1. The market for replacement parts, accessories, etc., as for an automobile, after its sale to the consumer. **2.** See **secondary market.**

AFTRA See **American Federation of Television and Radio Artists.**

Age Discrimination in Employment Act An act of Congress that prohibits job discrimination on the basis of age by employment agencies, labor unions with more than 25 members, and companies that employ more than 20 people.

agency 1. A legally binding association that exists when a principal party authorizes another (the agent) to act on his or her behalf, either orally, in writing, or (as in the transfer of real property) by power of attorney. See also **agent** (def. 2); **princi-**

pal (def. 2). **2.** A company, organization, or business whose primary activity is the provision of services to other companies (e.g., an advertising, public relations, real estate, or insurance agency).

agency of record The principal advertising agency chosen by an advertiser to coordinate and manage the activities of a media project involving a number of subordinate agencies.

agency recognition A written or oral statement given to an advertising agency by appropriate officials of a client company testifying that the agency meets required standards and is entitled to agency commissions.

agency shop A unionized workplace that collects union dues from union members and also from nonunion employees who benefit from any agreements that result from negotiations between employer and union.

agent 1. A person who acts as an intermediary in a business transaction and for such service receives a percentage (generally from 10 to 25%) of the fee negotiated. **2.** Any person who acts for another (as a broker for an investor, a trustee for a bondholder, a fiduciary for an heir).

age of majority The age (varying among states) at which an individual acquires full legal rights and responsibilities (e.g., to sue and be sued).

aggregate demand 1. The total dollars spent on goods and services in an economy during a specified period of time. **2.** The total demand for all of a firm's products and services during a specified period of time.

aggregate planning Preparation of an intermediate-range production schedule, together with a plan for providing the capacity needed to meet that schedule.

aggregate supply The total amount of goods and services produced in an economy during a specified period of time.

aggressive Emphasizing maximum growth and capital gains over quality, security, and income.

aging schedule A list, often issued quarterly, of outstanding accounts receivable, in which accounts are grouped according to the age of overdue amounts: a ''strong'' aging schedule indicates a lower percentage of accounts receivable on old sales than on recent sales.

AIA See **Business and Professional Advertisers Association.**

AIDA process (*acronym for a*ttention, *i*nterest, *d*esire, *a*ction) The process of increasing involvement through which prospective customers go while being influenced to buy a product.

AIDCAS process (*acronym for a*ttention, *i*nterest, *d*esire, *c*onviction, *a*ction, *s*atisfaction) An expansion of the AIDA process to include the customer's conviction that the product's benefits are better than those offered by other products and satisfaction with the purchased product.

algorithm A series of instructions to be followed or steps to be taken to solve a particular problem.

alien corporation A corporation chartered in a foreign country but operating in the United States (e.g., Toyota, Volkswagen).

allocation 1. Dispersal of a supply of a product in multiple small containers for transporting. See also **bulk breaking. 2.** The assignment of a frequency and broadcast signal to a radio or television station by the Federal Communications Commission.

allonge A separate form attached to a negotiable instrument to provide space for multiple endorsements.

allowance for doubtful accounts Also called **allowance for bad debts; reserve for bad debts.** A contra asset account in which the amounts of accounts receivable that may not be collected are recorded (the balance thus deducted from accounts receivable yields the net book value of receivables).

allowed time The amount of time that hourly and part-time employees are permitted to absent themselves from the job on personal breaks.

all-purpose revolving account See **revolving charge account.**

alphanumeric Consisting of both numbers and letters (e.g., ''x305PS6'').

alternate sponsorship 1. Sponsorship of a television program by two advertisers on alternate weeks. **2.** The sharing of commercial time by two advertisers who provide programs on alternate weeks during the same time slot.

AMA 1. See **American Management Associations**. **2.** See **American Marketing Association**.

amalgamation A merger of two or more companies brought together by an outside interest, such as an investment bank.

American Academy of Advertising (*abbr* ACA) An organization composed of individuals in the advertising field who are interested in furthering their own and other members' education in advertising.

American Accounting Association (*abbr* AAA) An association of accountants, accounting teachers, and accounting researchers formed to develop accounting theory and techniques, conduct research, and promote understanding of accounting principles; publishes *Accounting Review.*

American Arbitration Association (*abbr* AAA) A nongovernmental, nonprofit organization founded in 1926 to promote the use of arbitration in the settlement of disputes.

American Association of Advertising Agencies (*abbr* AAAA) An organization founded in 1917 to foster, strengthen, and improve the advertising agency business, and to aid its members in operating more effectively and profitably.

American College of Life Underwriters A professional organization that awards certification to practice insurance underwriting, upon the passing of examinations and fulfillment of experience requirements.

American Federation of Labor (*abbr* AFL) A national federation of craft unions, which joined in 1955 with the CIO to become the AFL-CIO. See also **Congress of Industrial Organizations.**

American Federation of Television and Radio Artists (*acronym* AFTRA) A performers' union that lobbies for improvements in benefits and working conditions for its members and offers standard union services.

American Institute of Certified Public Accountants (*abbr* AICPA) An association of CPAs that carries on wideranging programs encompassing professional development, the establishment of accounting standards and procedures, continuing education, publication of the *Journal of Accountancy*, and administration of the uniform CPA examination (though each state sets its own requirements for certification).

American Management Associations (*abbr* AMA) A professional nonprofit organization of business professionals that conducts study courses, training programs, and management seminars, conducts research, and issues numerous publications on business subjects.

American Marketing Association (*abbr* AMA) A professional organization devoted to its members' continued improvement in the marketing arena and to the setting and upholding of ethical standards for the marketing profession as a whole; publishes *Journal of Marketing, Journal of Marketing Research,* and other periodicals.

American Production and Inventory Control Society (*acronym* APICS) A society of professionals in production and inventory management who have joined together to establish professional standards, research new ways to improve production and inventory management, develop and offer educational programs, publish journals, and provide research grants.

American Society of Woman Accountants (*abbr* ASWA) An association of female accountants; joint publisher, with the American Women's Society of Certified Public Accountants, of *The Woman CPA,* a bimonthly journal.

American Stock Exchange (*abbr* ASE) Also called **AMEX.** The second largest stock exchange in the U.S., located in New York City.

American Women's Economic Development Corporation (*abbr* AWED) A corporation set up by the federal government to train women entrepreneurs in basic business practices.

American Women's Society of Certified Public Accountants (*abbr* AWSCPA) An association of female certified public accountants; joint publisher, with the American Society of Woman Accountants, of *The Woman CPA,* a bimonthly journal.

AMEX See **American Stock Exchange.**

amortization The scheduled periodic repayment of a debt or loan at a rate sufficient to meet current interest and to extinguish the debt at the point of maturity; interest is usually charged only on the unpaid balance of the loan, though generally all payments are equal.

analytic process The process of breaking down a raw material into its component parts in order to extract one or more products, which may or may not resemble the original material in form and function. See also **synthetic process.**

anchor 1. A catchy phrase used by consumers as a rule of thumb to guide purchasing decisions (e.g., "You get what you pay for"). **2.** A major store in a shopping center.

announcement Also called **commercial.** A sponsor's message broadcast by television or radio, either between programs or during a brief break in a program, for the purpose of advertising a product, service, or idea. See also **advertisement.**

annual percentage rate (*abbr* APR) The annual rate of interest; the total interest to be paid in a year divided by the balance due.

annual report A corporation's financial and organizational report prepared by its officers on a yearly basis, as required by law, stating the corporation's assets, liabilities, earnings, general financial condition, profits, and losses and other information that may provide evidence to shareholders, customers, and creditors of the corporation's ability to pay its debts, and indicating the officers' goals and assessment of performance potential.

annuitant A person who receives an annuity.

annuity An income payable in equal installments at fixed intervals, either for life or for a specified number of years.

annuity depreciation Depreciation of an asset by a method that allows for a return of imputed interest on the undepreciated balance of the value of the asset, such interest being subtracted from the amount of current depreciation before that amount is credited to the accumulated depreciation accounts.

anthropometric data Data on the physical dimensions of various parts of the human body that serve as a basis for the design of products and tools.

anticipation The payment of an account before

the due date, normally for the purpose of receiving a discount.

anticipatory breach The breaching of a contract before the time specified for performance, as by notifying the other party that the terms of the contract will not be fulfilled, such that the other party to the contract has the legal right to sue for damages.

Antitrust Improvement Act An act of Congress passed in 1976 requiring companies to give advance notice of planned mergers and empowering state attorneys general to bring suit on behalf of state residents harmed by failure to comply with its provisions.

antitrust laws The body of legislation passed by Congress to maintain competition, prevent monopoly, and outlaw price discrimination. See also **Antitrust Improvement Act; Antitrust Procedures and Penalties Act; Celler-Kefauver Act; Clayton Act; Federal Trade Commission; Robinson-Patman Act; Sherman Antitrust Act; Wheeler-Lea Act.**

Antitrust Procedures and Penalties Act An act of Congress passed in 1974 to increase the penalties for failure to comply with the provisions of the Sherman Antitrust Act to a maximum fine of $100,000 for an individual or $10 million for a corporation.

appellate court A court that has the power to affirm, repeal, or modify a decision of a lower court upon appeal by either plaintiff or defendant on any of various grounds (e.g., denial of fair trial, judicial error).

application 1. The use of concepts and/or devices, such as those of science and technology, to define and solve real problems (e.g., engineering is the application of science, technology, art, and economics for practical ends). **2.** A computer program designed for a specific kind of task, such as word processing.

applied behavior analysis A behavior-change technique characterized by a functional combination of systems analysis, feedback systems, and reinforcement (e.g., analysis of a worker's job performance, decision-making ability, and competence to evaluate situations carried out by the worker's peers and/or supervisors for the purpose of determining any need for further training of the individual).

applied cost A cost allocated to a certain department or project before the expense has been incurred.

applied overhead Overhead costs for a specific department.

applied research Investigation or experimentation with the aim of developing practical applications of the knowledge thus gained.

appraisal 1. A professional estimate of the market value of an asset or liability. **2.** Evaluation of an employee's job performance.

appreciation An increase in the value of an asset, the amount being listed on the balance sheet as a capital gain or other form of income only when the asset is sold. See also **capital appreciation.**

apprenticeship A system by which a novice learns a skill while practicing it under the guidance of an experienced person.

appropriated retained earnings Also called **surplus revenue; suspense reserve.** A portion of retained earnings that a board of directors has designated for a special purpose and that thus is not available for dividends or other purposes.

appropriation An amount of money designated for the payment of known or anticipated costs.

APR See **annual percentage rate.**

a priori (*Latin*) From the former; based on accepted definitions or assumptions rather than on factual evidence.

arb (*informal*) Arbitrageur.

arbitrage 1. The simultaneous purchase and sale of the same security or of equivalent securities for the purpose of profiting from differences in market prices (as between New York and Paris). The practice tends to equalize prices by boosting them in the depleted cheaper markets and driving them down in the glutted expensive markets. **2.** See **risk arbitrage.**

arbitrageur Also called **arbitrager.** A person who engages in arbitrage. Also known, familiarly, as an ''arb.''

arbitration Also called **mediation.** Mediation of a

dispute by a person chosen by the parties to the dispute or appointed under statutory authority: a right guaranteed by most union contracts. See also **compulsory arbitration; conciliation.**

arbitrator A disinterested person who individually or as a member of a group mediates a dispute between labor and management, with powers defined by contract and whose ruling is the final resolution of the conflict.

area of choice and chance See **action-event area.**

Area Redevelopment Program A federal program initiated under the Area Redevelopment Act of 1961 to stimulate business growth and employment in depressed areas.

arithmetic mean The sum of all items divided by the number of items.

ARM See **adjustable-rate mortgage.**

ARO After receipt (of) order.

array (*statistics*) An arrangement of items by value, size, etc., from either smallest to largest or largest to smallest.

arrears 1. The state of a bill or invoice unpaid past its due date, which may be subject to interest or the loss of any discount allowed for prompt payment. **2.** The state of an as yet undeclared dividend on cumulative preferred stock.

arrival rate The average rate at which customers arrive for service, expressed in terms of customers per time period.

articles of association A written affiliation agreement entered into by a nonprofit organization.

articles of copartnership A written partnership agreement that includes the names of the parties; the specific business and its intended duration; the amounts of the original investments; any arrangements concerning future investments, salaries, profits, and other financial matters; and procedures to be followed in the event that a partner wishes to withdraw from the agreement.

articles of incorporation A written agreement embodying the terms and conditions of the incorporation of a business entity in accordance with the laws of the state in which the entity seeks to be incorporated: upon approval by the state becomes the corporation's charter.

artificial intelligence (*abbr* AI) The capacity of a computer to perform operations similar to the learning and decision-making abilities of human beings. Advances in AI have led to the increased use of computers in product design and in the manufacturing process.

artisan's lien Also called **mechanic's lien.** A legal claim against property pending payment to a worker for services rendered or materials supplied.

ASCII (*acronym for American Standard Code for Information Interchange*) A standardized code in which characters are represented for computer storage and transmission by the numbers 0 through 127.

ASE See **American Stock Exchange.**

asked price The lowest price a securities dealer will accept for a given stock. See also **bid and asked; bid price.**

assemble-to-order A type of manufacturing in which standard-design components or modules are produced for stock and subsequently assembled to meet the specific needs of each customer.

assembly line An arrangement of tools, machines, and workers, as in a manufacturing plant, so that a product can be assembled as it passes through a succession of workers and work stations.

assertiveness training A developmental program designed to help participants to experience and diagnose their own behavior for the purpose of improving their ability to influence other individuals and groups by stating their ideas and opinions with assurance.

assessment 1. An official valuation of property for the purpose of levying a tax; an assigned value. **2.** An amount assessed as payable.

assessment center A place where individuals are brought together, either voluntarily or at the request of an organization seeking to fill a position, and administered a series of tests and simulations to determine their mode of reaction in certain situations for the purpose of assessing their appropriateness for a given position.

asset Anything owned that has a value. See also **liability.**

asset accounting The total resources and property of a person or organization, as listed on a balance sheet.

asset allocation The apportioning of investments among broad categories of investments, such as stocks and bonds.

asset depreciation range (*abbr* ADR) The length of time within high and low limits established by the Internal Revenue Service for the useful life of an asset, within which the owner of the asset may depreciate it without offering evidence in justification.

assignee An individual or organization to whom property or a right under a contract has been transferred. See also **assignment.**

assignment The transfer of property or a right, as to collect money or to receive a performance, specified by the terms of a contract, such transfer being exercisable only after the assignee has given the party who owes money or services written notification of the assignment.

assignor An individual or organization that transfers property or a right under a contract. See also **assignment.**

associated buying office A cooperatively supported resident buying office established in a central buying area.

associated independent An independent retail store associated with other stores for the purpose of gaining merchandising benefits.

Association of Industrial Advertisers (*abbr* AIA) Former name of the Business and Professional Advertisers Association.

assortment plan A merchandising strategy whereby a carefully selected variety of merchandise is held by a retail store to meet its customers' needs. See also **basic stock; model stock.**

ATM (*abbr for automated-teller machine*) An electronic machine that provides banking services when activated by insertion of a plastic card.

attached Subject to a security interest; seized by virtue of a writ to be held to satisfy a judgment. See also **perfected.**

attachment The seizure of an asset by a legal process to satisfy a judgment against a debtor who has failed to discharge an obligation.

at-the-market price A retail price generally agreed upon by area store owners. See also **market-minus pricing; market-plus pricing; price leader.**

attitude survey 1. A questionnaire used to gather data on the opinions of individuals or groups for any legitimate purpose. **2.** A survey of employees' opinions about the organization that employs them, intended to reveal trends in such variables as feelings toward supervisor, pay, and work itself.

attrition 1. Staff reduction due to the customary causes of resignation, firing for cause, retirement, transfers, etc. **2.** Forcing the resignation of an undesirable employee by constant criticism, pressure, etc.

audimeter A mechanical device that records the amount of time a radio is operated and the station or stations to which it is tuned.

audit 1. A review of the accuracy and validity of the financial and/or operations records, reports, and statements of a company for the purpose of verifying that the firm has conformed to established accounting procedures and principles. **2.** To conduct such a review.

Audit Bureau of Circulation (*abbr* ABC) An independent organization that collects and provides data on the number of copies of U.S. publications distributed at each printing.

audit committee A group appointed by a board of directors to select an external auditor and to serve as liaison between the auditor selected and the board, handling such problems as audit procedures and differences of opinion between the auditor and management.

audit opinion Also called **auditor's opinion.** Part of an audit report in which the auditor states whether or not the financial statement was prepared according to generally accepted accounting principles and is consistent with previous financial statements.

auditor An individual, group, or company qualified to perform an audit. See also **external auditor; internal auditor**.

audit program A description, agreed upon by management and auditor, of the objective of an audit and the procedures to be followed to reach those objectives.

audit report Also called **auditor's report; accountant's report**. A written statement by the outside auditor, accompanying a financial statement and addressed to the executives, board members, shareholders, etc., expressing his or her opinion as to the accuracy of the statement in setting forth the company's financial position for the period specified.

audit trail A sequence of financial evidence, consisting of codes, cross-references, documentation, account balances, and previous calculations, which an auditor follows in order to verify balances and to locate and correct errors.

authoritative leadership Leadership that depends on formal authority backed by the power of the organization.

authoritative power See **legitimate power**.

authority 1. The legitimate power attached to position, office, or rank. 2. The right granted by an organization and acknowledged by its employees to issue orders, make decisions, and command the activities of subordinates. See also **functional authority** (def. 2); **line authority; staff authority**.

authorized dealership A retail outlet that has been given exclusive right by a manufacturer to sell a specific item or line of goods in a defined geographical area (akin to a franchise on a manufacturer's product).

authorized stock The maximum number of shares a corporation is entitled to issue, as stated in the corporate charter.

autocratic style A management style characterized by the direct exercise of authority over subordinates.

automated-teller machine See **ATM**.

automatic data processing (*abbr* ADP) The systematic and orderly analysis, sorting, gathering, and processing of data by a mechanical or electrical device, with little human intervention. See also **electronic data processing**.

automatic markdown A price reduction based on the length of time merchandise has been in stock in a retail store.

automatic reorder The ordering of goods or materials in accordance with a system based on levels of stock on hand.

automatic selling Retailing by vending machine.

automation The efficient use of mechanical or electrical devices to perform tasks previously accomplished by human action. See also **robotics.**

autonomous work group A group of workers given total responsibility to meet a specific level of production, its members determining and therefore handling much of the management activity involved in their work. See also **job enrichment.**

autonomy 1. Freedom from arbitrary control. **2.** A quality of freedom evident in the performance of individuals with well-defined job activities and relationships.

auxiliary memory Also called **secondary storage.** Computer memory, as on disk or tape, supplemental to and slower than main memory, and not under the direct control of the CPU.

average collection period ratio Total accounts receivable divided by average daily sales: a formula used to determine the amount of daily sales revenue locked up in unreceived payments. See also **activity ratio.**

average cost The sum of the costs of beginning inventory and subsequent additions to inventory divided by the total number of units available during the time period.

average gross sales The dollar amount of all sales divided by the number of sales transactions.

average tax rate Allowable expenses divided by pretax net income.

avoidable cost A variable cost that can be avoided if production is not permitted to reach the level at which additional expenses will be incurred.

awareness (*marketing research*) The level of information about a product possessed by individuals being researched. See also **perceptions.**

B

backdating The practice of placing on a statement, order, or check a date earlier than that on which the document is prepared.

back-door financing The financing of a program of a governmental agency by borrowing from the U.S. Treasury when Congress fails to appropriate the requested funds.

back-haul allowance A price reduction granted to customers who pick up their goods from a seller's warehouse to reflect the seller's savings in freight costs.

backlog The aggregate of production orders that have been processed through a company's records as sales but have not been shipped to customers.

back office Functions performed in a service organization by personnel who have little or no contact with customers.

back order An order or part of an order waiting to be filled.

backup stock Merchandise in excess of that needed for retail display, usually kept in an easily accessible stockroom.

backward integration The acquisition by a firm of ownership or control of facilities that provide raw materials or parts for products that the firm produces and sells.

backward scheduling A method of preparing a schedule by starting with the desired completion date and working backward to schedule earlier activities in time to meet the completion date.

backward vertical merger See **vertical merger**.

bad check A check written either against a bank balance that is insufficient to cover the amount specified or against a bank in which the drawer has no account. See also **NSF check**.

bad title A legal document assigning ownership of land or goods which is in some way improperly executed.

bafflegab Unintelligible, often deliberately confusing jargon.

bailment lease A security agreement by which a

buyer rents goods from a seller with the understanding that when the sum paid for rental equals the purchase price, the buyer may take possession of the item for an additional nominal sum.

bailout period The time until the total net cash inflows accumulated from a project, including the potential salvage value of all assets at periodic points in time and the present value of cash to be received after the termination date of the project, equal the total cash spent on the project. See also **payback period.**

bait and switch A system of publicizing exceptional prices or terms in a deceptive effort to attract customers; the advertised product (the bait) is either unavailable or disparaged to the customer, who is encouraged to buy a more expensive product (the switch).

balance 1. The remainder; the part left untouched or unpaid. **2.** The sum of all debits less the sum of all assets in an account. See **credit balance; debit balance. 3.** The book value of an asset or liability. **4.** The total to date of a revenue or expense account. **5.** The amount in a checking or savings account. **6.** To calculate any difference between debits and credits in an account. **7.** To cause debits and credits in an account to be equal.

balanced economy An economy in which the value of imports equals the value of exports in monetary terms.

balanced fund A mutual fund that must keep a certain percentage of its assets invested in senior securities.

balanced scale (*marketing research*) A questionnaire design that includes categories calling for equal numbers of favorable and unfavorable responses.

balanced stock A stock of goods at all prices sufficient to meet customers' demands, maintained as a long-range inventory strategy.

balanced tenancy A mix of stores in a geographical area adequate to meet the needs of the population of the area, as determined by a needs assessment.

balance of payments The net flow of money in and out of a country, including the value of imports and exports, loans and investments, foreign aid, income from tourism, deposits of foreign currency in domestic banks, and withdrawals of such deposits.

balance of trade 1. The net value of a country's total imports and exports. **2.** The net value of a country's import and export transactions with a given country. See also **favorable balance of trade; unfavorable balance of trade.**

balance sheet Also called **statement of financial position.** A statement of a company's financial position on a given date, usually at the end of a calendar or business year, including all of the elements in the accounting equation and the details of the financial transactions that back it up, specifying the type and amount of assets, liabilities, and owners' equity on the given date.

balloon loan Also called **balloon mortgage.** A relatively short-term loan, usually at a fixed rate of interest, in which the entire balance is due at the end of the term. Attractive because of generally low monthly payments, though these may pay off only the interest, with all or most of the principal coming due with the final payment.

ballpark pricing The practice of estimating a dollar value or price for a product to be produced or a job to be done by comparing the prices of similar projects or by adding the estimated costs of completing the project.

bandwagon effect An infectious buying climate in which the buying enthusiasm of some people spreads to others.

bangtail A detachable offer of merchandise on the back of a self-addressed envelope accompanying a monthly billing statement, usually supplied by a merchandise syndicator. See also **syndicator.**

Bank Deposit Insurance Act of 1934 Federal legislation enacted to protect depositors against loss in the event of bank failure by insuring bank deposits for amounts up to a specified maximum.

bank draft A check drawn by a bank on funds deposited to its account in another bank.

banker's acceptance A promissory note drawn on and accepted by a bank (commonly used in import/export transactions involving foreign banks and currencies), which by its endorsement accepts the obligation to pay the note on the due date, drawing the amount of the note plus interest from a deposit made by the debtor.

Banking Act of 1933 The first major banking legislation leading to significant changes in banking law, including the creation of commercial banking loans and credits, with or without collateral, and the development of branch banking services.

bank reconciliation An analysis that brings into agreement the amount in a bank account, as calculated by the depositor on the basis of canceled checks and stubs, and a different amount reported on the bank's statement; lists outstanding checks, deposits recorded after the statement date, bank service charges, and any other items that explain the difference.

bankruptcy A court action that cancels the debts of an individual, business, or corporation whose liabilities exceed its assets or that is otherwise unable to meet its financial obligations by dividing the debtor's available assets among the creditors. See also **Chapter 11; involuntary bankruptcy; voluntary bankruptcy.**

Bank Secrecy Act of 1970 Federal legislation requiring banks to maintain records of all transactions with depositors, and to report transactions over $10,000 to the Treasury Department.

bantam store Also called **vest-pocket supermarket.** A small convenience store generally open 24 hours a day.

bar chart A graph consisting of bars of uniform width but varying lengths proportional to the numbers they represent, permitting comparison of amounts of items or variables.

bar code A series of lines of varying width, printed on a product, package, etc., that can be read by an optical scanner to determine charges for purchases, destinations for letters, etc. See also **Universal Product Code.**

bargain and sale deed A deed transferring title to real property with no guarantee of the title or of the use of the property.

bargaining strategy A plan devised to permit two negotiating parties with differing opinions to reach agreement within the limits imposed by their organizational objectives.

bargaining unit A group of employees within an organization who are represented by a particular labor union.

barter An exchange of goods and/or services by two or more parties without the use of money, credit, or formal documents.

barter plan A trading arrangement (often found in the communications industry) by which advertising time on television or space in a publication may be paid for in merchandise or services rather than money.

base pay Pay received for a given work period, as an hour or week, but not including additional pay, as for overtime work.

base period A period of time selected as a reference point to define a time frame, so that changes in prices or other economic indicators over the designated interval can be assessed.

base-point pricing The calculation of freight charges on the basis of distance from a geographical location that differs from the point of origin of the goods shipped (often a place within a state where a major competitor is located) for the purpose of reducing freight fees charged and thus enhancing the shipper's competitive position or of charging customers for freight costs not paid by the seller. See also **phantom freight.**

base-stock method A method of costing inventory (no longer acceptable for tax purposes) which assumes a minimum inventory that must be kept on hand, valued at its acquisition cost; items added to this base stock are valued on the basis of last in, first out.

BASIC (*acronym for* Beginners' All-Purpose Symbolic Instruction Code) An easy-to-use computer programming language, developed in the 1960's. See also **COBOL.**

basic research Investigation or experimentation for the purpose of increasing knowledge or understanding. See also **applied research.**

basic stock A retail store's stock of merchandise consisting of items that the store intends to keep on hand for approximately a year and lists in a form that indicates when stock is nearly depleted and should be reordered.

basis The acquisition cost or book value of an asset, which is subtracted from the selling price of that asset to determine capital gain or loss.

basis point One hundredth of one percent, as of interest rates or investment yields.

basket purchase Also called **lump-sum purchase.** The purchase of several assets for a single price; for accounting purposes, each asset is assigned a cost to be entered into the proper account, the sum of all such costs equaling the cost of the basket purchase.

batch processing The processing of all related materials or documents at one time; in computers, the execution of programs by sets, so that each program within a set is completed before the next is begun.

battleground map A map designating all branch stores and competitive stores within a retailer's trading area.

bean counter (*informal*) A person who makes judgments chiefly on the basis of numerical calculations.

bearer bond A bond payable to any person who presents it, such person being presumed to be its owner. See **bond** (def. 1).

bearer instrument A legal instrument that is not registered and is negotiated merely by delivery.

bear hug A takeover offer in which a company is willing to pay a price significantly higher than the target company's market value.

bearish 1. Pessimistic, especially about stock prices. **2.** (of stock prices) Generally declining.

bear market A stock market characterized by a general decline in prices. See also **bull market.**

BE cluster See **belief-evaluation cluster.**

beginning inventory The value of an inventory at the beginning of an accounting period.

behavioral modeling A training technique in which a trainee role-plays a situation calling for particular skills; a trainer then evaluates the effectiveness of the skills demonstrated and shows the trainee how to adopt a new pattern of behavior demonstrated by a model, in the hope that the new behaviors can be transferred to the individual's work situation.

behavioral science 1. The body of disciplines (psychology, sociology, anthropology) encompassing the study of human behavior. **2.** A branch of experimental psychology that emphasizes the influence of the immediate consequences of actions on subsequent learning and performance.

behavior analysis See **applied behavior analysis.**

behavior modification A program of systematic reward for desired behavior and withholding of reward for undesired behavior, for the purpose of increasing desired behavior and reducing or eliminating undesired behavior. See also **coercive reward and punishment system.**

belief-evaluation cluster (*abbr* BE cluster) The collection of impressions, ideas, and judgments, subject to change with new information and experience, which make up an individual's attitude toward a subject.

below par Below face value; (a stock) offered for sale at a price lower than the amount appearing on the face.

below-the-line 1. Referring to an expense or source of income that is unique or unusual. **2.** (*motion pictures*) Referring to the production costs of a film (e.g., settings and costumes, camera crews, sound effects). See also **above-the-line.**

benchmark Also called **yardstick. 1.** Anything that serves as a standard against which other things are compared and measured; a reference point. **2.** (*advertising, marketing research*) A variable (e.g., brand awareness) that is measured before and after an advertising campaign to help determine the campaign's effectiveness in influencing the target audience to buy the product.

beneficial interest The right to receive a benefit from property that one does not own.

beneficiary 1. A person who receives benefits or income. **2.** A person who will legally receive an amount of money or property at the death of another person, as stipulated by a contract or will. **3.** One who benefits from the act of another.

benefit 1. Financial or other assistance offered to employees in addition to salaries and wages. See also **compensation; employee benefit plan; fringe benefit. 2.** A significant advantage that a customer can expect to enjoy as a result of purchasing a product (emphasized in consumer-oriented selling).

benevolent leadership Also called **system 2 management.** A style of leadership that emphasizes the formal roles of superiors and subordinates, discourages interaction between them, maintains strict control, and initiates any communication, while fostering a psychological closeness to subordinates that maintains discipline through apprehension and sometimes fear.

bequest A gift of property bestowed by a will.

best-case scenario The best possible outcome of a situation.

beta Also called **Beta Factor.** A measure of a stock's volatility, based on the volatility of the market as a whole. A stock having a beta of 1.1 would be considered 10 percent more volatile than the market average.

Better Business Bureau A nonprofit organization established by business leaders to promote ethical business practices, investigate complaints of unethical practices, and expose unethical businesses to the public: branches in most major cities.

betterment An improvement made to an asset in order to enhance its performance or productivity or to prolong its useful life, the cost of which is added to the asset account for later depreciation.

bid 1. To elicit prices from a number of competitive vendors. **2.** To offer a price or prices for a job to be done for a potential client or for a stock.

bid and asked The amount offered (bid) for a stock by a prospective buyer and the amount asked for that stock by a prospective seller, reported in over-the-counter stock quotations. See also **asked price; bid price.**

bid peddling The practice of reporting a low bid to potential suppliers of goods or services in an attempt to elicit an offer lower than the one reported.

bid price Also called **quoted bid.** The highest price a securities dealer will pay for a given stock. See also **asked price.**

big bath A write-off of extensive asset costs for

the purpose of shedding an unprofitable line of business or of eliminating the need for gradual write-offs in future periods.

big board The enormous wall of the New York Stock Exchange where quotations and other information are displayed; by extension, the New York Stock Exchange itself.

big-ticket item An item that commands a very high price.

big-ticket sales Sales of big-ticket items. See also **megaselling.**

bilateral Affecting two parties reciprocally.

bilateral contract A contract by whose terms two parties are bound by reciprocal obligations. See also **unilateral contract.**

bill An invoice submitted to a purchaser detailing the costs of products sold or services rendered, applicable taxes, total amount due, and due date.

billing cycle See **cycle billing.**

bill of exchange Also called **draft.** A written order (e.g., a check) signed by one person (the drawer) requiring that a sum of money be paid to a second person (the payee) by a third party (the drawee), who indicates his or her willingness to pay by writing "Accepted" on it and signing it.

bill of labor A list of the standard times required in each work center to produce one unit of a specific product.

bill of lading A receipt for goods accepted for shipment given by a transportation company to a shipper. See also **order bill of lading.**

bill of materials A list of the quantities of all parts and material needed to complete the production of one unit of a specific product.

bill of sale A written statement of the transfer of ownership of personal property or of the rendering of services, proving past title to property transferred but not proving present ownership.

binary system A system consisting of two components or offering two alternatives (e.g., yes/no, go/no-go). See also **bit.**

binder 1. A temporary insurance policy that extends coverage to an applicant for a policy until the regular policy can be issued, such coverage generally being in effect from the moment that the insurance agent accepts the application. **2.** Money or a receipt for money paid to the owner of real estate for the exclusive right to purchase the property at terms agreed upon or to be agreed upon by buyer and seller.

bingo card A prepaid postcard inserted in a magazine by its publisher that a reader can return to order free information about advertisers' products.

bird dog A person who is paid by a salesperson to identify prospective customers (a practice considered all but unethical in some industries).

birdyback The transportation of goods by truck in a trailer that is then loaded directly onto an air carrier for delivery to an airport near its destination.

bit (*from b*inary dig*it*) A single digit, either 0 or 1, used in a binary system of numeration; the smallest unit of information storage for a computer.

blacklist A secret list circulated among employers to prevent union organizers and other antagonistic employees from obtaining work.

black market 1. The illicit buying and selling of goods in violation of legal price controls, rationing, etc. **2.** A place where such activity is carried on.

Black Monday October 19, 1987, when the Dow Jones Industrial Average fell a record 508 points in trading on the New York Stock Exchange.

Black Tuesday October 29, 1929, when stock values on the New York Stock Exchange collapsed and, after frantic selling, many shares became virtually worthless.

blad (*informal*) A flier or other promotional piece distributed by a company to sell a product.

blank endorsement An endorsement of an instrument (e.g., a check) which does not specify any person to whom payment is to be made, thus making the amount named in the instrument payable to any person who presents it without further endorsement.

blanket agreement An agreement reached by collective bargaining that applies to workers throughout an organization, industry, or geographical area.

blanket lien A lien that gives a creditor the right to seize any or all of a debtor's real property in order to cover an unpaid loan. See also **lien** (def. 2); **specific lien.**

blanket order Also called **open-end order; yearly order.** A purchase order issued by a buyer to cover a year or some other specified period, eliminating the need to issue routine releases and redundant purchase orders throughout the time frame covered.

blanket policy An insurance policy that covers multiple properties, locations, or shipments under one contract.

blind check A system in which a form used for verifying invoice data is circulated between the receiving clerk and the accounting department as a systematic way of double-checking inventory.

blind entry An accounting entry that indicates only the accounts and the amounts debited and credited, without supporting information or explanation.

blister packaging A type of clear packaging that forms a protective bubble of plastic about a product while permitting visual inspection.

block A large holding of stock, commonly considered to be more than 10,000 shares.

blocked need satisfaction Inability to satisfy a need or reach a desired goal, resulting in a state of tension which the individual attempts to reduce by coping behavior that others may interpret as trial-and-error problem-solving behavior. See also **need satisfaction.**

blow-in A piece of advertising inserted in but not attached to a magazine or newspaper, usually printed on stiff card stock.

blowout A quick sellout of securities being offered to the public due to heavy demand.

blue chip A stock issue of a company with a consistent history of earnings and dividend payments, leadership in an established industry, and good prospects of future stability and growth, such that its stock tends not to be subject to sudden or great changes in price and is generally expensive.

blue-collar Belonging or relating to wage-earning workers who wear work clothes or other specialized clothing on the job, as mechanics, longshoremen, and miners.

blue-sky Unsound or of no value; applied to ideas that are beyond the realm of the possible (sometimes interpreted as ideas that are ahead of their time).

blue-sky laws Federal laws designed to protect investors from investing in securities that have no value by empowering such federal agencies as the Securities and Exchange Commission and the U.S. Postal Service to enforce state laws requiring public disclosure of the issuing corporation's financial status and the way in which the money collected from the sale of stocks is to be used.

blurb A brief advertisement or notice, as on a book jacket, especially one expressing praise.

board of directors The group of persons (at least three in most states) at the highest level of organizational responsibility in the modern corporation, with the authority to guide corporate affairs and make general policies.

board of governors The governing body of the Federal Reserve System.

bodily injury liability insurance Insurance that protects the insured against claims and lawsuits resulting from accidental injury or death caused by the insured person's negligence, as in the operation of a motor vehicle.

boiler room A slang term for a roomful of telephone operators who phone prospects, giving sales pitches for investments and investment schemes.

bond 1. An interest-bearing instrument issued by a corporation or governmental body as evidence of a long-term debt, usually incurred for a specific purpose. See also **bearer bond; convertible bond; corporate bond; coupon bond; government bond; municipal bond. 2.** An agreement under which an insurer agrees to indemnify the insured for losses caused by the act, negligence, or default of a third party, or by circumstances over which the third party has no control. **3.** The state of goods being manufactured, transported, or held in the care of an agency covered by such a bond pending payment of taxes ("in bond").

bonded warehouse 1. A warehouse in which goods stored are insured against loss or damage. **2.** A warehouse in which goods stored are in bond to the government pending payment of taxes. See also **bond** (def. 3).

bond fund A mutual fund that invests primarily in specialized corporate bonds or in municipal bonds, usually charging an initial sales fee (included in the offering price) plus an annual management fee that seldom exceeds 1 percent of the fund's net asset value. See also **bond** (def. 1).

bondholder The current owner of a bond.

bonding company An organization that insures a party against loss caused by a third party. See also **bond** (def. 2).

bond rating Evaluation of a corporation's or state or local government's ability to honor the debt represented by the bonds it issues, made on the basis of the issuer's debt level and past payment record, the coupon rate, the security of the assets backing the bonds, and any other relevant data. Bond ratings are usually classified as follows: AAA (highest quality), AA (high quality), A (upper medium grade), BBB (medium grade), BB (mostly speculative), B (low grade, speculative), CCC (poor), CC (highly speculative), C (lowest quality), D (in default).

bond refunding Issuance of additional bonds (and thus the incurring of additional debt) for the purpose of acquiring the funds needed to redeem outstanding bonds.

bond table A schedule for determination of the current value of bonds as a function of their coupon rates, times to maturity, and effective yields until maturity.

bonus A payment to an employee in addition to the regular wage or salary, intended as motivation for increased productivity, an incentive to remain with the company, or as a supplemental reward.

bonus circulation Copies of a publication distributed in excess of the number guaranteed to advertisers by the publisher.

bonus method A method of calculating partners' shares in a business whereby a new partner is credited with an amount in excess of the capital he or she has actually contributed by transfer of capital from the accounts of the old partners to that of the new. See also **goodwill method.**

book inventory The amount of stock shown to

be on hand by a perpetual inventory method; total purchases to date less sales, markdowns, and discounts.

bookkeeping The keeping of account books or systematic records of money transactions: distinguished from accounting, which is the analysis of such records. See also **double-entry bookkeeping; single-entry bookkeeping.**

book of original entry See **journal.**

books The financial records of a business.

book value 1. The value of a share of common stock calculated by subtracting all liabilities (including liquidation value of outstanding preferred stock) from total assets and dividing the result by the number of outstanding common shares. See also **market value. 2.** The current value of equipment or other depreciable capital asset after all accumulated depreciation has been subtracted from its acquisition cost.

book-value shares Shares of stock offered to executives at a price equal to their book value rather than at their market price, with the understanding that when the book value has risen, the company will buy back the stock at the increased book-value price or will make payments in stock equal to the appreciation in book value.

boom Any period of economic prosperity (opposite of *bust*).

boondoggle Any wasteful, inefficient, and generally useless program or activity.

booster A shoplifter.

boot Also called **boot money.** An amount of cash paid along with an asset traded for another, more valuable asset.

bootlegging 1. Illegal movement of goods and materials for the purpose of avoiding payment of taxes. **2.** Movement of illegal goods.

borrow to carry inventory To borrow money in order to pay the costs of seasonal inventories that must be purchased substantially in advance of sales.

bottleneck Any operation whose capacity is insufficient to meet requirements, resulting in reduced system output and often the buildup of inventory prior to that operation.

bottom line 1. The sum or result of all items listed above the last line of a balance sheet or financial statement; thus, final profit or loss. **2.** The final result. **3.** The ultimate objective or the critical issue.

bottom management Collectively the people who hold lower-level supervisory positions in a company but do not become directly involved in major corporate decision-making, marketing, or forecasting activities. See also **management pyramid; top management.**

boundary-spanning unit An informally organized group created to meet a short-term objective or to work on a special problem unique to the organization that called it into being. See also **ad hoc committee.**

bounded rationality A tendency to choose facile and easily workable solutions to problems over more difficult courses of action that might be of greater long-term value but that would be more immediately costly in time and money.

bourse A stock exchange, esp. the stock exchange of certain European cities.

boutique agency An advertising agency that specializes in a specific service or phase of advertising (e.g., copywriting).

boycott 1. An organized refusal to buy or handle a company's products or use its services, as well as an attempt to persuade others not to do so in order to express disapproval or exert pressure. **2.** To engage in such a concerted action.

BPI (*abbr for* bu*y*ing-*p*ower *i*ndex) See **consumer price index.**

bracket creep Also called **tax-bracket creep.** The gradual movement of a wage earner into a higher federal income-tax bracket as a result of wage increases intended to offset inflation. Since tax rates also tend to increase during inflation, the individual is often left with no corresponding increase in real income.

brainstorming A technique for solving a specific problem by which group members gather together and spontaneously offer as many ideas as possible in a nonthreatening atmosphere, each idea offered generating others.

branch accounting The keeping of records by a

branch office, until they are combined with those of all other branches and of the main office in a single financial statement.

brand The name or symbol of a product or service; an identifying mark intended to differentiate a product or line of products from those offered by competitors. See also **trademark.**

brand awareness Conscious knowledge by consumers that a particular brand of merchandise is available.

brand image The impression of a brand held in the minds of consumers or conveyed by the physical and qualitative characteristics of the product or products with which it is associated and by advertising and publicity.

brand leader A brand that is the leading seller in its field.

brand loyalty Marked preference for a product of a particular brand over similar products of other brands.

brand name 1. A word, name, symbol, etc., especially one legally registered as a trademark, used by a manufacturer or merchant to identify its products distinctively from others of the same type and usually prominently displayed on its goods, in advertising, etc. 2. A product, line of products, or service bearing a widely known brand name.

brand switching Ceasing to buy a product of a brand that one has been accustomed to using and shifting to another, similar product of a different brand.

breach of contract Failure to carry out the terms of a contract without legal justification, or compliance in an unsatisfactory manner, such that the injured party may sue for damages or for specific performance. See also **anticipatory breach.**

break-even analysis Calculation of the relationship between production costs, both fixed and variable, and income (revenue) generated by that production. See also **break-even point.**

break-even point 1. The amount of sales a business must generate in order to cover the costs of operation. 2. The point on a graph at which the vector for total revenues (usually plotted against the horizontal axis) meets the vector for total costs (usually plotted against the vertical axis).

breaking bulk The process of dividing a large shipment into smaller lots. See also **bulk breaking.**

bribery The act of promising or giving a monetary or other reward to gain an improper advantage.

bridge loan Also called **swing loan.** A temporary, short-term loan, as for making the down payment on a new house while one's present house is being sold.

broadcast 1. To transmit television or radio signals from a transmitting station to remote terminals. 2. A television or radio program as it is received by an audience. 3. To mail promotional material to all dealers simultaneously.

broad-form insurance Insurance that provides more comprehensive coverage than the ordinary policy.

broadside A promotional advertisement, usually very large and inexpensively printed, distributed in quantity as handouts or from door to door.

brochure A pamphlet designed to promote a company's products or services.

broken lot 1. A quantity of manufactured goods insufficient to fill a boxcar or standard container. 2. See **odd lot.**

broker 1. Also called **registered representative.** An agent, especially a stockbroker, who for a fee or commission negotiates a transaction between a buyer and seller of securities, commodities, or real estate without personally taking title to or possession of the subject of the transaction. 2. A person who acts as an agent to negotiate on behalf of a principal in the making of a contract with a third party.

brood hen A buyer employed by the main store of a retail chain who buys merchandise for all stores in the chain.

bubble diagram A graphic plan designed for use in structuring environmental space allocated to a department of a company, which may be manipulated before actual construction in order to determine the most desirable locations of line officers and staff.

bucket shop 1. The illegal practice by a broker of accepting an order for stock but not executing the order until the price is more advantageous to the broker. 2. The practice of selling stocks, usually by phone, but never actually placing the orders. **3.** Any overaggressive brokerage house dealing usually in highly speculative stocks.

budget A plan or schedule detailing income and allocation of expenses, which when complete includes a production budget, a materials budget, a cash budget derived from the production and materials budgets, and pro forma accrual-based income statements and balance sheets.

budget variance 1. The difference between the amount budgeted and the net amount of actual expenditures and receipts. **2.** In a standard cost system, the amount by which overhead exceeds the amount budgeted for it.

buffer stock See **safety stock**.

bug An error in a computer software program. See also **debug**.

built-in obsolescence. See **planned obsolescence**.

bulk breaking The dividing up of large quantities of goods for sale.

bulk discount A price reduction based on volume of purchases.

bulk freight A large quantity of items transported uncrated or unpackaged.

bullion Gold or silver that has been processed, refined, and formed into bars or ingots.

bullish Optimistic.

bull market A stock market characterized by generally rising prices. See also **bear market**.

bundle To offer or supply related products or services in a single transaction at one all-inclusive price.

burden The portion of the cost of manufacturing or business that does not contribute directly to production or operations (e.g., employee fringe benefits, overhead).

bureaucracy An administrative system characterized by diffusion of authority among many departments or divisions and strict adherence to inflexible rules and procedures.

bureaucrat A manager who demonstrates strict conformity to rules and prescribed routines, characterized by a lack of flexibility and initiative, indifference to the needs of others, and a proclivity for referring decisions to superiors.

Bureau of Labor Statistics (*abbr* BLS) A research agency of the U.S. Department of Labor that develops and disseminates statistics on a variety of matters related to employment.

buried position A position in a publication considered unfavorable for an advertisement because the surrounding material either has little attraction to the target audience or distracts attention from the ad.

burn-rate The rate at which start-up capital is used to bring a product to market, usually budgeted to carry over until the product begins to show a profit.

burst A graphic design, usually a notched circle, printed on a product package, cover, or label, or on a direct-mail envelope, and bearing a brief sales pitch.

business Any activity, enterprise, or transaction designed to provide consumers with goods or services for a profit.

Business and Professional Advertisers Association An association of marketing and advertising executives in the industrial goods field.

business cycle A fluctuating pattern of business conditions characterized by successive periods of prosperity, crisis, recession, and recovery which cannot be predicted with assurance by any theory.

business development center A local office of a federally funded program that provides research and consulting services to small businesses.

business environment All of the phenomena and conditions that directly or indirectly influence business.

business ethics A set of principles that guides business practices to reflect a concern for society as a whole while pursuing profits.

business film A film or tape conveying information on a product, service, or other subject of interest to business, professional, or technical audiences. See also **sponsored film; training film.**

business game A training and educational technique designed to improve participants' business skills, incorporating such activities as simulations, action mazes, in-basket experiences, card-sort and functional games concentrating on management principles, long-range planning, decision making, and time management, in which participants engage either individually or as members of a team, the particular activity engaged in being determined by the objectives sought.

business indicator See economic indicator.

business interruption insurance Insurance that protects a business against loss in the event of a fire, flood, or other disaster that forces it to suspend operations temporarily.

business market A sphere of business activity in which goods and services are sold to businesses rather than to the general public.

business park 1. See office park. 2. See industrial park.

business plan A proposal prepared by an entrepreneur for prospective investors, explaining a new business idea, indicating why it represents an attractive investment opportunity, and often outlining ideas for marketing, financing, and operations.

business reply A form of mail, usually sent as an enclosure, which can be mailed back by respondents without their having to pay postage. Business reply cards are often used for sales promotions. Business reply envelopes are used for orders, payments, etc.

business year See fiscal year.

bust A sudden severe decline in business and economic activity (opposite of *boom*).

buyback The buying back by a company of its own stock (a) when the market price is low or (b) usually at an inflated price, in an attempt to thwart a takeover.

buyer 1. Any person who makes or seeks to make a purchase. 2. A person employed by a department store to select, purchase, and price merchandise to be sold in a specific department of the store, and often to supervise the personnel of the department.

buyer's market A market in which goods are available in large quantities and in great variety, so that prices tend to fall as sellers compete for buyers. See also seller's market.

buyer's wheel A pocket-size disk marked with

figures representing costs, attached to another disk marked with figures representing selling prices, such that when a specific cost is aligned with a specific selling price, the resulting profit margin is shown.

buying by specification Purchasing materials or goods in accordance with requirements precisely described in writing.

buying committee A group of buyers who jointly select products to be purchased, usually for sale in a retail store.

buying on margin Purchasing securities by paying half or more of the purchase price, the remainder being financed as a loan by the broker.

buying power Also called **purchasing power**. The total amount of money available for spending and consumption (liquid assets plus available credit).

buying-power index (*abbr* BPI) See **consumer price index.**

buy out To purchase all of the assets of an existing business or partner.

buzzing Brainstorming as a training technique.

by-bidder An individual who deceptively bids at an auction for the purpose of generating higher bids.

bylaws Rules and regulations devised by a corporation to specify and govern its methods of doing business, generally dealing with matters not covered by local, state, or federal statutes and more unchanging than policies and general operating procedures.

by-product A product created incidentally while manufacturing the main product (e.g., sawdust as a by-product of lumbering), with a sales value insignificant compared with that of the main product; no value is attached to the anticipated sale of a by-product, but for accounting purposes, any income realized from its sale is deducted from the cost of the main product.

Byrnes Act Federal legislation enacted in 1936 to prohibit the use of strikebreakers.

byte A string of eight binary digits (bits) that are processed as a unit by a computer: one byte equals one alphanumeric character. See also **bit.**

C

CA See **chartered accountant.**

CAA See **Civil Aeronautics Administration.**

cable television A system of transmission of television signals from distant stations via a master antenna and thence by a cable to the television sets of individual subscribers.

CAD See **computer-aided design.**

cafeteria plan A group benefit plan under which employees may choose among various benefits offered those that best fit their own individual needs and situations, up to a specified maximum dollar value. See also **fringe benefit.**

CAI (*abbr for* *c*omputer-*a*ssisted *i*nstruction) See **programmed instruction.**

call 1. a. Also called **call option.** An option to buy a stock or commodity at a specified price (call price) within a specified period, purchasable for a premium of a percentage of the current market price of the stock or commodity; if the price rises during the option period, the owner of the option can either buy the shares or commodity for the (lower) price specified or sell the option at a profit. See also **put. b.** To exercise such an option. **2. a.** A notice to a holder of a bond or of preferred stock that the issue is to be redeemed before its normal maturity. See also **callable bond. b.** To issue such a notice. **3. a.** A notice to a stockholder or subscriber that an assessment or subscription to capital is to be paid. **b.** To issue such a notice.

callable bond Also called **redeemable bond.** A bond that the issuing corporation reserves the right to redeem before maturity, as when the general market interest rate has dropped below the interest rate payable on the bond.

callback pay A premium wage paid to a worker who is called back to work after completion of his or her regular work shift.

call option See **call** (def. 1a).

call premium The percentage of a bond's face value that a company must pay in addition to the face value in order to redeem (call) a callable bond.

call price 1. Call premium plus face value. **2.** The specified price at which the owner of a call option may buy stock during a specified period.

CAM See **computer-aided manufacturing.**

cancel 1. To close an account by crediting or paying all outstanding charges. **2.** To eliminate or offset a debit or credit with an entry for an equal amount on the opposite side of a ledger, as when a payment is received on a debt.

canceled check A check that has been redeemed by a bank and then usually returned to the issuer.

cancellation 1. Termination of a contract. **2.** Elimination of a particular business activity.

cap 1. A maximum limit set by law or agreement on prices, wages, spending, interest rates, etc. **2.** See **capitalization.**

capacity The number of units that can be processed in a unit of time; for accounting purposes, capacity can be used to allocate fixed costs for normal amounts of goods to be produced.

capacity costs Fixed costs, consisting of standby costs and enabling costs, incurred to give a company the capacity to produce or operate.

capital 1. a. Long-term assets in which a corporation has invested for the production of goods or services. **b.** The money raised to invest in such assets. **c.** Funds in the form of investments, profits, or loans necessary to finance the operation of a business. **2.** The equity interest of the owners in a company.

capital appreciation An increase in the value of capital assets, usually reflected in the market value of a corporation's securities.

capital assets Land, buildings, machinery, and other major items owned by a business for use in its operations.

capital budget A budget that lists the amount needed to purchase capital items and indicates the source from which the money is to be obtained.

capital expenditure An addition to the value of fixed assets, as by the purchase of a new building.

capital gains Income from the sale of capital assets, formerly subject to special tax breaks, but now taxed as ordinary income. See also **capital losses.**

capital goods Items that usually are treated as long-term investments because of their substantial value and life.

capital-intensive Requiring a greater expenditure for capital assets per unit of production than for labor. See also **labor-intensive**.

capital investment Funds that have been invested in capital goods.

capitalism An economic system, first defined by Adam Smith in 1776, that is based on the law of supply and demand and relies on the institutions of private property, competitive markets, free consumer choice, and minimal government interference. See also **classical economics; invisible hand; law of supply and demand**.

capitalization 1. The total amount of long-term debt (preferred and common stock, bonds, promissory notes, debentures, etc.) and owners' equity. **2.** See **market capitalization**.

capitalization rate The interest rate used to calculate a single present value of a series of future payments, receipts, or earnings or to evaluate the worth of an asset on the basis of its income stream.

capitalize To record as a capital or long-term asset an expenditure that will benefit future periods, permitting depreciation of the asset thus created.

capital lease Also called **financing lease; sales-type lease.** A lease agreement extending over at least 75 percent of the leased asset's useful life and allowing the lessee to buy the asset either for a bargain price or by assuming ownership at the end of the lease period.

capital losses Losses resulting from the sale of capital assets. See also **capital gains**.

capital market A securities market in which securities with maturities of more than one year are traded, so called because such securities (most corporate, municipal, and government bonds, mortgages, and some preferred stocks) ultimately represent claims against capital assets.

capital rationing A capital budgeting measure used to constrain or restrict the total amounts of capital expenditures.

capital shares Shares of stock in a dual-type closed-end investment company which earn no dividends but gain or lose value as the net assets of the company rise or fall. See also **dual distribution**.

capital stock The entire stated value of the shares of stock issued by a corporation.

capital structure The long-term financial foundation of a corporation, consisting of long-term debt, preferred stock, and the net worth of common stock and retained earnings.

capital surplus Also called **additional paid-in capital; paid-in surplus.** The money that comes into a corporation beyond the amount raised by the par or stated value of common and preferred stock issued; the difference between the par value of shares issued and the price actually paid for them plus capital otherwise contributed, as by gifts or donations (part of owners' equity).

capital turnover The rate at which the assets of a business are converted into cash.

captive insurance company An insurance company established by a business or a group of businesses for the purpose of providing low-cost coverage to the organizations involved.

cardmember A person authorized to use a credit card.

career development See **life planning**.

career-path planning A technique for motivating an employee to consider the company's long-range goals in concert with his or her expectations of personal growth and occupational desires, for the purpose of clarifying the relationship between the employee's chosen career steps and increased responsibility within the organization.

carload lot A shipment of goods that completely fills a rail freight car (and usually costs less per unit of goods to send than a partial carload).

carrier's lien A legal claim against goods pending payment to a carrier for transportation of the goods.

carry-over Also called **carry-back; carry-forward.** Deduction of corporate operating losses from taxable income during the past three years (carry-back) or the next five years (carryforward) in order to reduce overall taxable income when income fluctuates drastically: not applicable if 50 percent of the corporation's securities have changed hands in the last two years or if the corporation changes the business in which it engages.

carry-over effects The long-range effects of a short-term advertising campaign.

cartel 1. A group of people, organizations, or nations joined to limit competition and regulate prices. **2.** A written agreement of trust between two dispassionate parties.

cartouche A decorative frame, frequently oval, enclosing a brand name or symbol.

case divider A divider strip used to organize food sections in a store display, often designed to allow an advertising message to be carried on it.

case method A teaching method that presents for discussion and analysis actual instances of the problem being studied and encourages students to arrive at practical solutions.

case study An intensive analysis of a person, group, community, or other social unit stressing the interaction of developmental and environmental factors.

cash accounting The recording of expenses when they are actually paid and of revenues when they are actually received. See also **accrual accounting.**

cash-and-carry wholesaler A wholesaler who provides goods from a warehouse but no transportation, credit, or other services, and whose prices reflect the savings in expenses thus effected.

cash audit An examination and analysis to determine that all cash has been properly accounted for.

cashbook A journal or ledger used in a simple accounting system to record and keep a balance of all receipts and disbursements of cash.

cash budget A projection indicating expected receipts and expenditures and consequent anticipated need for or surplus of cash.

cash cow A slow-growth company that invests little money in research and development because its existing product lines sell steadily and produce a good profit. See also **dog; star.**

cash discount A deduction from the selling price offered for prompt payment.

cash flow Also called **gross received.** The

amount of money generated by a special activity after payment of expenses.

cash-flow cycle The financial process from the time a company buys raw materials until the finished goods have been sold and payment for them has been received.

cashier's check A check issued by a bank, usually in exchange for cash, that is signed by the cashier or other official and that represents an obligation of the bank. See also **certified check**.

cash machine. See **ATM**.

cash surrender value Also called **surrender value.** The actual value of a life insurance policy; the money that the insured will receive if the policy is canceled or cashed in, which increases with the age of the policy as long as the premiums are paid.

cash trading See **futures trading**.

cash up To total up receipts at closing time, the end of a shift, etc.

casualty insurance Insurance that protects the policyholder against losses resulting from accidents or from such disasters as fire, flood, and wind.

casualty loss A financial loss caused by an unexpected or unusual disaster, such as fire or flood.

catalyst A person who provokes or precipitates action without exercising direct control or influence over the outcome.

causal model A model used in business forecasting, as in regression analysis, that describes the reaction of a variable factor to changes in one or more explanatory variables.

cause-and-effect diagram A diagram that graphically shows the relationship between a problem and its major potential causes as well as the contributory causes: often used in an effort to improve quality.

caveat emptor (*Latin*) Let the buyer beware.

caveat venditor (*Latin*) Let the seller beware.

CD See **certificate of deposit**.

Celler-Kefauver Act An act of Congress passed in 1950 to close loopholes in the Clayton Act by forbidding mergers through the acquisition of a competitor's assets and by other means not covered by the Clayton Act, and authorizing the Federal Trade Commission to approve or deny proposed mergers before they occur.

centerfold Also called **center spread.** An advertisement or other material that occupies the two facing pages at the center of a magazine. See also **double-page spread; double-truck spread.**

central corporate expenses The overhead expenses of operating a corporate headquarters and its activities, exclusive of manufacturing overhead.

centralization Concentration of power in the hands of executives, who delegate only limited decision-making authority to lower-level managers.

centralized functional design An organizational design in which decision-making power is concentrated at the top of the system, with each department or division (e.g., marketing, production, sales, personnel) headed by an executive, usually a vice president, who is accountable to a chief executive officer, who in turn is responsible for strategic planning and coordination of the divisions or subsystems of the organization.

central limit theorem An important statistical theorem that the distribution of the sums of a large number of samples of random variables will, when plotted, fit a normal, or bell-shaped, curve, regardless of the type of distribution from which the samples were obtained.

central processing unit (*abbr* CPU) The main internal part of a computer, encompassing a control unit, an arithmetic-logic unit, and a main or internal memory, which controls all operations of the system, provides primary storage of data, and transfers data.

cents-off promotion A promotion of merchandise through a price reduction of less than $1, advertised on the product's package either alone or in combination with other advertising.

CEO chief executive officer (of a company).

Certificate in Management Accounting (*abbr* CMA) A certificate awarded by the National Association of Accountants' Institute of Management Accounting after the candidate has passed an examination and met other requirements.

certificate of deposit (*abbr* CD) A deposit account in a bank or savings and loan association, usually for a minimum of $1000 and with a maturity of from 30 days to several years, from which money usually cannot be withdrawn without loss of interest or other penalty and which earns interest at a rate established by law for accounts of less than $100,000 or at a rate that may be negotiable for larger accounts.

certificate of incorporation A document issued by a state government authorizing an organization to operate as a corporation.

certificate of indebtedness A note that specifies the amount of a debt and the time limit or repayment schedule.

certified check A depositor's check drawn on a bank and bearing the words "certified" or "accepted" and the signature of a bank official; in effect, the bank certifies that money to cover the check is on deposit and will be set aside until the check is presented by the payee. See also **cashier's check**.

certified financial statement A set of financial papers that generally carry a CPA's acknowledgment that they are fairly presented, usually as a result of extensive review and testing.

certified internal auditor (*abbr* CIA) An auditor who has satisfied the experience, ethics, educational, and examination requirements established by the Institute of Internal Auditors.

certified public accountant (*abbr* CPA) A person who has satisfied the requirements for education and/or experience established by the state in which he or she practices and who has passed the Uniform Certified Public Accountants' Examination and met other statutory requirements, and thus is authorized to express an audit opinion on the fairness of corporate financial statements and to perform other work reserved to CPAs.

CFO chief financial officer (of a company).

CFP Certified Financial Planner. See also **financial planner**.

chain of command The path of authority from the lowest-ranking worker to the highest-ranking supervisor/manager; a pattern of authority and responsibility.

chairman of the board The presiding officer of a corporation's board of directors, who manages its activities and delegates responsibilities to its top officers (i.e., the president and/or the chief executive officer), on either a full-time or a part-time basis.

change agent A person who is responsible for mobilizing an organization's resources; an expediter or facilitator.

channels of distribution The paths goods follow from the producer through intermediaries, if any, to the consumer, including all transportation systems and storage facilities used.

Chapter 11 A section of the Bankruptcy Reform Act of 1978, under which a company unable to pay its debts may petition a court for permission to retain its assets while reorganizing in an effort to regain profitability; continued failure to pay debts following reorganization may result in liquidation of the company by distribution of its assets first to its creditors and then, if any assets remain, to its common stockholders.

charge 1. (*bookkeeping*) **a.** A debit to an account. **b.** To enter such a debit. **2.** To buy on credit, thus incurring a debit in one's charge account in the seller's ledger.

charge and discharge statement A trustee or fiduciary's periodic report on the resources received and their disposition.

charge card See **credit card.**

charge off To treat what was originally assumed to be an asset as a loss or expense: usually an indication that the charge (debit) is not equal to its earlier stated value.

charismatic power Power derived from the ability to inspire and motivate by force of personality. See also **expert power; legitimate power.**

charter A written instrument of a state government granting an organization the rights, privileges, and immunities of a corporation. See also **articles of incorporation.**

chartered accountant (*abbr* CA) The British equivalent of the certified public accountant in the United States.

chartered financial analyst (*abbr* CFA) An individual who has passed a series of examinations and demonstrated expertise in securities investing.

chartered life underwriter (*abbr* CLU) An individual who has met the standards established by the American College of Life Underwriters.

chart of accounts A company's list of all bookkeeping accounts and their assigned codes.

chattel mortgage An agreement by which a car, truck, agricultural machine, or other movable equipment becomes collateral for a loan of money to purchase it; until or unless the lender must seize the property for nonpayment, the borrower retains ownership of it with attendant risk of damage or loss.

checking account A bank deposit against which checks can be drawn by the depositor. Cf. **savings account**.

checking copy A copy of a magazine supplied to an advertiser for the purpose of gaining approval of the position and appearance of the advertiser's ad.

checkoff The authorized withholding of union dues and assessments from employees' wages for transmittal to the union that represents them.

check register **1.** A written record of issued checks detailing check number, date, payee, amount, and purpose of payment, with a running balance maintained for the account. **2.** A format for the keeping of such records, as a series of check stubs or journals or a program for computer printouts.

cherry picking Selection by a buyer of only a few items out of a vendor's complete line.

chief executive officer (*abbr* CEO) A manager (usually chairman of the board or president) who occupies the most powerful position in a corporation, with responsibility for setting company policies under the guidance of the board of directors and for supervising the executives who carry out those policies.

chief financial officer (*abbr* CFO) The company executive empowered to make the financial decisions necessary to carry out company policy.

chief operating officer (*abbr* COO) A manager responsible for administering and supervising the day-to-day operations of a company under the direction of the chief executive officer and/or the board of directors.

chip Also called **microchip**. A tiny slice of semi-conducting material (usually silicon) on which an integrated circuit is formed.

chronological stabilization Also called **spread-loss plan**. Periodic repayment to an insurance company of a sum received under the terms of a policy; a method of risk management that allows an insurer to assume a higher degree of risk than would be the case under regular insurance.

churn (*stock market*) To trade a customer's securities excessively in order to earn more commissions.

CIF (*abbr for* cost, insurance, freight) An indication that the price quoted in a shipping contract includes the cost of freight and insurance until delivery at the port whence the goods will be shipped.

CIM See **computer-integrated manufacturing**.

circularization An auditor's confirmation of the validity of accounts payable and receivable by direct contact of customers and suppliers involved in those accounts.

circulation 1. The approximate number of copies of a newspaper or magazine that are distributed at each printing. 2. The number of homes in which a particular television show is regularly viewed.

civil action A lawsuit filed by an individual who seeks to recover damages resulting from an invasion of his or her personal rights.

Civil Aeronautics Administration (*abbr* CAA) A governmental agency established in 1940 to regulate nonmilitary aviation.

Civil Rights Act of 1964 Federal legislation enacted to promote equal opportunity by prohibiting discrimination against any individual on the basis of race, creed, or national origin.

claim 1. A demand for payment, reimbursement, or compensation, as under the terms of contract or an insurance policy. 2. A statement, usually included as the final paragraph of a patent specification, that clearly explains and describes the unique nature of an invention as created by the applicant, and which ultimately serves as the protection conferred by the patent.

classical administrative theory A theory of high-level management functions that emphasizes five fundamental components of managerial activity (planning, organizing, commanding, coordinating, controlling), each subdivided into a specialization of tasks, chain of command, unity of direction, tenure, and centralization of authority.

classical economics The economic concepts developed in 18th and 19th-century England by Adam Smith, David Ricardo, and John Stuart Mill, which constituted the first formulation of the capitalist system and were generally held in England and the United States until the Great Depression of the 1930s demonstrated a lack of correspondence between the theory and reality. See also **Keynesian economics.**

classical theory of motivation The theory that the individual worker is motivated primarily by money and therefore will perform tasks according to company standards only if payment is made contingent on performance.

classification 1. Collectively, all items of a given category or use or sharing common characteristics. **2.** A system, method, or act of categorizing.

classified ad Also called **classified advertisement, want ad.** A brief advertisement in a newspaper, magazine, or the like, dealing with offers of or requests for jobs, houses, apartments, used cars, etc.

Clayton Act An act of Congress passed in 1914 to discourage monopolies by declaring illegal such business practices as tying contracts, interlocking directorates, purchase of large quantities of a competitor's stock, and discriminatory pricing.

Clean Air Act Federal legislation enacted in 1970 to require emission controls on sources of air pollution and to establish air-quality standards that the states must meet within a specified time limit.

clearing account An account (e.g., an income summary account) in which money accumulates until it is transferred to another account (e.g., retained earnings) at the end of the fiscal year or accounting period.

clearinghouse An institution where representatives of member banks meet to exchange checks, drafts, notes, and other instruments drawn on each other's banks.

client bank A treasury of customers or users of one's services or products, related or unrelated, which encompasses the total inventory of accounts of the organization or individual providing such services or products.

client rough A preliminary layout of an ad or other promotional material that is shown to a client for approval before the material is prepared in final form.

client system A system (organization, unit, group) that is the object of a change strategy by a consultant or other professional.

close 1. The end of the selling process; the conversion of a prospect into a customer. See also **objection. 2.** To finalize the transaction in which a property is sold to a new owner.

closed corporation A corporation owned by a few individuals who seldom sell their stock and so retain control.

closed display A merchandising display case, usually covered by glass, that permits no access to goods by customers. See also **open display.**

closed-end credit 1. Credit, such as a bank loan, that is limited to a specified amount, so that any further money sought can be obtained only in the form of a new loan. **2.** A loan payable in monthly installments or by a specified date. See also **open-end credit.**

closed-end investment company An investment company that is capitalized by a public offering of usually common stock, which is traded on an exchange or over the counter. See also **open-end investment company.**

closed-end mortgage bond A corporate bond backed by property that is guaranteed not to back another bond issue or otherwise be used as collateral. See also **open-end mortgage bond.**

closed shop A place of business where by agreement with a union the employer hires only union members and keeps in employment only union members in good standing (illegal under the provisions of the Taft-Hartley Act). See also **union shop.**

closed system A method of decision making that takes into account only the system under observation, without regard to the influence of environmental factors on its activity.

closely held Referring to a corporation whose

stock is held by a few individuals. See also **closed corporation.**

closing 1. The accounting activities performed at the end of a period of time, generally one year, including the preparation of closing entries and financial statements. **2.** The final act in securing a sale or purchase: the delivery of final payments and the transfer of title.

closing date 1. The latest date on which an advertisement can arrive at a publisher or broadcaster to be eligible for appearance in the next scheduled issue or program. **2.** The date on which a real estate transaction is to be finalized.

closing inventory See **ending inventory.**

closure 1. An act or instance of finishing or bringing to a conclusion. **2.** Perception of incomplete figures, objects, or situations as though they were complete by the process of ignoring missing parts or filling them in from experience, whether consciously or unconsciously; a manifestation of the human tendency to seek wholeness.

cluster analysis A marketing procedure involving the sorting through of quantities of information on consumer behavior and the grouping of similar behaviors and attitudes in regard to a product, with the object of identifying patterns that may indicate typical responses to a product among various population segments.

cluster sampling A random sampling method involving the grouping (clustering) of items according to time period, type, or some other identifiable characteristic, the random selection of some of those clusters, and the subsequent analysis or examination of the clusters chosen.

CMA See **Certificate in Management Accounting.**

coalition bargaining Negotiation with an employer by two or more unions acting in concert, with the expectation that together they will have greater bargaining strength than any one of them alone.

COBOL (*acronym for* Common Business-Oriented Language) A computer programming language that uses common English business terms. See also **BASIC.**

COBRA (*acronym for* Consolidated Omnibus

Budget Reconciliation Act) See **continuation of benefits.**

c.o.d. (*abbr for cash on delivery*) A method of purchasing goods whereby the customer agrees to pay for the purchase in full when it is delivered.

codetermination Participation by workers in such decision-making activities as planning for modernization and expansion, selection of production methods, hiring and firing of management personnel, and planning of mergers, layoffs, investments, and declaration of dividends.

codicil A formal addendum to a legal document, usually a will, which may take the form of an addition to the original document or a separate paper, and which must be developed with all the formalities of the original document.

coercive power The capacity to dominate others by controlling punishment, withholding information or membership, and demoting or firing.

coercive reward and punishment system A motivational technique that employs coercion in the form of punishment for objectionable behavior and rewards for acceptable behavior. See also **behavior modification.**

c.o.g. (*abbr for customer-owned goods*) Goods already paid for.

cognitive approach An approach to the acquisition of knowledge characterized by the gathering of facts and the application of logic.

cognitive dissonance Incongruity between two related perceptions or opinions, resulting in a state of tension that the individual tries to reduce by altering one of the perceptions.

cognitive style A style of learning based on teacher-directed activities, lectures, and readings. See also **experimental learning.**

coinsurance **1.** A form of casualty insurance in which the insured is required to maintain coverage on the property insured at a certain minimum percentage of its estimated replacement value in order to avoid a penalty in the event of loss. **2.** The percentage of total property value covered by fire insurance, agreed upon and maintained by the insured, which the insurer will pay in the event of loss by fire. **3.** A form of major medical insurance in which payments for hospital and medical treatment for illness or injury are shared by the insurer and the insured in a prescribed ratio.

COLA (*acronym for* cost-of-living *a*djustment) See **cost-of-living escalator.**

cold call A visit or phone call to a prospective customer without an appointment or a previous introduction.

cold canvassing Systematic coverage by cold calls of a geographical area by a salesperson.

Colgate doctrine A Supreme Court decision incorporated in the Robinson-Patman Act (1936), acknowledging the seller's right to conduct business or to refuse to conduct business with any dealer or other person.

collar (*stock exchange slang*) Official restrictions imposed on computerized program trading when the Dow Jones rises or falls 50 points or more in one day's trading.

collateral Also called **collateral security.** An asset that a lender is entitled by law to seize from a borrower if the loan is not repaid in accordance with the terms agreed upon.

collection 1. The presentation of a draft, check, etc., for payment. **2.** The process of receiving or compelling payment of a debt.

collective bargaining Negotiation by representatives of an employer and a union of the terms of a contract covering wages and working conditions of union members.

comaker A person who formally agrees to repay a loan made to another person if the borrower fails to pay.

COMEX Commodity Exchange, New York.

comfort letter A CPA's letter to an underwriter or legal counsel attesting that financial statements submitted in regard to a securities offering are not false or misleading.

commercial See **announcement.**

commercial bank A bank chartered by a state government or by the federal government to offer a full range of financial services, including checking and savings accounts, short-term business and personal loans, foreign currency exchange, and the discounting of promissory notes and drafts.

commercial goods Goods and services used by companies in carrying on their businesses.

commercial paper 1. Collectively, negotiable instruments in the form of drafts or notes. **2.** Collectively, short-term notes with maturities of less than a year, usually in amounts of $15,000 or more, issued by corporations to provide working capital and purchasable at a discount (below face value) or on an interest-bearing basis and sellable before maturity.

commercial paper house A company that buys commercial paper from corporations for resale, either on order from a customer or on its own account.

commercial protection See **product protection.**

commission A percentage of the price charged for a good or service paid to a salesperson or agent.

commission house An agency that negotiates the sale of goods and receives payment on the basis of volume of goods sold.

committed cost The fixed, long-term cost incurred when an asset is bought, leased, or modified, which cannot be readily reduced or liquidated and is not affected by short-term fluctuations in production levels.

committee An advisory group, ideally made up of people with a vested interest in the organization, responsible for identifying the needs of a unit or subsystem. See also **ad hoc committee.**

committee buying Selection of merchandise to be ordered for sale in a retail store by a group rather than by an individual buyer. See also **buying committee.**

committee organization An organizational structure in which authority and responsibility are held jointly by a group, usually consisting of high-level officers of the corporation, rather than by one executive.

Commodities Futures Trading Commission (*abbr* CFTC) An independent federal agency that regulates the commodities futures markets in the United States.

commodity A product of agriculture, animal husbandry, lumbering, or mining, in contrast to services, and usually excluding manufacturing.

commodity approach A method of studying marketing that focuses on the means by which products move from producers to consumers. See also **functional approach; institutional approach.**

commodity exchange A trading facility similar to a stock exchange, such as the Chicago Board of Trade or the New York Mercantile Exchange, where members meet to trade commodities up to a year or more in advance of their delivery dates.

common carrier A company that offers transportation services for goods or people to the general public at uniform rates.

common cost See **joint cost.**

common law The system of unwritten law governing the rights and duties of individuals, based on principles established by judicial decisions, such that all new decisions or interpretations set precedents for future decisions, but which in the absence of a precedent is capable of being modified and adapted to new circumstances. See also **public law.**

common market 1. An economic alliance that provides for common tariffs and attempts to bring the trade rules of all participating governments into agreement. **2. Common Market** See **European Economic Community.**

common share See **common stock.**

common-size statement A financial statement in which amounts are expressed in percentages of some base figure, usually total assets or revenues, which is listed as equaling 100 percent.

common stock Stock issued by a corporation with no guarantee of dividends, which if declared are distributed after the holders of preferred stock have received their guaranteed share of corporate profits, but with the right to vote on matters presented at the corporation's annual meeting. See also **preferred stock.**

common stock fund A mutual fund that invests only in common stock, as a result of either a decision made or a policy set forth in its charter.

community-planning legislation Legislation empowering a local government to develop and implement plans to control community growth.

comp (*abbr for comp*rehensive layout) A presumably final version of a printed advertisement presented to the client for approval.

company loan A loan or guarantee of a bank loan, often at a low interest rate and with generous repayment terms, made by a company to an executive, usually to enable the executive to exercise a stock option.

company-sponsored tax shelter A limited partnership organized usually by a privately held company to provide its executives with a means of sheltering income from taxes.

comparable worth The belief or practice that (1) employees having identical responsibilities or performing identical tasks should receive comparable or identical wages, and (2) that women should receive comparable wages to men for the same work. See also **two-tier wage plan.**

comparative advantage theory A theory of foreign trade that holds that all trading partners would benefit if each country were to specialize in the products that it can produce most cheaply (those in which it has a comparative advantage) and trade them for the specialized products of other nations (in which they have a comparative advantage).

comparative financial statement A comprehensive financial statement that provides detailed figures for both the current and preceding periods, so that they may be compared. See also **historical summary.**

compensating balance The minimum amount of a line of credit that a customer of a bank is expected to maintain.

compensation A benefit in the form of money or an equivalent beyond the basic salary or wage paid for time on the job (e.g., employee services, health insurance, time off with pay, retirement benefits).

competition Also called **competitive market.** A market condition in which a large number of independent buyers and sellers vie with each other for identical goods and services, trade with each other without restriction, and freely enter and leave the market.

compiler A computer translation program that

converts programs from the programmer's language (e.g., BASIC, FORTRAN) into a language of binary numbers (machine language).

complementary products Products that are generally used in combination (e.g., shampoo and hair conditioner, razors and blades).

completed-contract method An accounting method in which the profits from a long-term project are not entered on the books until the project is completed.

composite estimate A prediction of total sales based on the collective estimates of all district managers, each assessing future sales in his or her own territory on the basis of past events. See also **correlation; time series analysis.**

compound interest Interest calculated on the basis of principal plus interest previously credited.

compound journal entry A journal entry that requires more than one debit and one credit, as in the instance of revenue received partly in cash and partly in securities.

comprehensive advertising Advertising in which the advertised brand is compared with competitive brands.

comprehensive insurance Insurance that covers loss of or damage (e.g., to a motor vehicle) as a result of theft, fire, flood, windstorm, vandalism, rain, or lightning.

comprehensive major medical insurance Employee health insurance characterized by high maximum benefits, a low deductible, and a coinsurance feature.

comp time Time off from work, granted to an employee in lieu of overtime pay; compensatory time.

comptroller See controller.

compulsory arbitration Mediation of a labor dispute, initiated by the federal government or another outside agency with the power to require both labor and management to accept the arbitrator's decisions. See also **arbitration.**

computer A complex electronic machine that can be programmed to perform computations and to analyze, sort, compare, store, and edit huge quantities of information. See also **hardware; software.**

computer-aided design (*abbr* CAD) The use of computers, especially computer graphics, to develop new products, packaging, manufacturing processes, etc.

computer-aided manufacturing (*abbr* CAM) The use of computers in the manufacturing process, especially to control the operation of an assembly line. See also **robotics**.

computer-assisted fraud (*abbr* CAF) Illegal entry into and use of a confidential data base. See also **fraud**.

computer graphics Images created on a display screen by the use of a computer linked with additional electronic devices.

computer-integrated manufacturing (*abbr* CIM) The use of computers to control, on a real-time basis, the complete manufacturing cycle, including design, planning, and manufacture.

computer-output microfilm (*abbr* COM) Microfilm in either roll or card form on which materials are printed by computer to reduce the amount of space required to store them.

COMSAT (*acronym for Com*munications and *Sat*ellite *Corporation*) A cooperative communications network of businesspeople who supply management and satellite expertise to government representatives upon request.

concentration A clustering of production plants, factories, or warehouses within a designated geographical area. See also **dispersion**.

conciliation Intervention in a labor dispute by a third party who has no power to compel the opposing parties to reach agreement but relies on persuasion.

conditional sale A sale that is subject to the fulfillment of a stated condition (e.g., full payment of the selling price) before title to the merchandise is passed from seller to buyer.

condition precedent A condition that must be fulfilled before title to merchandise can pass from seller to buyer.

condition subsequent A condition that must be fulfilled after title to merchandise has passed from seller to buyer (e.g., a warranty).

condominium 1. An apartment house, office

building, or other multiple-unit complex, the units of which are individually owned, with each owner receiving a deed to the unit purchased, including the right to sell or mortgage that unit, and sharing in joint ownership of any common grounds, passageways, etc. **2.** A unit in such a building.

conduit A channel through which something is transmitted, such as untaxed dividends passed along to investors by an investment organization. Fannie Mae Remics, for example, are "real estate mortgage-investment conduits."

conference call A telephone call that interconnects three or more phones simultaneously.

confidential disclosure Divulgation of information under the terms of a disclosure agreement.

confirmation A detailed description of the terms of a securities transaction supplied by a broker to a customer.

conflict management Judicious use of disagreements between individuals or factions to produce beneficial results in place of an attempt to eliminate disagreement.

conflict resolution Management of interpersonal conflict by either (*a*) adoption of a passive role, (*b*) facilitation of a win-lose situation, or (*c*) facilitation of a win-win or integrative solution.

confrontation Face-to-face opposition as a method of resolving an issue or difference.

conglomerate A corporation made up of companies that produce significant quantities of output in several industries.

conglomerate merger Absorption by a corporation of another in an industry distinct from that of the parent company.

Congress of Industrial Organizations (*abbr* CIO) A national federation of labor unions organized according to industry, formed in 1935 by a dissident faction of the American Federation of Labor to represent unskilled and semiskilled workers; merged with the AFL in 1955 to become the AFL-CIO.

congruent innovation Also called **me-too.** Imitation of an innovation already introduced.

connect time The time that elapses between the

signing on of a computer user and the moment of that user's signing off.

consent order An order issued by a government agency by whose terms a respondent agrees not to engage in a specified business practice proscribed by statute and/or regulation, without admitting to having actually engaged in such activities previously.

conservative focus An orientation to problem solving characterized by a tendency to identify alternative solutions to a problem one at a time and to alter one's views accordingly.

consideration Anything of value, including the relinquishing of a legal right, exchanged as a binder between parties to a contract.

consignment A quantity of goods delivered to a dealer with the agreement that title remains with the shipper until the goods are sold and that the dealer will remit the proceeds of sales less a commission and return goods unsold.

consolidated financial statement A financial statement in which information in regard to a parent company and its subsidiaries is presented as a unified whole, with like accounts combined and some eliminated as balances offset each other.

consolidation The combining of the accounts of a parent company and all subsidiaries into a consolidated financial statement.

consortium An international business or banking combination organized to carry out a large project.

conspicuous consumption The purchase of goods and services well beyond basic material needs.

constant dollars Current dollars valued as a percentage of their buying power in a specified previous year, as determined by the net change in the consumer price index.

constraint Any restriction imposed on the decision-making process that eliminates certain alternatives. See also **feasible solution.**

constructive receipt A ruling by the Internal Revenue Service specifying that receivable but unreceived income (e.g., reinvested dividends from mutual funds) is taxable in the year in which it could have been received if the taxpayer had elected to receive it.

consultant See **external consultant; internal consultant.**

consultative leadership Also called **system 3 management.** A leadership style characterized by discussion with subordinates for the purpose of giving them a sense of responsibility for productivity and decision making.

consumer advisory board A group of consumers whose opinions and advice are sought by a company in the early stages of marketing a new product or service, which need not be of potential use or interest to the consumers consulted. See also **consumer panel; idea-development interview.**

consumer credit Credit extended to an individual for the purchase of personal products or services.

Consumer Credit Protection Act Federal legislation that releases consumers from obligations under contracts with obscure credit terms and affords other protections of their rights.

consumer jury See **consumer panel.**

consumer movement Also called **consumerism.** A movement begun in the 1960s for passage of laws to protect consumers against unsafe and misrepresented products, unfair and misrepresented credit terms, and other business abuses. See also **consumer rights.**

consumer-oriented marketing See **target marketing.**

consumer panel A carefully selected group of people, representative of a population of potential users of a product or service, who are hired on an ad hoc basis to help advertising and marketing research companies pretest and evaluate products or ads before they are presented to the public.

consumer price index (*abbr* CPI) Also called **cost-of-living index.** An index issued periodically by the Bureau of Labor Statistics that expresses the cost of goods and services purchased by typical wage earners as a percentage of the cost of the same goods and services in some base period.

Consumer Product Safety Act Federal legislation enacted in 1972 requiring that manufacturers (1) have documented proof that their products have been tested for reliability before being placed on the market, (2) have means of recalling their products if necessary, and (3) reply to valid customer complaints.

Consumer Product Warranties Act See **Magnuson-Moss Act.**

consumer rights A concept, put forward by President John F. Kennedy and subsequently enacted into law by Congress, that encompasses consumers' rights to safety, to be heard, to choose, and to be informed. See also **Consumer Product Safety Act; Magnuson-Moss Act; Truth-in-Lending Act; Wheeler-Lea Act.**

consumer sovereignty The economic power exercised by consumers in the marketplace by virtue of their ability to select or reject products and services.

consumer's risk The risk run by a consumer that a defective item from a lot will be accidentally purchased. See also **producer's risk.**

contact person See **account executive.**

containerization Packaging of goods in sealed containers before shipment for the purpose of minimizing damage and transportation costs. See also **birdyback; fishyback; piggyback.**

contingency approach A method of analyzing the activity of an organization that focuses on the causal relationships of four factors: (*a*) the degree of openness of the system, (*b*) the system as the sum of its parts, (*c*) the boundaries of the system, and (*d*) the various paths by which the system can reach its goals.

contingency management See **situational management.**

contingency theory An organizational theory that seeks to explain the idiosyncratic nature of each organization's response to similar situations by focusing on organizational patterns and the degree to which management methods are appropriate to specific situations.

contingent business-interruption insurance Insurance that covers the risk of a business loss resulting from interruption in the delivery of supplies necessary to the conduct of business.

contingent liability A possible or likely liability that will be incurred only in the event of some specific occurrence (e.g., an unfavorable court decision) and that is noted in parentheses or footnoted in financial statements but is not added to total liabilities unless the unfavorable event is fully expected to occur.

continuation of benefits The right of an employee and his or her spouse and dependents to continue participation in an employee health plan after coverage has been terminated due to layoff, divorce, etc. This right was conferred by a federal law commonly referred to by the acronym COBRA, which stands for Consolidated Omnibus Budget Reconciliation Act.

continuous compounding The calculation of compound interest on an ongoing basis rather than at specific points in time. See also **compound interest; discrete compounding.**

continuous innovation A gradual improvement in a product already in the marketplace, usually with little measurable effect on established buying patterns.

continuous inventory See **perpetual inventory.**

continuous process A production operation that turns out finished products with little or no change in procedures or equipment over a period of days, months, or years, as in the production of steel and the refining of petroleum.

contra account A separate bookkeeping account in which sums are accumulated for eventual subtraction (deduction) from a main account, with attendant elimination of the need for constant subtractions from the main account (e.g., discounts on bonds payable, allowance for doubtful accounts, accumulated depreciation).

contra asset An account balance that is deducted from an asset account to arrive at a net book value.

contract A legally enforceable agreement, either oral or in writing, between two or more mentally competent adults, one or more of whom voluntarily accept a legitimate offer voluntarily made, and who exchange something of value (e.g., money, goods, services, or the relinquishing of a legal right).

contract carrier A person or company that enters into a contract with an individual shipper or other person to transport goods or people.

contraction 1. A restriction or withdrawal of currency or funds available to be lent. **2.** A decrease in economic and industrial activity.

contracts administration Management of purchase orders and other contracts involved in procurement, including maintenance of contract files and oversight of the carrying out of the terms of such agreements.

contract to sell A contract to sell goods at a future date. See also **future goods.**

contractual liability An obligation assumed under the terms of a contract.

contrarian A person who rejects the majority opinion. This term is often applied to an investor who buys when others are selling, and vice versa.

contributed capital See **paid-in capital.**

contribution income statement An operations report in which the contribution margin is determined by subtraction of variable costs from revenues and the further subtraction of fixed costs to yield net income.

contribution margin The amount by which the revenues of a given company, branch, department, or project exceed its total variable costs; the unit's contributions to profit and fixed costs.

contributory pension plan A pension plan financed by contributions from both employees and employer. See also **noncontributory pension plan.**

control account An account that contains the total of transactions that are recorded in detail in a subsidiary ledger (e.g., the accounts receivable account contains the total of the balances of all subsidiary accounts receivable).

control chart A graph used for plotting the measured quality of samples of completed work and comparing these observed quality levels against predetermined limits (**control limits**) to decide whether the process quality is acceptable or indicates the need for corrective action.

controllable cost A cost that to some extent is under the control of a manager or otherwise affected by the way business operations are conducted.

controlled-circulation publication A periodical publication consisting of no less than 25 percent editorial material sent free of charge to members of an association by virtue of their paid membership.

controller Also called **comptroller.** The chief accounting officer or financial vice president of a company, in charge of designing and directing the accounting information system, including such matters as internal control, cost accounting, financial accounting, tax planning, and financial reporting.

control limits See control chart.

controlling interest Ownership of enough stock in a company to exert control over policy and management.

convenience goods Products, generally moderately priced, that can frequently be purchased in conveniently located outlets (convenience stores).

convergent marketing The marketing of all of a company's products by a single marketing team. See also **divergent marketing.**

convertible bond A corporate bond that the holder can at any time exchange for shares of the corporation's common stock at a specified ratio of shares per bond.

convertible preferred stock Preferred stock that the holder can at any time exchange for shares of the corporation's common stock at a specified ratio.

COO chief operating officer (of a company).

cooling-off law An FTC ruling that allows customers to cancel sales contracts with door-to-door salespeople within three days.

cooling-off period 1. A period of 80 days during which, under the terms of the Taft-Hartley Act, a strike that endangers the national health or safety may be halted by an injunction obtained by the president of the United States. **2.** A period of 60 days following submission by an employer or a union of a notice of termination of contract, mandated by the TaftHartley Act, before a strike or lockout may be called.

co-op See cooperative.

cooperative 1. An association of people or small

companies, predominantly in the agricultural field, who join together in order to increase their bargaining power in the marketplace and divide profits among members. **2.** Also called **co-op.** A building or apartment owned and managed by a corporation in which shares are sold, entitling the shareholders to occupy individual units in the building.

cooperative advertising Also called **dealer tie-in.** The sharing by local merchants and national advertisers of the costs of product promotions appearing locally.

cooperative buying Purchasing by customers or buyers who have joined together to increase their bargaining power.

copay Also called **copayment.** A fixed amount, or a percentage of the usual and customary fee for a medical service, required by a health insurer to be paid by the patient to the health-care provider.

coping behavior Behavioral adjustment to an unsatisfied need, usually in the form of a trial-and-error search for an alternative goal that is more realistically attainable than that to which access has been blocked.

copy 1. The part of an advertisement that delivers the advertiser's message, exclusive of illustrations. **2.** See **transfer** (def. 4).

copyright Legal protection offered for a fee by the Library of Congress to the creator of any printed, taped, filmed, or recorded material against infringement of the exclusive right of the creator or of his or her heirs to copy or adapt the material during the creator's lifetime and for fifty years thereafter.

copywriter A writer of copy for advertisements, news releases, etc.

corporate bond A promissory note issued by a corporation, usually in multiples of $1000 and yielding a specified rate of interest until a specified expiration date, at which time the corporation must return the loan represented by the bond. See also **bond** (def. 1); **convertible bond; coupon bond; government bond; municipal bond.**

corporate purpose A corporation's stated goals, objectives, quality of management, community responsibility, and manner of doing business.

corporate raider See raider.

corporate welfare Financial assistance, as tax breaks or subsidies, given by the government esp. to large companies.

corporation An entity formed and authorized by a state charter to act as an individual (i.e., to own, buy, and sell property, to enter into contracts, and to sue and be sued), with the right of succession; to issue shares of stock, which represent shares of ownership of the corporation; and to have legal liability for damages and debt only to the limit of the stockholders' investments.

correction A reversal of the trend of stock prices, especially temporarily, as after a sharp advance or decline in the previous trading sessions.

correlation The relationship or interdependence between two random variables, used in predicting or forecasting events.

correspondent bank A bank that acts on behalf of another bank in a business transaction.

cost A (usually initial or long-term) payment or sacrifice, direct or indirect, tangible or intangible, that is incurred or will be incurred to acquire, produce, or provide goods or services. See also **acquisition cost; expense; fixed cost; incremental cost.**

cost accounting 1. A branch of management accounting that clarifies, summarizes, measures, accumulates, controls, allocates, and reports on current or predicted costs, especially those of production. **2.** The recording, reporting, and allocation of current and forecast expenses for labor, equipment, supplies, and utilities.

cost basis The original cost of an asset, used in calculating depreciation and capital gains or losses.

cost-benefit analysis A financial management technique developed to explore alternative courses of action in order to determine the one that will produce the optimum benefit at the minimum cost.

cost-benefit worksheet A worksheet used by a project team to compute the costs and benefits of its recommendations in regard to materials, work force, machines, reduction of error, time needed for processing, etc.

cost center A part of a company (division, department, branch, plant, territory, project, product) that is important enough to accumulate its own accountable costs.

cost depletion The depletion of a natural resource calculated by multiplying the estimated total value of the resource by a fraction representing the amount consumed during a certain period. See also **percentage depletion.**

cost-effective Also called **cost-efficient.** Producing benefits or revenues in excess of the total cost.

costly time Work time for which the employer must pay a premium wage or otherwise divert resources in order to complete a task. See also **crash time; expediting time.**

cost of goods manufactured The total cost of producing goods during a certain accounting period, including materials, labor, and overhead, but excluding the ending work-in-progress inventory.

cost of goods sold The sum of all expenses incurred in the manufacturing and/or purchasing and selling of goods that were actually sold during an accounting period, calculated by adding beginning inventory and cost of goods purchased or manufactured and from that sum subtracting ending inventory adjustment.

cost-of-living escalator Also called **COLA** (*cost-of-living adjustment*). A clause in a union contract guaranteeing that wages will be adjusted to reflect changes in the consumer price index whenever inflation reaches a specified rate, so that employees' buying power will be maintained.

cost-of-living index See **consumer price index.**

cost overrun Cost in excess of that originally estimated or budgeted, especially in a government contract. Often caused by delays in starting, resulting in higher costs of labor, materials, etc. Such costs are usually borne by the client.

cost per minute (*abbr* cpm) The cost charged advertisers per 1000 viewers of a television program or 1000 listeners to a radio program divided by the number of minutes of commercial time made available on the program.

cost per thousand (*abbr* cpt) The cost charged advertisers for each 1000 homes reached by a television or radio program or for each 1000 copies of a publication distributed.

cost-plus pricing The practice of basing the selling price of an item on its cost plus a percentage of that cost, so as to recover selling expenses and make a reasonable profit.

cost-push inflation Inflation due to increased production costs, such as labor and parts, although demand remains the same. See also **demand-pull inflation.**

cost sheet See **job cost sheet.**

cost trade-off The allocation of more money for some marketing activities than for others, with the goal of creating the most effective overall campaign.

cost-volume-profit analysis (*abbr* CVP analysis) A form of break-even analysis in which the effect on cost of changes in volume are compared with consequent changes in profit: done for the purpose of evaluating the possibility of a change of price, introducing a new product, or expanding capacity or sales territory.

Council of Economic Advisers (*abbr* CEA) A group of economists who advise the President of the United States on matters pertaining to the economy.

counteradvertising FTC-approved advertising by a public group warning consumers of potential harm that can result from the use of a product or class of products.

counterdependent One who continually resists the authority and leadership of others, creating a lack of unity in an organization or subsystem.

countervailing powers Two opposing authorities (as of big business, labor, or government) that are equally strong and mutually influential.

coupon bond A corporate bond from which coupons entitling the bearer to payment of interest may be detached for presentation to the issuing company at the specified time.

couponing The practice of offering a discount on or partial refund of the purchase price of a product upon presentation of a coupon clipped from a publication, received through the mail, or acquired with a previous purchase.

coupon rate The rate of interest designated on a bond certificate.

covenant A provision or reservation specified in a

legal agreement restricting the actions of one or both parties.

CPA See **certified public accountant.**

CPI See **consumer price index.**

cpm See **cost per minute.**

cpt See **cost per thousand.**

CPU See **central processing unit.**

craft union A labor union that represents skilled artisans of a particular trade, who band together to establish a fair price for their services, regulate working hours, and restrict entry into the trade in order to maximize their bargaining power.

crash A sudden general collapse of a business enterprise, the stock market, etc.

crashing Shortening the time it takes to complete an activity by assigning additional resources to it.

crash time Also called **red rush.** Work time during which a product or service is rushed to completion with special handling or attention.

credit 1. The dollar amount of goods or services a person may receive for payment in the future. See also **closed-end credit; line of credit; open-end credit. 2.** The balance in a person's account. **3.** An amount of money placed at a person's disposal by a bank or other lending institution. **4.** (*abbr* cr.) An entry on the right side of a balance sheet, indicating a decrease in assets (in asset accounting) or an increase in equity (in equity accounting). See also **debit.**

credit balance 1. An excess of credits over debits in an account. **2.** The amount by which the sum of credit entries in an account exceeds the sum of debit entries in that account. See also **debit balance.**

credit card A plastic card bearing a customer's name and account number and usually an expiration date evidencing a firm's willingness to extend credit to the customer named for the purchase of goods or services.

credit life insurance Insurance on the life of a borrower that guarantees payment of the amount due on a loan installment contract in the event of the borrower's death.

credit line 1. A line of type accompanying a photograph, illustration, published article, or television program acknowledging its source. **2.** See also **line of credit.**

creditor An individual or organization that is owed money by a borrower or customer.

credit rating An estimate of the amount of credit that may safely be extended to an individual or a company, usually made by an agency that specializes in such services on the basis of financial resources and responsibilities and history of repayment of past loans.

credit sale A sale of goods or services for which the purchaser agrees to pay in the future in accordance with specified terms.

credit union A cooperative group that makes loans to its members at low rates of interest.

crime insurance Insurance that covers losses resulting from the commission of a crime by a person other than the insured.

criminal law The body of laws and court decisions dealing with violations of public law.

crisis management The techniques used to deal with or avert crisis situations, especially strikes or violence.

critical incident An incident or experience that constitutes a turning point in one's life or way of thinking about a subject (the recall and description of which are thought to be helpful in management training). See also **incident pattern.**

critical path Also called **critical activity.** The order of operations in a manufacturing process, usually expressed in a diagram using arrows to indicate the flow: used as a basis for scheduling. See also **PERT.**

critical path method (*abbr* CPM) A project-planning method by which the sequence of activities involved in a planned project is plotted and timed for the purpose of determining the minimum time the project can be expected to require for completion.

cross-elasticity of demand A relationship between two products, often those that are substitutes for each other, such that a change in the price of one product affects the sales of the other.

crossfoot To add figures across a row rather than up and down. See also **foot.**

cross-ruff promotion A coupon, premium, or cents-off promotion in which products of two or more companies are promoted jointly.

cross-train To train (an employee) to be proficient at different, usually related, skills, tasks, etc.

culture The body of beliefs, attitudes, values, patterns of behavior, social forms, language, and material adjuncts of a social group; by extension, the consistent habits, values, and customs of an organizational environment.

cum dividend With dividend: applied to shares of stock traded when payment of a declared dividend is pending, indicating that the price of the stock includes the value of the declared dividend, to which the buyer is entitled. See also **ex dividend.**

Cummins Amendment An amendment to the Interstate Commerce Act of 1877, affecting the liability of carriers for loss or damage of freight transported across state lines.

cumulative preferred stock Stock that carries with it a guarantee that in the event that a dividend is not declared in any year, such dividend will be added to the next dividend declared and paid before the holders of common stock receive any dividend.

cumulative voting 1. The practice of combining stockholders' votes in elections of members of a board of directors, thus increasing the influence of small holders. **2.** The practice (required in 22 states and permissible in 18 others) of multiplying the number of shares owned by one stockholder by the total number of candidates for membership in a board of directors to determine the number of votes that may be cast by the stockholder, who may divide them among the candidates in any proportion he or she wishes or cast them all for one candidate.

current assets All assets currently owned, including cash and that which can or will become cash within a year (e.g., cash on hand and in checking and savings accounts, inventories, prepaid expenses, marketable securities, accounts receivable, notes receivable).

current liabilities Money owed by a company and payable within one year.

current ratio Current assets divided by current liabilities; a rough indication of a company's ability to meet its obligations. See also **liquidity ratio.**

current value 1. The value of an asset estimated by reference to recent transactions involving similar assets, as by reference to market value or replacement cost. **2.** The value of a long-term asset or inventory calculated as replacement cost multiplied by the fraction of acquisition cost not yet depreciated.

current yield The ratio of the annual interest or dividend to the actual market price of a bond or stock.

curriculum vitae (*abbr* CV) See **résumé.**

custodian A bank or corporation authorized to safeguard the securities and other properties of an investment portfolio.

customer A person who buys or leases some product or employs some service, especially one who does so frequently or regularly.

customer's man See **broker** (def. 1).

custom manufacturing The production of goods in accordance with customers' orders, with resultant short production runs and frequent shutdown of machinery. See also **assemble-to-order; intermittent process; make-to-order.**

customs Duties or taxes imposed by a government on goods imported from foreign countries.

customs union An economic alliance of nations that establish a free-trade area for members and place uniform tariffs on trade with nonmember nations.

cutoff test An audit procedure to ascertain whether transactions executed shortly before or after the closing of an accounting period have been recorded consistently and in the correct period.

CV See **curriculum vitae.**

CVP analysis See **cost-volume-profit analysis.**

cybernetics The study of control systems, especially the analogy between human reasoning processes and mechanical and electronic systems designed to replace them.

cycle billing The practice of billing a portion of a firm's customers on each working day of the month, the specific day for each customer being determined by the initial of the last name, to equalize the work involved.

cycle stock Inventory resulting from periodic replenishment or production of an item in batches or lots.

cycle time The time allotted to each work station on an assembly line to perform the assigned tasks for each successive unit.

cyclical stock A security that rises and falls in value in accordance with business fluctuations.

cyclical unemployment Unemployment attributable to a temporary disruption of the economy (as during the energy crisis of the 1970s) or to a low level of aggregate demand (as during a recession).

cyclical variation A fluctuation in business conditions seen as part of a recurrent cycle characterized by initial prosperity followed by crisis, recession, and recovery.

D

data (*Latin, plural; sing. datum*) Individual facts, statistics, or items of information. See **primary data; secondary data**.

database **1.** A body of information, usually factual and from a primary source, which serves as a foundation for future decisions, discussions, or operations. **2.** Also called **data bank**. Information entered and stored in a computer to serve as the primary data source for other operations.

data-based intervention Also called **action research**. The gathering and evaluation of information for the purpose of formulating appropriate plans to improve the operations of an organization.

database management system (*abbr DBMS*) A set of software programs for controlling the storage, retrieval, and modification of organized data in a computerized database.

DBMS See **database management system**.

DDB See **double-declining-balance depreciation**.

dead-cat bounce (*slang*) A temporary recovery in stock prices after a steep decline, often resulting from the purchase of securities that have been sold short.

deadhead To move an empty truck, rail car, airplane, or the like, to a destination to pick up freight, passengers, etc.

deadline A time limit set on the completion of a project; the time by which a product must be finished or material for publication must reach the publisher. See also **closing date** (def. 1).

dealer brand See **private brand**.

dealer tie-in See **cooperative advertising**.

death benefit **1.** An amount of money paid to a beneficiary upon the death of a person covered by life insurance. **2.** An amount of money paid from Social Security funds to a spouse or child to help pay for the funeral expenses of a person who has been receiving Social Security benefits.

debenture A corporate bond or long-term loan that is secured only by the general credit rating of the issuing company. See also **mortgage bond**.

debit (*abbr dr.*) An entry on the left side of a balance sheet, indicating an increase in assets or expenses and a decrease in liabilities or income accounts (depending on the accounting system used). See also **credit.**

debit balance 1. An excess of debits over credits in an account. **2.** The amount by which the total debits in an account exceed the sum of the credits in that account (asset, expense, and some contra accounts normally have debit balances). See also **credit balance.**

debit card A plastic card through which payments for purchases are made electronically from the bank account of the cardholder.

debt See **liability.**

debt capital Capital raised by the sale of bonds or the borrowing of money. See also **equity capital.**

debt-equity ratio The ratio of either total liabilities or long-term debt (depending on context) to owners' equity: an indication of the extent to which investors or lenders are financing a company's assets.

debtor An individual or organization that is obligated either to repay money borrowed or to make payment for goods or services received on credit.

debt-service cost The amount that must be paid annually for the use of borrowed money, including interest, required payments of principal, and contributions to sinking funds.

debt-to-assets ratio A measure of a company's ability to sustain debt, determined by dividing its total liabilities by its total assets.

debt-to-equity ratio A measure of a company's ability to sustain debt, determined by dividing the total liabilities by the owner's equity.

debug To locate an error in a software program and make the appropriate corrections; by extension, to eliminate any technical problem.

decapitalize To withdraw financing from (a company).

decay rate The approximate percentage of customers who cease to buy a product in the course of a year.

decentralization Delegation to middle and supervisory managers of authority to make decisions in regard to financial, production, and personnel matters. See also **centralization**.

decentralized divisional design An organizational structure in which each division of a company is semiautonomous, specializing in a particular product or responsible for a regional market, and whose head is given all but total authority to coordinate operations within the division, to make decisions, and to establish strategy under the overall coordination of the chief executive officer at the organization's headquarters.

decertification Revocation of a labor union's authorization to serve as bargaining agent as a result of a vote conducted among workers under the supervision of the National Labor Relations Board.

decision-making process A rational thought process involving the identification and evaluation of two or more alternatives, selection and implementation of one, and evaluation of the effectiveness of the alternative chosen.

decision rule A guideline selected to express the conditions under which a decision to proceed with a recommended course of action will be made (e.g., "If 55 percent of our test market favor the new design, we'll go ahead with it.").

decision tree A graphic representation of a network of hypothetical actions and events indicating the probabilities of success and failure of each action that might be taken in the situation under study, designed to facilitate the decision-making process. See also **action-event area**.

declaration 1. Disclosure of income, property, or items to customs agents or other governmental or legal authorities. 2. A written but unsworn statement, as by an applicant for a patent.

declining-balance depreciation A method of accelerated depreciation by which each year's depreciation is calculated as a percentage of current book value. See also **double-declining-balance depreciation**. The calculation is made by means of the following formula, in which L is the useful life, s is the salvage value, and c is the acquisition cost:

$$1 - \frac{L}{s/c}$$

deductible A specified amount of a loss that an insurance policy does not cover (e.g., a $100 deductible policy means that the insurance company deducts $100 from each claim that is paid).

deed A legal document by which title to real property is passed to a new owner. See also **quitclaim deed; warranty deed.**

deed of trust A deed transferring ownership of property to a third party, such as a bank, until a mortgage or other indebtedness is fully discharged, at which time the trustee transfers the deed to the purchaser.

deep discount A discount far larger than normally offered.

default Failure to fulfill a contract or other obligation, especially to pay a debt or interest due.

defendant A person who must answer a criminal charge or a civil action in a court of law. See also **plaintiff.**

deferred annuity An annuity providing for payments to begin at some specified future date.

deferred charge Also called **deferred cost; deferred debit; deferred expense.** An expenditure, as for an advance payment or an insurance premium, which is regarded as an asset to be depreciated over future periods rather than as a charge in the period in which it is made.

deferred compensation Payment made to an employee in the form of a stock option or by other means designed to bring the employee income in the future and encourage long-term commitment to the employer.

deferred income See **advance from (by) customer.**

deferred income-tax liability See **interperiod income-tax allocation.**

deferred revenue See **advance from (by) customer.**

deficit 1. The amount by which a sum of money falls short of the required amount. 2. A loss, as in the operation of a business. 3. The amount by which liabilities exceed assets.

deficit financing Expenditures, especially by a government, in excess of public revenues, usually made possible by borrowing.

deficit spending The practice, especially by a government, of spending funds in excess of income, usually financed by borrowing.

deflation 1. A decline in the general price level, or an increase in the value of money; a reversal of inflation. 2. (*economics*) A decrease in the amount of money in circulation. See also **disinflation**.

defraud Deceptively or improperly to take or withhold something that belongs to another.

dehire A euphemism for "discharge" or "dismiss": often used of executive layoffs.

Delaney Amendment A 1958 amendment to the Food, Drug, and Cosmetics Act of 1938 authorizing the Food and Drug Administration to remove from the market any food or food additive that has been shown to cause cancer in animals or humans.

delegate To assign, commit, or entrust to another, as authority, responsibility, or a task.

delivered cost The price at which goods are billed, including the cost of transportation.

Delphi technique The practice of seeking the opinions of experts on likely future events and trends that would affect business.

demand 1. The desire to purchase a particular product or service by those who have the means to do so. 2. The quantity of a good or service that buyers will take at a particular price. See also **law of demand; law of supply and demand.**

demand-backward pricing See **market-minus pricing.**

demand curve A graphic representation of the quantities of a good or service that will be purchased at various prices at a specific time.

demand deposit A checking account in a bank.

demand loan A loan that has no specified maturity date but is payable whenever the lender demands payment.

demand-pull inflation Inflation resulting from increased demand. See also **cost-push inflation.**

demarketing A temporary reduction in purchasing activity in the marketplace resulting from a supply of goods inadequate to meet the demand for them.

democratic leadership Also called **participative leadership; system 4 management.** A style of leadership characterized by group involvement in decision making, a free flow of information and communications, and delegation of authority to qualified members of the group.

demographics The study or aggregate of definable characteristics of a population, including sex, race, religion, health, age, income, education, and homeownership. See also **RACORNOS**.

demotion Reassignment of an employee to a position of lesser status and responsibility than the position the employee previously held.

demotivator Also called **demotivating factor**. An aspect of one's employment that, if diminished or downgraded, tends to inhibit peak performance.

demurrage The holding of a rail car, barge, or ship beyond the time allowed for loading and unloading.

demurrer A plea that a legal action be dismissed on the grounds that although the facts presented by the opposing side are true, either they are insufficient to support the claim based on them or the pleadings suffer from some other defect in law sufficient to call for a judgment that the case should not proceed further.

denominator value The expected volume of units to be produced in the current period, which when used as the figure by which budgeted fixed costs are divided yields fixed cost per unit of production.

dental and vision insurance Insurance covering a percentage of an employee's expenditures for eyeglasses, contact lenses prescribed by a physician, and dentistry, often excluding bridgework and children's braces.

department A group or section of employees who work together in a specific area of a company. See also **departmentation**.

departmentation Also called **departmentalization**. The grouping or departmentalizing of employees in accordance with type of work done, territory served, product produced, type of customer dealt with, etc.

dependency The state of an organization, subsystem, or individual that requires support from other organizations or persons.

dependent demand Demand for component

parts and raw materials that is determined by or dependent upon requirements for products and can therefore be calculated rather than forecast.

dependent variable (*statistics*) A value that can be predicted as a result of knowing the value of one or more independent variables.

depletion The reduction in value of capital that results from the exhaustion or using up of an asset. See also **amortization; depreciation** (def. 1).

depletion allowance The amount by which the Internal Revenue Service permits taxable income to be reduced to reflect the exhaustion of such assets as oil wells, mines, and quarries.

deposit in transit A bank deposit made and recorded but not yet reported on a bank statement.

deposition Written testimony given under oath by a witness for use in a court trial.

depreciation 1. A decline in the value of an asset attributable to wear, use, or the passage of time. **2.** The amount by which taxable income is or may be reduced to reflect such a decline in value, based on the asset's estimated or allowable useful life. **3.** A fall in the value of one currency in relation to another. See also **devaluation.**

depression 1. A drastic drop in business with resultant high rates of unemployment and business failure; the bottom of a business cycle. **2.** A severe and long-term recession during which unemployment exceeds 10 percent of the work force and profits drop sharply enough to cause widespread bankruptcy; a chronic aberration in the normal business cycle, not easily rectified by the normal dynamics of supply and demand.

deregulation The removal of existing state or federal regulations governing such industries as airlines, railroads, and trucking, with the objective of stimulating business competition and lowering consumer costs. See also **price war.**

derivative A financial contract whose value derives from the value of underlying stocks, bonds, currencies, commodities, etc.

derived demand Demand for a product that is directly or indirectly related to the demand for another product, as the demand for tires is related to the demand for automobiles.

descriptive billing A billing system that incorporates a description of the charges rather than copies of the original invoices.

designated market-area rating (*abbr* DMA rating) The number of homes in which a television program is being viewed in a defined market area at a given time.

design review Inspection of a completed or planned product design by representatives of each segment of the operation for the purpose of confirming the producibility of the product and of identifying errors that may be rectified.

desktop publishing The design and production of publications by means of specialized software enabling a microcomputer to generate typeset-quality text and graphics.

devaluation A reduction in the exchange value of a currency by a lessening of its equivalency in gold or in some other currency, with resultant decreases in the prices of the country's goods in foreign markets. See also **depreciation** (def. 3).

developing Designating a nation or region having a standard of living or level of industrial production well below that possible with financial or technical aid; not yet highly industrialized.

development 1. The process of making usable and commercially available a product or process discovered or perfected by applied research. **2.** The process of mutual adaptation by which an individual pursues his or her career goals within an organization that guides the individual's training and performance in light of its own objectives.

development training Training in skills required for job performance and advancement appropriate to an individual's motivation and capabilities.

diagnosis Assessment of strengths and weaknesses, dependent on the perceptions and interpretations of those reviewing the data.

Dictionary of Occupational Titles (*abbr* DOT) A reference book published by the U.S. Department of Labor that lists and describes 20,000 jobs.

die-cut Cut by a set of tools or devices that produce a desired form, usually for assembly with other components into a more complex product (e.g., an automobile).

differential advantage An advantage enjoyed by one marketer, retailer, or nation over competitors (e.g., lower cost, better product features, location).

differential cost See **incremental cost** (def. 2).

differential threshold See **just noticeable difference**.

diffusion process The process by which a new product or service comes into general use.

digital Involving the use of a code consisting of numerical digits, recognized and read by a computer or other electronic device.

Dilbert A syndicated 1990's comic strip character created by Scott Adams. The comic strip satirizes business activities and management techniques.

dilution A decrease in the percentage of ownership of a corporation represented by a quantity of stock resulting from issuance of additional shares.

diminishing returns A rate of return on investment that at some future date fails to increase in proportion to additional investment. See also **law of diminishing returns**.

direct-action advertising Advertising designed to elicit some action from the target audience (e.g., sending money for a sample, writing for additional information).

direct confrontation An aggressive strategy to limit reliance on other organizations by seeking a monopolistic position or by initiating an exchange of services.

direct cost Also called **direct expense.** The costs of overhead, materials, and labor that can be directly attributed to the production of a specific number of units of product, an organizational unit, or a project.

direct costing Also called **marginal costing.** The charging of variable manufacturing costs only (the costs of labor, materials, and variable factory overhead costs) to the cost of a product. See also **absorption costing**.

direct deposit The use of electronic funds transfer to deposit wages directly to an employee's bank account each payday.

directed interview A structured interview in which the interviewer follows a prepared form or list of questions (often used to select a candidate for a specific job).

direct expense See **direct cost.**

direct exporting The shipping of goods from a company in one country directly to a company in another country, without the use of intermediaries.

direct labor Factory labor that is clearly responsible for the production of a specific number of units or batches of product. See also **indirect labor.**

direct mail Mail, usually consisting of advertising matter, appeals for donations, or the like, sent to large numbers of people.

direct marketing Marketing direct to the consumer, as by direct mail or coupon advertising. Also called **direct selling.**

direct materials Raw materials that can be associated with an identifiable amount of units or batches manufactured.

direct posting The making of accounting entries directly in ledger accounts without prior entry in journals.

direct supervision Management characterized by direct interaction between supervisor and subordinates.

disability benefit An insurance payment made to an employee who is unable to work as a result of illness or injury.

disability income insurance Insurance that protects an employee against loss of income while partially or totally disabled by illness or injury.

disbursement A payment made by cash or check, often recorded in a separate cash disbursements account.

discharge 1. Permanent involuntary termination of employment. 2. To pay (a debt) or perform (an obligation).

disciplinary action A penalty (e.g., loss of privileges, a fine, demotion, suspension, oral or written reprimand, discharge) imposed on an employee whose behavior on the job is unacceptable to management, illegal, or contrary to union regulations.

disciplinary practices Formal procedures to be followed in the taking of disciplinary action, specified in a document that outlines offenses that warrant disciplinary action and stipulates the sequence of penalties and the steps to be taken in carrying them out.

disclaimer Refusal of a certified public accountant to permit an audit opinion to be included in a financial statement because (1) he or she was not independent of the company, (2) the information available was insufficient to support an opinion, or (3) the outcome of the audit was too inconclusive to justify an opinion.

disclosure agreement A written agreement whereby one party promises to keep secret information that is to be divulged by another.

discount 1. A price reduction given to a customer in the form of cash, a reduction of the list price, or merchandise. See also **cash discount; quantity discount; trade discount. 2.** The percentage by which a price is reduced. **3.** To purchase a promissory note before its due date for the face value of the note less a service charge. **4.** To take into account the present value of a sum of money or other asset having a known value at a certain time in the future.

discount broker 1. An agent who discounts commercial paper. **2.** A stockbroker who charges discount commission fees.

discount rate 1. The rate of interest charged in discounting commercial paper. **2.** The interest rate charged by Federal Reserve Banks on loans to their member banks, usually against government securities as collateral.

discount store A store that sells a variety of goods below market price, usually because of large volume of sales and a small profit margin.

discrete compounding The periodic calculation of compound interest at specific points in time. See also **compound interest; continuous compounding.**

discretionary account An investor's account with a broker or agent who, within specified limitations, is free to buy, sell, or retain securities at times and in amounts the agent deems to be in the best interest of the investor.

discretionary income Also called **discretionary spending power.** The amount of money remaining after essential expenses are met. See also **disposable income.**

discretionary order An order to buy issued with the proviso that the broker is to judge whether to execute the transaction immediately or to wait for a better price.

diseconomy 1. A lack of economy. **2.** Something that adds costs, as opposed to something that contributes to economy or efficiency.

disemploy To cause to be unemployed: often a tactful reference to large-scale layoffs.

disinflation A slowing down of the inflation rate, when prices are still going up, but at a lesser rate than before. See also **deflation.**

disinvestment The withdrawal of invested funds or the cancellation of subsidies or other financial aid.

disk Any of several types of media for storing electronic data consisting of thin, round plates of plastic or metal. See also **floppy disk; hard disk.**

diskette See **floppy disk.**

dispatcher A person who is responsible for issuing work orders to all people working together on a job on the basis of a list prepared by a supervisor or department head. See also **dispatching.**

dispatching A phase of production control, usually managed by supervisors and department heads, in which tasks required to be completed in a work center are listed, assigned priorities, and routed; from this list a dispatcher in each work area issues work orders to employees.

dispersion The degree to which plants, factories, or warehouses are scattered over a large geographical area. See also **concentration.**

display 1. (*data processing*) **a.** The visual representation of the output of an electronic device. **b.** The portion of the device, such as a screen, that shows this representation. **2.** (*advertising*) A presentation of promotional material in a store.

display ad An advertisement in a newspaper, magazine, or on a billboard that includes a picture or special graphics in addition to a verbal message.

disposable income Personal income after income and social security taxes have been withheld; the amount that a person has available for living expenses, clothing, entertainment, etc. See also **discretionary income.**

dissatisfier Also called **hygiene factor**. A factor whose presence, according to Frederick Herzberg's motivation/hygiene theory, does not motivate an employee but whose absence leads to employee dissatisfaction (e.g., attractive work space, well-kept washrooms).

dissolution The liquidation and disbanding of a corporation, usually as a result of bankruptcy, as a consequence of which all stock is rendered value-less except for shareholders' claims against resid-ual assets.

distressed Designating merchandise that is dam-aged, out-of-date, or used, or real estate that is foreclosed and offered for sale.

distribution 1. The marketing, transporting, mer-chandising, and selling of any item. 2. The division of the aggregate income of any society among its members. 3. The parceling out of a decedent's es-tate to the beneficiaries. 4. The paying out of cor-porate profits to shareholders in the form of divi-dends, or the total amount of money involved. 5. The sale of a large block of stock. 6. The allocation of a bankrupt's assets to creditors.

distribution expense The expense of sales, marketing, and delivery of goods to the market-place.

distributor Also called **service wholesaler**. An in-dependent wholesaler who sells assorted goods to all users, including other wholesalers, retailers, and the industrial market, and provides such services as displays, delivery, and extension of credit.

divergent marketing The marketing of each line of a company's products by a separate market-ing team. See also **convergent marketing.**

diversification 1. The act or process of increas-ing the variety of products manufactured or of services offered. See also **merger.** 2. The process of spreading investments among various kinds of securities.

diversified investment company An invest-ment company that is required by law to invest 75% of its assets in such a way that no more than 5% is invested in any one company and that it holds no more than 10% of the voting securities of any one company.

divestiture The process of selling one or more small companies (usually companies that bear only a tenuous relationship to the parent organization's primary business or that have been marginally profitable) in order to raise cash or increase borrowing capacity.

dividend A distribution of a corporation's earnings to its shareholders.

divisible contract A document specifying two or more dissimilar obligations that are unrelated to each other.

divisionalization The dividing of an organization into separate sections that operate in an autonomous or semiautonomous manner. See also **decentralized divisional design.**

document of title A written document, either negotiable or nonnegotiable, signed by a titleholder and certifying to legal ownership of property specified (e.g., a car).

dog A company or product whose prospects are poor. See also **cash cow; star.**

dollar averaging Also called **dollar-cost averaging.** An investment technique whereby an investor invests a fixed number of dollars in stocks at regular intervals, so that more shares are bought when the price is low than when the price is high, with the expectation of profiting by selling all stock when the price is above the average cost paid per share.

domestic corporation A corporation that conducts its business in the state in which it was incorporated. See also **foreign corporation.**

dominant coalition An informal structure within an organization made up of top-level management, such as the chief executive and others in strategic decision-making positions. See also **inner circle.**

dormant partner A business partner who takes no active role in running a business and whose association with the firm is not public knowledge. See also **silent partner.**

DOS (*acronym for* **d**isk-**o**perating **s**ystem) A computer cataloging device that provides the user with a directory of information or programs on a disk and also acts as the mechanism by which these data may be accessed.

double-bill To bill two different customers for the same charge.

double-declining-balance depreciation (*abbr* DDB) A method of accelerated depreciation by which the annual depreciation charge is a percentage of the remaining book value equal to twice the percentage that would be calculated under the straight-line method; thus an asset bought for $1000 with a useful life of 10 years, which would be depreciated at a rate of 10% a year under the straight-line method, would be depreciated at a rate of 20% of recent book value under the double-declining-balance method.

double-entry bookkeeping A bookkeeping system that recognizes both what is received and what is given up in each business transaction by crediting one account and debiting another, the total debits always balancing the total credits.

double indemnity A provision in a life or accident insurance policy that entitles the beneficiary of the policy to receive double the face value of the policy if the insured dies an accidental death.

double-page spread Also called **double spread.** An advertisement or other material that occupies two facing pages of a magazine. See also **centerfold; double-truck spread.**

double T-account A T-account with double horizontal lines, used to record a change in an account balance during the preparation of a statement of change in financial position.

double taxation The taxation of a corporation's profit twice, once under the corporate income tax and again under the personal income tax levied against stockholders to whom that profit has been distributed in the form of dividends.

double-truck spread An advertisement or other related material that occupies two facing pages of a newspaper. See also **double-page spread.**

Dow Jones average An index of the relative price of securities based on the average daily prices of common stocks issued by selected companies in the fields of industry and transportation and selected public utilities.

down payment An initial amount given as partial payment at the time of purchase, as in installment buying.

downsize To reduce a labor force in size or number; to cut back.

downstream **1.** In the future. **2.** Concerning a lower level of business activity or authority, such as a subordinate or a subsidiary.

downtick (*stock exchange*) A closing price slightly below that of the previous day or trading period.

downtime Time when workers are idle because machinery is shut down for some cause, such as equipment failure, routine maintenance, or a temporary plant closing.

Dow theory A market analysis theory that predicts that if either the Dow Jones industrial or Dow Jones transportation average exceeds a previous significant high or low price, a general market trend will follow in the same direction.

draft See **bill of exchange; trade draft.**

drawee A person who must pay another the amount specified on a bill of exchange or a trade draft.

drawer A person who draws up a bill of exchange or trade draft specifying an amount payable by the drawee.

drive time The rush hour, when commuters listen to car radios: perceived as a source of increased ratings for programs and a consequent increase in advertising revenue.

drop shipper A wholesaler who deals in shipments of goods sent directly to a retailer by a manufacturer without passing through the hands of the wholesaler who negotiated the transaction.

dry goods Fabrics, clothing, and the like, as distinguished from hardware and groceries.

dual distribution Sale of a product or service through more than one marketing channel.

dub See **transfer** (def. 4).

due bill A statement of charges for services rendered, specifying the nature and date of the services, the terms of payment, and the date by which payment is due.

due date The day by which a debt is to be paid.

due process of law The proceedings and limitations set forth in the U.S. Constitution and in state constitutions to protect the rights of individuals against incursions by branches and agents of government and before courts of law.

dues checkoff See checkoff.

dummy Also called **mockup.** A preliminary layout of a publication showing the intended concept and design.

dump bin A jumble display in which all products are alike. See also **jumble basket.**

dumping The practice of selling goods in a foreign market at a price lower than that charged in the domestic market.

Du Pont system A system by which the relationship of a corporation's activity ratio and profit margin is analyzed in order to determine the relationship of profitability and assets. A simplified formula expressing this relationship is

$$\frac{\text{Net profit}}{\text{Sales}} \times \frac{\text{Sales}}{\text{Total investment}} = \frac{\text{Return on}}{\text{investment}}$$

durable goods Also called **hard goods.** Automobiles, machinery, refrigerators, jewelry, etc., designed to be used over a period of time, usually at least three years.

Dutch auction A method of selling, in which the price of an item is gradually reduced until a buyer is found.

duty-free Exempt from customs.

dyad Any two individuals who have a close personal relationship, such as husband and wife.

dynamics The pattern of interaction and response between two people or among members of a group.

E

early retirement benefits Pension benefits received by an employee who retires before the age of 65, usually reduced in amount from benefits receivable at age 65.

earned income Income from wages, salaries, fees, or the like, accruing from labor or services performed by the earner. Cf. **unearned income.**

earned surplus (*obsolete*) See **retained earnings.**

earnings before interest and taxes (*acronym* EBIT) See **net operating income.**

earnings per share (*abbr* EPS) Net revenues for a specific period divided by the number of shares of common stock issued.

easement A legal right to use or have access to property belonging to another (e.g., the right of a public utility to install and service pipes or wires running under private property.)

EBCDIC (*acronym for* extended binary-coded decimal interchange code) An eight-bit code with 256 character combinations used on large computers for data representation and transfer.

EBIT (*acronym for* earnings before interest and taxes) See **net operating income.**

echelon A steplike formation of units or individuals; thus, a level of decision-making responsibility and power.

econometrician A specialist in econometrics.

econometrics The use of scientific techniques, especially of mathematics and statistics, to support or test economic theories, solve economic problems, etc.

economic externalities Costs (or benefits) of a market activity borne by a third party (e.g., the costs of air and water pollution, which do not appear on the financial statement of the polluting firm but are borne by society at large).

economic growth An increase in production of goods and services as indicated by real GNP.

economic indicator Also called **business indicator.** An economic factor that is considered to signal the general direction of economic activity by fluctuating either in advance of, concurrently with, or after the aggregate of economic activity. See also **lagging indicator; leading indicator; roughly coincident indicator.**

economic life The period over which an asset is expected to yield benefits.

economic order quantity (*abbr* EOQ) The most economically efficient amount of stock to order or produce when inventory must be replenished. This is calculated by the following formula, in which *D* is the amount needed for a given period, *P* is the cost of placing one order, and *C* is the cost of carrying one unit for the period, including lost return on investment:

$$EOQ = \sqrt{\frac{2DP}{C}}$$

Economic Recovery Act An act of Congress passed in 1981 to cut federal taxes for individuals and businesses in order to encourage business investment.

economics The science that deals with the production, distribution, and consumption of goods and services, or the material welfare of humankind.

economic system 1. A system devised to establish the nature and quantity of goods and services to be produced, the means by which they should be produced, and the means by which they should be allocated. **2.** A system by which limited resources are allocated among competing uses.

economies of scale Reductions in minimum average costs that result from increases in the size of plant and equipment.

economy 1. The management of the resources of a community, country, etc., especially with a view to its productivity. **2.** The prosperity or earnings of a place.

EDP See **electronic data processing.**

effective interest method Also called **scientific method.** A method of amortizing a bond discount or premium so that at the beginning of each period the interest expense for that period (calculated by multiplying the bond's original yield rate by the net liability at the beginning of the period) divided by the bond's net liability (its face amount plus premium or minus discount) is equal to the bond's yield rate as of its issue date.

effective interest rate 1. Also called **effective yield.** The yield to maturity of a bond as of its date of issue. See also **coupon rate. 2.** The simple annual interest rate that would yield the same amount as a stated compound interest rate, equal to $(1 + r/m) m - 1$, where r is the compound rate and m is the number of compoundings per year.

EFT See **electronic funds transfer.**

EFTA See **European Free Trade Association.**

e.g. (*Latin abbr for e*xempli gratia) For example.

ego motive An incentive to performance provided by assurance of one's importance and self-worth.

elasticity See **price elasticity of demand; price elasticity of supply.**

electronic data processing (*abbr* EDP) Collection, storage, and processing of information in a computer and retrieval of that information from any connecting terminal. See also **automatic data processing.**

electronic funds transfer (*abbr* EFT) The transfer of funds by debiting a bank account and crediting another account in the same or another bank by means of a computer.

electronic mail Also called **e-mail.** A system for sending messages via telecommunications links between computers.

electronic point of sale An automatic data-processing station located at a cashier's station in a retail store that enables a clerk or operator to verify customers' charge accounts, record sales, and process other information.

elimination An entry made on a worksheet used in preparing a consolidated statement in order to avoid a duplication of recorded assets, liabilities, owners' equity, revenues, or expenses in the summation of the records of a parent company and its subsidiaries.

e-mail Also, **E-mail. 1.** See **electronic mail. 2.** A message sent by e-mail.

embargo A prohibition of trade in either certain

specified products or all products of a foreign country.

embezzlement The act of appropriating for one's own use property entrusted to one's care by its owner (e.g., the theft of money by a bank employee).

emergent factor An informal condition or element in a work situation (e.g., consistency) that over time serves to indicate the nature and effectiveness of group interactions.

emerging market A market in a less developed country whose economy is just beginning to grow.

eminent domain The legal right of the government to appropriate property for public use.

empathy 1. Projection in imagination of a subjective mental or emotional state onto another person or an object. **2.** The capacity to experience vicariously another person's feelings, wishes, or thoughts.

employee benefit plan A plan encompassing pension, insurance, and other benefits offered employees. See also **cafeteria plan; compensation; fringe benefit.**

employee communications Company or departmental memos, newsletters, etc., circulated between departments and between management and staff as a means of keeping employees informed of new policies, promotions, hirings, and the like.

employee counseling The assessment and improvement of employees' skills and competencies as a means of enhancing job performance, production levels, morale, etc.

employee insurance Insurance coverage for life, accident, major medical, etc., usually provided by management as an employee benefit. See also **disability income insurance; employee life insurance.**

employee life insurance Insurance providing for payment of a specified multiple of an employee's annual salary to a surviving beneficiary upon the death of the employee. Usually paid for entirely by the employer.

employee maintenance A program for keeping able employees within the organization, as by insuring that wages and benefits are competitive.

Employee Retirement Income Security Act (*acronym* ERISA) An act of Congress passed in 1974, establishing the Pension Guaranty Corporation to insure the assets of pension plans, requiring disclosure of the provisions of employee pension and welfare plans, establishing standards of conduct for the trustees and administrators of such plans, and establishing requirements for funding of and participation and vesting in pension plans.

employee stock ownership plan (*acronym* ESOP) A program to encourage and aid employees to become shareholders in the corporation that employs them, thus contributing capital to the corporation, sharing in profits, and acquiring an incentive to help it reach its goals.

employers' association A cooperative alliance of employers (e.g., National Association of Manufacturers, U.S. Chamber of Commerce) who publicize the views of members on issues of concern to them and negotiate with labor unions on behalf of individual employers.

employment 1. Work performed for pay. **2.** The number or percentage of people who are employed of the nation's total work force. See also **unemployment. 3.** The process of recruiting and selecting qualified job applicants.

employment agency An independently owned agency that recruits and screens job applicants for employers for a variable fee (from 7% to 25% of the annual salary of the position filled) payable within a specified time of hiring by either the employer or the applicant in accordance with terms agreed upon, which vary over time with the state of the job market. See also **executive search firm.**

employment taxes See **payroll taxes.**

enabling costs Capacity costs incurred to permit production or operations to take place, and which cease when production ceases. See also **standby costs.**

encounter group An unstructured group in which members are encouraged to confront one another directly and express their feelings for the purpose of developing emotional ties and promoting understanding of themselves and others; a device used in organizational development.

ending inventory Also called **closing inventory.**

The cost of inventory on hand at the end of an accounting period: generally carried into the following period as beginning inventory and shown on the balance sheet as an asset at the end of the reporting period.

endorsement 1. Writing on the back of a negotiable instrument that transfers the property named in the instrument to a person specified or to the bearer. **2.** See **testimonial.**

endowment insurance Insurance that will pay the face value of the policy to a named beneficiary if the insured dies within a stated length of time, generally 20 or 30 years, or to the insured if he or she is still alive at the end of that time.

end user The ultimate user for whom a machine, product, or service is designed. Also called **end consumer.**

Engel's law The economic principle, proposed by Ernst Engel, that the lower a person's income, the greater the proportion of it he or she must spend on food and other necessities.

enterprise 1. Any corporation, public utility, firm, partnership, company, or other business organization. **2.** An investment venture or project.

enterprise fund A government fund used to support and account for the acquisition, operation, and maintenance of a government service intended to be self-supporting through payments and charges collected from users, such as those paid to water companies and airports.

entrepreneur A person who plans, organizes, manages, and owns a business and assumes the attendant risks of the enterprise.

entropy 1. The degree to which effort is determined to be lacking at the management and production levels of an organization. **2.** A tendency of a subsystem or work unit to remain stable and unchanging, especially at a low or unproductive level.

entry level The lowest position within a job category; usually the lowest job from which one can be promoted.

entry process 1. The series of events that take place when a new employee enters an organization to begin work. **2.** The process by which the expectations of a new employee and of the employing organization are adapted to the realities of the situation.

entry value The current fair-market acquisition cost of an asset, usually equal to replacement cost.

envelope stuffer A promotional piece (e.g., a printed announcement, a product sample) sent to customers along with an invoice or other correspondence at no additional mailing cost.

environment See **business environment**.

environmental impact statement A study detailing the possible effect on the environment of a specific proposed activity and discussing alternatives to the proposed action, required to be disseminated to federal agencies, state and local governments, and the public under the provisions of the National Environmental Policy Act before any process that might have undesirable environmental effects may proceed.

environmentally adaptive design An organizational plan that identifies potentially adverse conditions and proposes long and short-range activities responsive to and contingent on such conditions.

Environmental Protection Agency (*abbr* EPA) A federal agency created in 1970 to execute the policies of the Council on Environmental Quality, which conducts research studies and coordinates all federal programs dealing with industrial pollution.

environmental protection legislation A series of acts passed by Congress beginning in 1970 to regulate the use of air pollutants, water pollutants, pesticides, and other toxic chemicals. See also **Clean Air Act; Federal Insecticide, Fungicide, and Rodenticide Act; Federal Water Pollution Control Act; Toxic Substances Control Act**.

environmental turbulence An upheaval created by a change in the status of interacting dependent environmental systems (e.g., an increase in the relevance of one department to an organization's goals at the expense of other departments).

EOM dating (*abbr for* end-of-month dating) The practice of stating credit terms as of the end of the month in which the transaction occurred (e.g., "2/20 EOM" indicates that a 2 percent cash discount is given if the bill is paid within 20 days of the end of the month).

EPA See **Environmental Protection Agency.**

EPS See **earnings per share.**

Equal Credit Opportunity Act Federal legislation passed in 1975 prohibiting discrimination on account of sex or marital status in any transaction involving credit. See also **Regulation B.**

Equal Employment Opportunity Commission. An agency of the U.S. government instituted to establish guidelines for hiring and recruitment practices in order to reduce discrimination against members of minority groups and to encourage such people to apply for jobs they are qualified to fill.

equal opportunity Policies and practices in employment and other areas that do not discriminate against persons on the basis of race, color, religion, sex, age, mental or physical handicap, or national origin.

Equal Pay Act A 1963 amendment to the Fair Labor Standards Act of 1938, which provides that any employer who engages in business activities involved in interstate commerce or who receives federal funds must give women employees the same pay as men who perform the same job.

equity 1. An interest in the net assets of a corporation. **2.** The percentage of investment that an investor has contributed in a margin transaction. **3.** The value of a property in excess of the amount that the owner still owes on a mortgage or debt secured by a lien.

equity accounting The right of ownership to securities and investments made by an individual or organization, listed on a balance sheet.

equity capital Funds raised through the sale of stock or the conversion of one or more stock issues into a single new issue. See also **debt capital.**

equity real estate investment trust (*abbr* equity REIT) A mutual fund that buys real estate and distributes at least 90 percent of its income as dividends, issuing shares to meet demand at a low price per share and offering a choice of automatic reinvestment or periodic payment of dividends, thus permitting greater flexibility than a mortgage real estate investment trust.

equity turnover A ratio that indicates the relationship between sales and stockholders' equity.

ergonomics Also called **human engineering.** An aspect of technology that studies the application of engineering and biological data to the mutual adjustment of machines and the people who operate them, and seeks to improve physical working conditions.

ERISA See **Employee Retirement Income Security Act.**

escalator clause A contract provision calling for increased charges, wages, or other payments, based on increased production costs, the cost of living, etc.

escape clause A provision in a contract that enables a party to terminate contractual obligations in specified circumstances.

escheat The reversion to the state of property left by a deceased person who has no legal heirs at the time of death.

escrow 1. A bond, deed, sum of money, or article of property left in the care of a third party to be held until specified conditions are fulfilled. **2. in escrow** In trust as surety for payment or performance.

ESOP See **employee stock ownership plan.**

esprit de corps (*French*) Group spirit; a feeling among peers of satisfaction in group membership and enthusiasm for and commitment to the group's goals: the end product of team building.

estimation sampling Random selection of facts or examples in order to derive an estimated characteristic of the large group that includes those facts or examples (e.g., by checking at random 100 of every 100,000 invoices for arithmetic correctness, one can calculate an estimated percentage of incorrect invoices among all invoices).

estoppel A legal bar against making a statement of affirmation or denial that will contradict a statement one has previously made.

et al. (*Latin abbr for et al*ii) And (all the) others.

ethical pricing The practice of charging less than

the maximum price for products or services subject to price elasticity.

ethics A set of moral principles and values that govern one's actions. See also **business ethics.**

et seq. (*Latin abbr for et sequens*) And the following (one or ones).

euro A proposed single monetary unit for all European countries.

Eurocurrency Money and negotiable instruments of non-European countries held outside their countries of origin for use in European money markets.

Eurodollars U.S. dollars held in European banks and used as a medium of international credit, especially for foreign trade.

European Economic Community (*abbr* EEC) Also called **Common Market.** An economic alliance established in 1958 by Belgium, France, Italy, Luxembourg, the Netherlands, and West Germany (since joined by Great Britain, Ireland, Denmark, Greece, Spain, and Portugal) to adopt common import duties and expedite trade among member nations.

European Free Trade Association (*abbr* EFTA) An economic association established in 1960 and originally composed of Austria, Denmark, Britain, Norway, Portugal, Sweden, and Switzerland, that maintains free trade in industrial products among member countries.

evoked set (*marketing research*) The limited number of brand items that a consumer can mentally recall before making a product selection. See also **span of recall.**

Excel A powerful spreadsheet program developed by Microsoft Corporation for personal computers. It is known for its ease of use and its built-in routines for producing charts and graphs from the data.

excessive trading The practice of churning.

exchange See **stock exchange.**

exchange controls Regulations imposed by some governments to allocate, expand, or restrict the exchange of their national currencies into foreign currencies as a means of regulating foreign trade.

exchange gain (loss) 1. a. A difference caused

by the translation of a financial statement from one unit of currency to another when the exchange rate has changed during the period of that statement. **b.** An entry item that reconciles the difference caused by the translation. **2.** An amount gained or lost on foreign currency held when the exchange rate changes.

exchange rate The price at which a nation's money can be exchanged for another currency or for gold.

excise tax A tax on certain items or services, payable by manufacturers or consumers or both, imposed by a state or by the federal government in order to control the traffic in potentially harmful goods or to subsidize services related to the items so taxed.

exclusion clause A clause in an insurance policy detailing specific risks not covered by the policy.

exclusion ratio The portion of an annuity that is made up of nondeductible contributions and is therefore nontaxable.

exclusive marketing plan A business strategy whereby a product is offered to a limited number of retail firms in exchange for their agreement not to stock competitive products.

ex dividend (*abbr* ex div; XD) Exclusive of dividend: applied to a stock traded when payment of a dividend is pending to indicate that the price of the security does not include any dividend declared. See also **cum dividend.**

executive A person who assumes responsibility for the performance of others within a corporation. See also **middle management; top management.**

executive park See **office park.**

executive search firm An independently owned agency that recruits and screens top-level executives for prospective employers, who are charged a fee consisting of a percentage of the annual salary of the position filled.

executor A person named in a will to administer the estate of the deceased.

exemption An amount that an individual (noncorporate) taxpayer may deduct from his or her gross income before calculating income tax owed, based on the number of dependents claimed (including oneself).

exempt personnel An employee or the group of employees who are exempted from the provisions of the Fair Labor Standards Act, and thus are not required to be paid for overtime work: in general, administrative, executive, professional, and outside sales employees.

exercise price (*stock trading*) The price at which an open order is executed. See also **limit order.**

exit interview A meeting between resigning or terminated employees and a representative of the personnel department to determine employee perceptions and reasons for leaving, to settle final payments and disposition of benefits, and to ensure the return of company property.

expansion An increase in economic and industrial activity.

expected return The amount that is expected to be earned from an investment in securities or from a business venture.

expected value The weighted average outcome for a specific decision alternative, where the weights are the probabilities associated with each possible outcome.

expected yield The ratio of the expected return to the total amount invested.

expediting time Work time spent in locating a misplaced order and carrying out the tasks necessary for its fulfillment.

expense 1. A current charge incurred in order to generate revenues and sustain operations. **2.** A charge incurred by an employee in the course of conducting business outside the office, typically for transportation, meals, and lodging.

expense account An account of business-related expenses incurred outside the office by an employee and reimbursable by the employer. See also **expense** (def. 2).

experience curve See **learning curve.**

experience rating A determination of current charges on the basis of past costs and risks, used in insurance, especially unemployment insurance.

experimental learning A proactive method of learning whereby learners develop their own understandings of concepts on the basis of personal experience; learning by doing. See also **cognitive style.**

expert power Power derived from technical or professional expertise that is recognized by others. See also **charismatic power; legitimate power.**

exploitive leadership Also called **system 1 management.** A style of leadership that emphasizes the formal roles of superiors and subordinates, discourages interaction between them, leaves it to management to control all activities and initiate all communication, and makes no provision for teamwork, thus eliminating any possibility of influence by subordinates on the goals of the organization or the methods and activities of their work group and generating fear and distrust.

exponential smoothing A forecasting procedure that uses an exponentially weighted average of past observations as a basis for forecasts.

export 1. To sell goods or raw materials to a foreign country. **2.** A product sold to a foreign country.

express warranty A promise or statement of fact concerning goods made by a seller as part of a bargain with a buyer. See also **implied warranty.**

ex rights Without the right, enjoyed by current shareholders, to purchase a new issue at a special subscription price: applied to previously issued shares that are traded during the period when the special price is being offered to shareholders.

ex-rights date The date after which shares of stock are sold ex rights. See also **rights on.**

external auditor Also called **independent auditor.** An independent auditor engaged to scrutinize a company's accounting data and financial statements in order to determine whether the firm has conformed to accepted accounting practices and principles. See also **internal auditor.**

external consultant Also called **outside consultant.** An adviser who is hired by a company on a temporary basis to analyze a specific problem and suggest a solution.

external control The management and regulation of people within an organzation by those to whom power has been formally delegated. See also **first-order controls.**

external data Facts generated outside a company, as by surveys or by government or private sources.

externalities See **economic externalities.**

external reporting The reporting of a company's financial situation to shareholders, the public at large, or any audience outside the company (e.g., annual report, 8-K report). See also **internal reporting.**

external storage Computer memory storage not part of the computer but connected to it in such a way that it is accessible by the central processing unit.

extra dating Extension of time beyond the established limit for payment of an invoice.

extra dividend Also called **extra.** A dividend in cash or in additional shares paid in addition to regular dividends.

extra-expense insurance Insurance that covers the extra expenses of carrying on business in temporary quarters after a fire or other disaster.

extraordinary item Also called **extraordinary gain (loss).** An accounting entry or tax item reflecting a material expense or revenue that is neither frequent nor normal (e.g., a gain generated by the sale of a significant portion of the company at a profit, a loss incurred as a result of an earthquake).

extraordinary repair An accounting entry reflecting the cost of repairs not frequently or normally made (e.g., reconditioning or overhaul of a major piece of equipment to extend its useful life or utility).

extrapolation Projection or extension of known facts to an unknown situation.

extra terms Provisions of an agreement that allow a credit customer extra time for payment for a product or service.

extrinsic reward Satisfaction derived from salary, status, job title, and other recompense for work performed. See also **intrinsic reward.**

F

fabricating material A raw material (e.g., wood, cotton) that is processed into usable forms (e.g., lumber, fabric).

fabrication A form of manufacturing that involves machining, finishing, weaving, or some other treatment of raw materials.

face value The amount designated on the face of an instrument that is to be paid by the issuer or that represents its book value (e.g., the principal amount of a bond, the maturity value of a life insurance policy, the par value of a municipal bond).

facilitation 1. Provision of clear objectives to be attained in the accomplishment of a task. **2.** Coordination of assigned tasks and direction of effective performance in light of the goals to be achieved.

facsimile See **fax.**

factor 1. An agent who buys or sells goods for other persons on commission. **2.** A finance company or commercial bank that discounts accounts receivable for dealers and producers.

factoring 1. The practice of lending money on the basis of a company's accounts receivable. **2.** The purchase by a bank or other financial institution or group of a company's accounts receivable, after which customers make payments directly to the institution or group holding the accounts.

factor of production A resource used in the production of goods and services: land, labor, or capital.

factory outlet A store, operated by a manufacturer, that sells quality merchandise directly to consumers for less than current retail prices.

factory overhead Also called **manufacturing overhead.** Charges incurred in the manufacturing process exclusive of charges for raw materials and direct labor.

fact sheet A printed sheet listing all features of a product, intended to accompany the product when it is sold.

Fair Credit Reporting Act Federal legislation enacted in 1970 that includes among its provisions (enforced by the Federal Trade Commission) the requirement that consumers be permitted access to their personal credit records and given an opportunity to correct inaccurate data, and specifies the conditions under which such records will be maintained and disseminated.

Fair Labor Standards Act Also called **Wage and Hour Law.** An act of Congress passed in 1938 that regulates minimum wages, compensation for overtime work, and employment of minors, and designates employees exempt from its provisions.

fair market value The fair price that is likely to be paid for stock, real estate, or any other asset offered for sale on the open market when all existing factors are taken into consideration. See also **market value.**

fair-trade agreement An agreement or contract between a manufacturer and a retailer to sell a brand product at no less than a specified price: declared illegal in 1975.

false drop A descriptor or term that fails to describe the concept one is attempting to identify by means of a computer search of related terms.

family brand A brand name that is used on two or more products.

family group A group of individuals who are part of the same organization or are closely associated as an integral work group: applied to such a group undergoing training to improve interpersonal relationships with the aim of forming a cohesive unit.

Fannie Mae See **Federal National Mortgage Association.**

farming See prospecting.

f.a.s. (*abbr for free alongside ship*) An indication that the cost of transporting goods to a ship is borne by the seller, but that thereafter the transportation costs are to be paid by the buyer.

FASB statement An official decision policy or pronouncement issued by the Financial Accounting Standards Board that establishes a particular financial accounting practice as a standard and acceptable accounting principle.

fast track A career track in which a person advances more rapidly than usual.

favorable balance of trade An excess in value of exports over imports.

fax 1. Also called **facsimile. a.** A method or device (**fax machine**) for transmitting documents, drawings, photographs, or the like by telephone or radio for exact reproduction elsewhere. **b.** An exact copy or reproduction so transmitted. **2.** To transmit documents or the like by fax.

FCC See **Federal Communications Commission.**

FDA See **Food and Drug Administration.**

FDIC See **Federal Deposit Insurance Corporation.**

feasibility study Any of a series of studies, conducted principally by systems analysts, to determine the advisability of manufacturing a new product, revising a manufacturing process, etc., and if recommended, the steps necessary to implement such a course of action.

feasible solution A decision alternative that satisfies all constraints.

featherbedding The practice of requiring an employer to retain union members on a job when their skills are no longer needed, to hire more workers than are needed for an operation, or otherwise to pay full wages for unnecessary or nonproductive labor.

Fed See **Federal Reserve system.**

federal agency obligations Bonds or notes issued by the Federal National Mortgage Association, the Federal Home Loan Bank, the Government National Mortgage Association, and other federal agencies to finance their operations and available through commercial banks, generally at minimum values of $1000 to $5000 and at yields slightly higher than those of bills, notes, and bonds issued by the U.S. Treasury.

Federal Communications Commission (*abbr* FCC) A federal agency empowered to grant licenses to commercial broadcasters, assign frequencies, regulate interstate communications by radio, television, telephone, and telegraph, and set rates for wire communications.

Federal Deposit Insurance Corporation (*abbr* FDIC) A federal agency that insures up to a maximum amount deposits in all banks that belong to the Federal Reserve system.

Federal Energy Administration (*abbr* FEA) A federal agency instituted in 1973 to establish and implement a federal energy policy.

Federal Home Loan Mortgage Corporation A federally sponsored private corporation that purchases mortgages from banks, repackages them as securities, and sells them to private investors: primary purpose is to provide funds for residential mortgages.

Federal Housing Administration (*abbr* FHA) A federal agency established in 1934, now part of the Department of Housing and Urban Development, that insures mortgages on private and multifamily houses, housing for the elderly, nursing homes, and housing in urban renewal areas, and insures loans for property improvement.

Federal Insecticide, Fungicide, and Rodenticide Act An act of Congress passed in 1972 requiring that before a pesticide may be sold to the public it must be registered with the Environmental Protection Agency, which may refuse registration or restrict the sale of the product to specified types of customers.

Federal Insurance Contributions Act (*acronym* FICA) Also called **Social Security Act.** Federal legislation passed in 1935 to institute the social security system, under whose provisions a percentage of each worker's salary or wages is deducted by the employer and credited to the individual's social security account in order to create a fund for the provision of monthly benefits to retired and disabled workers and their dependents or survivors.

Federal Mediation and Conciliation Service A federal agency that may be called upon for aid in settling a labor dispute. See also **arbitration.**

Federal National Mortgage Association (*abbr* FNMA) A federally sponsored private corporation that purchases mortgages from banks for resale to investors, the purpose being to maintain a steady supply of funds for home mortgages.

Federal Reserve system (*abbr* Fed) A federal banking system created by the Federal Reserve Act of 1913 to set monetary policy and control the amount of cash and credit available by establishing reserve requirements, buying and selling government bonds, and setting the interest rates charged its member banks (now numbering 6000) in its 12 geographical districts when they borrow money from it.

Federal Trade Commission (*abbr* FTC) A federal agency created by the Federal Trade Commission Act (1914) with powers to enforce legislation banning unfair competitive practices among businesses and to guide businesses in avoidance of activities in restraint of trade. See also **Magnuson-Moss Act; Wheeler-Lea Act.**

Federal Water Pollution Control Act An act of Congress passed in 1972 establishing limits on the discharge of pollutants into national waterways.

federal withholding tax (*abbr* FWT) A percentage of an employee's gross earnings that is deducted from each paycheck and deposited with the federal government to offset the employee's income-tax liability, the percentage being dependent on the employee's income and number of exemptions.

fee A sum of money, either fixed by prior agreement or negotiated, paid by a client to cover the provision of services and materials used in the completion of a job.

feedback 1. Information on the results of any action, considered as influencing future decisions or performance. **2.** Reintroduction of part of the output of a computer system as input, especially for purposes of correction or control. **3.** Continuous, automatic furnishing of data concerning the output of a machine to an automatic control device so that errors may be corrected.

feedback system 1. A system of regular (daily or weekly) reports on production performance generated by computerized monitoring and/or supervisors. **2.** A system for continuous, automatic furnishing of data concerning the output of a machine to an automatic control device.

FHA See **Federal Housing Administration.**

FICA See **Federal Insurance Contributions Act.**

fidelity bond An insurance agreement providing for indemnification of an employer against losses sustained as a result of the dishonesty of an employee (as by embezzlement or theft).

fiduciary A person who has the legal power to act for another; a trustee (as of a pension fund or an investment plan).

fiduciary management system A formal system whereby an individual employee, work group, or supervisor can bring to management's attention any issue considered dysfunctional to the organization as a whole.

Fiedler's leadership contingency model A group contingency or interaction model developed by Fred E. Fiedler to measure leadership styles and permit evaluation of the effectiveness of a leader's style in relation to the makeup of the group.

Fiedler's LPC scale (*abbr for* least preferred co-worker scale) An eight-point scale developed by Fred E. Fiedler for evaluation of behaviors that either help or hinder successful completion of group tasks, the least preferred co-worker being rated low on such qualities as pleasantness, friendliness, helpfulness, enthusiasm, warmth, harmoniousness, and efficiency.

field salesperson A salesperson who visits clients and prospective clients at their business establishments.

field warehousing Storage of inventories used as collateral in a warehouse or area set apart on the borrower's property, usually to avoid the cost and difficulties of transporting awkward materials.

FIFO (*acronym for* first in, first out) A method of costing inventory that assumes that the stock acquired first will be sold first. Goods sold are therefore costed at the price of the earliest stock, and ending inventory is costed at the price of the most recent purchases (opposite of LIFO). See also **weighted average cost**.

file maintenance The process of periodically updating the information in computer memory files.

file wrapper A folder containing an application for a patent and all other documents pertaining to it.

final-goods recession Long-term erosion of consumer purchasing power due to a combination of inflation, increases in taxes and interest rates, and other factors. See also **inventory recession**.

finance 1. The management function of raising and using moneys. 2. To supply with money or capital; obtain money or credit for a purchase or enterprise.

finance charge Interest or a fee charged for borrowing money or buying on credit.

finance company An institution engaged in such specialized forms of financing as extending credit to retailers and lending money with goods as security.

financial accounting The area of accounting concerned with external reporting, as with financial statements and reports to government agencies.

Financial Accounting Standards Board (*abbr* FASB) An independent organization established by the certified public accounting profession to create and confirm accounting principles and financial reporting practices for adoption by the profession. See also **FASB statement; generally accepted accounting principles.**

financial lease A noncancelable lease that includes no maintenance service and is fully amortized (i.e., total payments equal or exceed the value of the property).

financial leverage The extent to which assets are supported or generated by debt, which acts as a sort of lever to raise income by providing funds for investment. See also **leverage.**

financial planner A professional who devises a program for the allocation of personal finances and capital through budgeting, investments, etc.

financial ratio A ratio expressing the relationship of any of various financial factors, including income, sales, expenses, and stock turnover, used as an indicator of a firm's economic condition and operating efficiency.

financial responsibility law A state law requiring automobile owners to provide evidence that they can pay for damages caused by accidents in which they are legally at fault.

financial risk Also called **speculative risk.** The probability that the return on an investment or the value of an asset will be unpredictably negative. See also **pure risk.**

financial statement Any of five reports on the operations or financial position of a business organization on a certain date or during a certain period, often in comparison with prior periods. See also **balance sheet; income statement; statement of changes in financial position; statement of changes in owners' equity; statement of retained earnings.**

financing lease See **capital lease.**

finder's fee 1. Payment to one who brings a buyer and seller together. **2.** Payment to one who secures a mortgage for a buyer, or who arranges a merger, finds an underwriter for a company issuing stock, etc.

finished goods inventory 1. The stock of finished products ready for sale. **2.** The dollar value of finished products ready for sale (a current asset).

firm order A written or verbal order that cannot be canceled by either buyer or seller without payment of a substantial penalty.

first in, first out See **FIFO.**

first-line management The lowest level of supervisory position in an organization, with responsibility for supervision of hourly production workers.

first-order controls Rules and regulations formally recognized by an organization and used to restrain or modify employees' behavior. See also **external control.**

first proof The first print of an advertisement, made for examination and correction.

fiscal policy The financial policy of a government, particularly in regard to debt and budgetary matters.

fiscal year Also called **business year.** The period of time, which may be less than 12 months but not more, and which may but usually does not coincide with a calendar year, from one balancing of accounts to the next; the period covered by an annual report.

fishbowl A training technique whereby participants take turns acting out solutions to organizational problems and observing and analyzing the solutions acted out by others.

fishyback Transportation of goods by truck in a trailer that is then loaded directly onto a ship for delivery to the port of their destination. See also **birdyback**.

five m's *M*anpower, *m*aterials, *m*oney, *m*achinery, *m*anagement: the basic resources of any organization.

fixed asset Also called **long-term asset; noncurrent asset.** A tangible asset with a useful life of more than one year (e.g., a building, land, furniture, manufacturing or transportation equipment) used in running a business and not usually converted into cash.

fixed asset turnover ratio Sales divided by fixed assets. See also **activity ratio.**

fixed cost Also called **fixed charge.** A cost that does not fluctuate with variation in production (e.g., interest, rent, payment to a sinking fund). See also **fixed overhead.**

fixed expense An expenditure (usually in connection with administration rather than manufacturing) that does not vary with short-term changes in production or sales.

fixed-income Gaining or yielding a more or less uniform rate of income, such as bonds that pay a fixed rate of interest until maturity or preferred stock that pays a fixed dividend.

fixed liability Also called **long-term liability; noncurrent liability.** An obligation that will not come due for a relatively long time, usually more than a year.

fixed overhead Factory overhead that does not change with normal increases or decreases in production (e.g., rent, most wages, utility costs).

fixed-rate mortgage A home mortgage for which equal monthly payments of interest and principal are made over the life of the loan, usually for a term of 30 years.

fixture An attachment to a building (e.g., a lavatory, a lighting fixture) that, though permanently installed, could be removed (a depreciable fixed asset).

flash sales report A daily report of the dollar value of sales made by each department of a retail store.

flat organization An organizational hierarchy that has relatively few levels and consequently is characterized by wide spans of management with a high degree of authority delegated to middle managers.

flat rate A standard or uniform rate charged for a product or service, with no discount given for any reason.

flat tax A tax applied at the same rate to all levels of taxable income.

flexdollars Money given by an employer that an employee can apply to any of various employee benefits.

flexible budget Also called **variable budget.** A budget in which alternative expense allowances are provided in conjunction with alternative levels of production and/or sales.

flexible manufacturing system (*abbr* FMS) A grouping of machines with reprogrammable controllers linked by an automated materials-handling system and integrated through a central computer, so that the system can produce a variety of parts that have similar processing requirements.

flexible-rate mortgage 1. See **variable-rate mortgage. 2.** See **renegotiable-rate mortgage.**

flextime Also called **flexitime.** A flexible schedule of work hours for employees, permitting them to arrive and depart within specified limits so long as they complete the required number of hours per day, week, etc.

flexweek Also called **flexiweek.** A four-day workweek.

flier A sales-promotion announcement, usually of one page, distributed to regular and prospective customers; a handbill.

flighting Also called **pulsing.** An advertising strategy that alternates periods of highly concentrated advertising with periods of no advertising at all.

float 1. To lay out an advertisement on a sheet much larger than any on which it will appear in print, leaving a large border. **2.** To offer (an issue of stock) for sale. **3.** The amount of money represented by checks that have been deposited in a bank but not yet collected from the banks on which they are drawn. The interest thus earned is often a bank's prime source of revenue. **4.** Also called **slack.** The amount of time an activity can be delayed beyond its earliest possible starting time without delaying the completion of a project. **5.** (*stock exchange*) The part of a new stock issue that has not been bought by the public. **6.** To let a currency or interest rate fluctuate in the foreign-exchange or money market.

floater An insurance policy to cover personal property taken with one, as on vacation.

floating rate note A note whose interest rate fluctuates in line with the money market, prime rate, etc.

floppy disk A thin plastic disk coated with magnetic material, for storing computer data and programs; diskette.

flow chart 1. A detailed diagram of the operations and equipment used to complete a manufacturing process. **2.** A graphic representation, using symbols interconnected with lines, used to show the successive steps in any procedure or system.

flow process chart A chart listing in detail each element involved in each step of a process, for use in analyzing and simplifying procedures.

fluid cash The cash and checks that are gathered by a company in the course of daily business.

FNMA See **Federal National Mortgage Association.**

f.o.b. (*abbr for free on board*) An indication that a seller will deliver goods to a shipper but thereafter freight charges are borne by the buyer.

f.o.b. destination (*abbr for free on board and to destination*) An indication that a seller bears the cost of transporting goods to a buyer and retains title to them until they are delivered.

focus gambling The process of focusing on alternative solutions to a problem or on alternative strategies for solving a problem. See also **scanning.**

focus group A representative group of people questioned together, usually in a controlled setting, about their opinions on product marketing or other issues.

follow-on experience An activity designed to reinforce concepts introduced in a training session and to support the lessons taught.

follow-up 1. A process of or system for taking additional action after an initial effort. **2.** The process of examining a past effort for any insights it may yield.

Food and Drug Administration (*abbr* FDA) A division of the U.S. Department of Health and Human Services that protects the public against impure and unsafe foods, drugs, and cosmetics.

Food, Drug, and Cosmetic Act An act of Congress passed in 1938 to prohibit the manufacture and interstate shipment of any food, drug, cosmetic, or health device that is mislabeled (bears a label that includes any false or misleading statement), adulterated (contains an admixture of another substance sufficient to dilute its strength), or injurious to health. See also **Delaney Amendment.**

foot To add figures in a vertical column. See also **crossfoot.**

forbearance The act of abstaining from doing or promising not to do something one has the legal right to do (e.g., the collecting of a debt).

forecasting The process of predicting future business conditions on the basis of study and analysis of available data for the purpose of making intelligent decisions in regard to promotions, advertising, plant expansion, development of new products, and other activities.

foreclosure The process of depriving a mortgagor of the right to own mortgaged property as a consequence of failure to pay by the due date, title to the property then passing to the mortgagee.

foreign corporation A corporation that conducts its business in a state other than the one in which it was incorporated. See also **domestic corporation.**

Foreign Corrupt Practices Act (*abbr* FCPA) An act of Congress passed in 1977 to outlaw payments of bribes to foreign officials for the opportunity to obtain lucrative contracts.

foreign exchange 1. The process of balancing accounts in transactions between individuals or firms in different countries. **2.** The currency of a foreign country or negotiable instruments payable in such currency.

foreign-exchange contract A contract by which two parties agree to an exchange of currencies on a specified future date at a specified rate, both parties thereby seeking to protect themselves against unforeseeable fluctuations in the exchange rate.

foreign-exchange rate The rate at which the currency of one country may be exchanged for another currency at a given time.

foreign-exchange service (*abbr* FX) Long-distance telephone service by means of a special (trunk) line run from a foreign or distant exchange to the subscriber's phone, on which calls may be placed at the rate in effect in the distant community.

foreign licensing A process by which a company authorizes a firm in a foreign country to produce and market its products in that country for a fee.

foreign-trade zone See **free-trade zone**.

forestalling The process of including anticipated objections in a formal sales presentation to a client, thereby retaining control over the presentation.

formal group A group of people, usually consisting of a supervisor and subordinates, assembled on a permanent or ad hoc basis to work toward common organizational goals and objectives. See also **ad hoc committee; informal group.**

formal integrative unit A group designated to facilitate and coordinate efforts to integrate various organizational units with specialized functions to meet the organization's specific goals.

formalization The process of establishing organizational standards to govern the behavior of employees.

formal leader A person selected by management to assume a position of leadership in the organization.

formal organization A company organized in accordance with a formal structural plan. See also **organization chart.**

formal search Systematized information retrieval through a process of data-based intervention.

format 1. The arrangement of data for computer input or output, such as the number of fields in a database record or the margins in a report. **2.** The programming featured by a radio or television station, such as talk show or classical music. **3. a.** To set the format of computer data input or output. **b.** To prepare a computer disk as required by the software that will be used.

form utility The value created through the transformation of raw materials and other inputs into finished goods.

FORTRAN (*acronym for For*mula *Trans*lation) A computer programming language designed for use in solving mathematical and scientific problems.

Fortune 500 An annual list compiled by Fortune magazine of the 500 largest industrial corporations in the U.S.

forward buying The practice of purchasing raw materials or other items required in manufacturing in large quantities far in advance of need for the purpose of securing a discount, ensuring needed supplies, and facilitating analysis of costs.

forward scheduling A method of preparing a schedule by starting with the first activity and working forward in sequence to schedule the later activities and derive a completion date.

forward vertical merger See **vertical merger.**

four-day week Also called **flexweek.** A workweek consisting of four days, usually of ten hours each.

401(k) A savings plan that allows employees to contribute a fixed amount of income to a retirement account and to defer taxes until withdrawal.

FPA See **Freight Paid Allowance.**

FPT See **freight-pass-through.**

franchise A right granted by a producer to sell or distribute the producer's products and use the producer's name, patents, trademarks, and processes in a specified location or territory in exchange for an initial fee plus royalties or commissions.

franchisee A person who has been granted a franchise.

franchisor Also called **franchiser.** A person who grants a franchise to another person.

fraud An act of trickery, deceit, or breach of confidence committed to gain an unfair or dishonest advantage.

Freddie Mac See **Federal Home Loan Mortgage Corporation.**

free enterprise Also called **private enterprise.**

An economic system that operates in accordance with the law of supply and demand, private businesses competing to satisfy consumers' demands, and government acting only to protect individual rights, not to regulate commercial activity.

freelance A self-employed specialist in some (usually creative) field who works on a temporary basis for various employers.

free-market system Also called **market economy.** An economic system that operates by free competition, the merchant setting his or her own prices and selling to anyone who will pay those prices, the consumer purchasing from any seller in accordance with his or her needs, desires, and ability to pay.

free-rein leader A manager who practices a policy of minimal supervision while delegating most decision making to subordinates.

free trade International trade unhampered by tariffs or other governmental restrictions. Free traders advocate the removal of all existing tariffs and restrictions on trade between countries.

free-trade area A geographical area consisting of nations (not necessarily contiguous) that agree to permit unrestricted trade in each other's products and commodities, with tariffs, if any, used only as a source of revenue and not as a means of limiting access to foreign goods or influencing their prices.

free-trader A person who opposes any restriction on foreign trade.

free-trade zone Also called **foreign trade zone.** A designated industrial area into which foreign goods (usually raw materials or parts) can be imported without payment of customs until the goods leave the zone as finished products, or with no such payment at all if the finished products are exported to a third country.

freeze 1. To fix rents, prices, etc., at a specific amount, usually by government order. **2.** To prevent assets from being liquidated or collected.

freeze rate Also called **rate stop.** A minimum rate established by a trucking company for transportation of goods that is essentially independent of the distance traveled.

freight allowed See **postage-stamp pricing.**

freight forwarder Also called **package-**

consolidating agency. An independent person or company that arranges for transportation of goods within a country or between countries.

freight in See **transportation in.**

freight out See **transportation out.**

Freight Paid Allowance (*abbr* FPA) An agreement whereby the shipper pays a specified percent or part of shipping costs, such as an agreement between publisher and bookstores.

freight-pass-through (*abbr* FPT) A special discount given a retailer for paying the freight charge on a shipment of merchandise: the charge is then passed along to the consumer by an increase in the product's suggested retail price.

frequency distribution An arrangement of a set of statistical data showing the number of times each item appears in each of the categories, intervals, or values into which the data are classified.

frictional unemployment Brief periods of unemployment, unrelated to basic inadequacies of supply or demand, experienced by people entering the job market or moving between jobs.

friendship, commerce, and navigation treaty (*abbr* FCN treaty) An international agreement by which each signatory nation permits nationals of the treaty partner to conduct business in its domestic market under conditions specified.

fringe benefit Compensation extended to employees (e.g., a pension plan, health and life insurance, vacations and sick leave with pay) in addition to basic salaries and wages. See also **cafeteria plan.**

front end Any location inside or outside a store where customers pay for goods.

front-end bonus A payment made usually to an executive at the time of hiring to compensate for bonuses or other payments the individual would have received in the job he or she is leaving and as an incentive, in preference to a higher salary, which might cause resentment among company veterans.

front-end checkout The placement of checkout counters near store exits rather than near sales areas.

front-end load The sales commission and other

fees taken out of the initial payments when an investor contracts to purchase shares of certain mutual funds.

front money **1.** Money paid in advance, as for goods or services, to a commission agent or the like. **2.** Capital necessary to begin a business enterprise. **3.** Money furnished by a company to a financier under a promise to procure funds for it.

front office Collectively, the offices of top management within a company.

frozen See **freeze.**

FTC See **Federal Trade Commission.**

fulfillment The process or business of handling and executing customer orders, as packing, shipping, or processing checks.

full costing See **absorption costing.**

full employment The lowest rate of unemployment compatible with price stability, variously estimated at between 5 and 6 percent.

full endorsement Also called **special endorsement.** Writing on the back of a negotiable instrument, consisting of the name of the person or persons to whom it is being transferred and, underneath, the signature of the payee.

full-service agency An advertising agency that provides accounting and marketing services, does product research and development, and works with clients from product conceptualization to market testing and full-scale launching, in addition to creating and placing advertisements.

full warranty A manufacturer's guarantee that a defective product will be repaired free of charge within a specified time after purchase, and that after a reasonable number of attempts to repair the product, the purchaser may elect either a refund (less an amount for depreciation) or replacement. See also **limited warranty; Magnuson-Moss act.**

fully diluted earnings per share The smallest earnings per share of common stock that would be paid if all convertible bonds and preferred stock and other convertible securities were converted to common stock, and which must be reported on the company's income statement if the figure represents less than 97 percent of total earnings available to an average number of outstanding common stocks.

fully managed fund A mutual fund with an investment policy that allows the fund's management to act with reasonable discretion in the buying and selling of any securities in any combination or quantity.

functional authority 1. The formal power exercised by the manager of a specific unit or subsystem of an organization. **2.** A right to direct the activities of others based on possession of specialized knowledge, skill, or ability. See also **authority.**

functional departmentalization A homogeneous grouping of jobs into a single department, major division, or subsystem.

functional discount See **trade discount.**

functional management The administration and control of a specific unit of an organization.

functional organization An organizational structure (common today only in the film industry) in which direct authority over each task or function resides in a manager who is considered a specialist, and each employee below the level of top management reports to more than one superior in accordance with a specific phase of his or her activity.

fund 1. funds **a.** Money; working capital. **b.** Assets, especially cash or marketable securities, set aside for a specific purpose. See also **sinking fund. 2.** A mutual fund. See also **closed-end investment company. 3.** A self-balancing account, as requested by a donor to a nonprofit organization or as required of a governmental agency by policy restrictions.

fund accounting A system of accounting in which each account is self-balancing. See also **fund** (def. 3).

fund balance In the fund accounting system of a nonprofit organization or governmental agency, the difference between assets and liabilities (including any reserves).

funding The acquisition and allocation of money needed to operate a business or to finance a venture.

funds statement See **statement of changes in financial position.**

fungible goods Products that consist of like

units that can be replaced by other units similar in weight and number.

furlough 1. A temporary layoff, usually due to lack of business. 2. A leave of absence from work or other duties due to an employee's desire for time to take care of personal business.

future goods Products that are allocated for sale before they have been manufactured, as crops that are not yet grown. See also **contract to sell; identified goods.**

futures trading Also called **cash trading.** Contract agreements that promise the buying and selling of commodities or securities for delivery at a later date, often a year or more in the future.

FWT See **federal withholding tax.**

FX See **foreign-exchange service.**

G

game plan A strategy or design for the achievement of an objective or goal.

game theory A mathematical theory that deals with strategies for maximizing gains and minimizing losses within prescribed constraints, applied to the solution of business problems and to the training of employees to deal with conflict, the decision-making process, leadership struggles, and group norms.

Gantt chart A chart on which work activities are plotted against a time scale.

garbage in, garbage out See GIGO.

garnishment A legal notice requiring the person addressed to hold money or property of another person in his or her possession pending the outcome of litigation over an unpaid debt owed by the owner of the money or property.

gatefold A magazine cover or page that is larger than the regular pages, being folded so as not to extend beyond the edges. Gatefolds are used for advertisements.

gatekeeping Regulation of communication patterns among individuals by a group facilitator, who encourages some to speak and others to listen.

gateway The point at which a shipment is transferred from one carrier to another or at which goods enter the transportation system.

GDP See **gross domestic product.**

General Agreement on Tariffs and Trade (*abbr* GATT) An international treaty and the autonomous agency established in 1967 to administer its provisions, with headquarters in Geneva, Switzerland, which provides a forum for settlement of trade disputes and negotiation of trade liberalization among nearly 90 signatory nations plus 30 de facto members.

generally accepted accounting principles (*abbr* GAAP) Standards, conventions, and rules established by the Financial Accounting Standards Board (in FASB Opinions), by the Accounting Principles Board (in APB Opinions), and by the American Institute of Certified Public Accountants to be followed in the preparation of financial statements.

generally accepted accounting standards
(*abbr* GAAS) Rules established by the American Institute of Certified Public Accountants to be followed in audits of financial statements.

general partner A partner in a firm who plays an active role in management of the company, is publicly known as a partner, and has unlimited liability for the company's financial commitments. See also **dormant partner; limited partner; secret partner; silent partner.**

generic product A product that bears no brand name, is packaged inexpensively, is not advertised, and generally is priced lower than comparable brand-name products.

gentrification The buying and renovation of houses and stores in deteriorated urban neighborhoods by upper- or middle-income families or individuals, thus improving property values but often displacing low-income families and small businesses.

GERT (*acronym for* graphical evaluation and review technique) A method of network planning, introduced in 1966 to overcome shortcomings of the PERT method, encompassing activities that have probability of occurrence, an option of being performed, and variable completion times.

gestalt theory A theory that views the human mind as having the capacity to perceive an event or occurrence as a unified whole having specific qualities that cannot be derived from the sum of its component parts or individual elements.

gift tax A federal tax on gifts above $10,000. Gifts up to this amount may be given annually to a child of any age.

GIGO (*acronym for* garbage in, garbage out) Data that are incorrect or incorrectly entered in a computer will yield useless results.

gilt-edged security Any security, especially a blue-chip bond, that has a good record of regular interest payments and redemption and a high likelihood of continued high performance. United States Treasury bonds are the best examples of gilt-edged securities.

Ginnie Mae See **Government National Mortgage Association.**

giveback A concession by unions that represents a cut in wages or benefits, usually demanded by a management in order to avoid large-scale layoffs, factory closings, etc.

glamour stock A stock, as in a new or rapidly developing industry, that captures investors' fancy and tends to rise quickly in price.

glass ceiling An upper limit to professional advancement, especially as imposed upon women, that is not readily perceived or openly acknowledged.

global firm, A business that has production and distribution facilities, as well as R & D and strategic decision-making authority, in more than one country.

GNMA See **Government National Mortgage Association.**

GNP See **gross national product.**

goal An objective of a system, subsystem, or group established to give its members direction, a common purpose, and a unique position in their environment, to facilitate accountability and resolution of conflicts, to provide a means of measuring performance and rating success, and to challenge and motivate individuals by stimulating commitment and involvement in a mutually beneficial direction.

goal setting The process of creating and revising realistic objectives for a system, subsystem, or group.

goal succession The process of establishing a set of new organizational goals or objectives to replace those goals that have been achieved or abandoned.

going concern A company expected to continue its business operations into the indefinite future, paying its debts on time and generating revenues at profitable levels.

golden handcuffs A succession of raises, bonuses, perks, etc., given or promised at specified future intervals or tied to length of employment, so that an executive would find it extremely difficult to leave a company.

golden handshake Dismissal of an employee with generous benefits, cash bonus, etc.

golden parachute A package of benefits, as severance pay and bonuses, guaranteed a key executive in case of job loss due to a merger or takeover. See also **tin parachute**.

gold fixing Also called **gold fix**. **1.** The procedure by which the price of gold is established. **2.** The price itself, esp. as established daily in the gold market.

go/no-go gauge A standard by which defective products or parts are distinguished from those that are acceptable.

good A product or commodity that is manufactured or otherwise made available for sale (distinguished from *service*): usually used in plural.

good delivery A correct, legal transaction of an order involving a security in accordance with the terms agreed upon (usually a precondition of payment).

good faith Absence of intent to deceive; a belief in the honesty of one's purposes and actions.

good-till-canceled order See **open order**.

goodwill **1.** The business advantage acquired by a firm as a result of reputation for good business dealings. **2.** The excess in purchase price for a firm over the value of its net assets. **3.** The capitalized value of a firm's anticipated profits in excess of the rate of return considered normal in the industry in which the firm operates.

goodwill method A method of calculating partners' shares of a business whereby the capital account of a new partner is credited with an amount of goodwill equal to the amount of money he or she has contributed to the partnership. See also **goodwill** (def. 3).

go public To abandon the policy or position of having a limited number of stockholders and issue shares of stock for sale to the general public.

government bond A promissory note issued by the U.S. government (i.e., a Series E or Series H bond, a bill, note, or bond issued by the U.S. Treasury, or an obligation of a federal agency), technically not guaranteed but considered to be the highest quality bond available. See also **bond** (def. 1); **municipal bond**.

Government National Mortgage Association (*abbr* GNMA) A federally owned corporation that buys mortgages, especially those on low-rent housing, and raises funds by selling bonds guaranteed by the Veterans Administration and the Federal Housing Administration.

grace period A period of time after a payment becomes due, as of a loan or life-insurance premium, before one is subject to penalties or late charges or before the loan or policy is canceled.

graduated tax See **progressive tax.**

grandfather clause A clause exempting certain people or firms from a regulation by reason of circumstances or conditions that existed before the regulation went into effect.

grant A transfer of real property from one owner to another by means of a deed.

grapevine An informal communication system that is present in all organizations and that operates outside the formal communication channels.

graphical evaluation and review technique See **GERT.**

graveyard shift A work shift, usually from midnight until 8 a.m.

gravure A printing process whereby a desired design is cut into a metal plate, ink rolled onto the plate fills the grooves, and the design is transferred to paper. See also **intaglio.**

gray market **1.** A market in which scarce goods (e.g., computer chips) are traded at above-market prices through irregular channels or by methods not explicitly illegal but usually not considered ethical. **2.** The selling at bargain prices of goods one has bought covertly at an abnormally large discount. **3.** The market provided by senior citizens for special products and services.

greenmail The purchase, usually surreptitiously, of a large bloc of a company's stock, thereby signaling a possible takeover attempt, and ultimately forcing the company to try to thwart the attempt by buying back its stock at a much higher price.

Green River ordinance A local regulation that establishes standards for allowable door-to-door selling practices.

grid See **managerial grid.**

grievance A complaint of an employee or group of employees that an injustice is being suffered in a job-related matter.

grievance committee A group of representatives of employees, or of management and employees jointly, formed to discuss and seek to eliminate employees' grievances.

gross annual wages See **guaranteed annual wage.**

gross audience 1. The total number of households that tune in to a television show for at least six minutes, as measured by a random sample. **2.** The total number of people who are exposed to a publication at any time and in any manner, as measured by a random sample.

gross domestic product (*abbr* GDP) Gross national product excluding payments on foreign investments.

gross national product (*abbr* GNP) The total market value of all final goods and services produced in a country in a given period of time (usually a year).

gross profit Also called **gross margin.** Net sales less cost of goods sold.

gross profit method Evaluation of ending inventory by means of the estimated gross profit ratio.

gross profit ratio Gross profit (net sales less cost of goods sold) divided by net sales.

gross rating points (*abbr* GRP) A percentage of homes containing television sets where sets are tuned to a specific program at a designated time, used as a measure of the number of people reached by the program.

gross received See **cash flow.**

gross sales The dollar amount of all sales before deduction of discounts, returns, and allowances.

gross weight The total weight of a shipment, including the item shipped, the packing material, and the container.

gross working capital The capital available for ongoing operations of a business, calculated by determining the excess of current assets over liabilities.

group See **formal group; informal group.**

group depreciation Accounting for the simultaneous loss in value of several assets that have similar useful lives by a single figure representing their combined loss of value in each accounting period.

group development 1. A process for increasing the effectiveness of a team or work group. 2. Establishment of a working team through a process designed to bring the group closer together in commitment to goals and objectives.

group discount A special discount given in connection with the purchase of large quantities of an item or service at one time or of air time on several radio or television stations simultaneously.

grouping Perception of clusters of figures, objects, or facts as related rather than as discrete units. See also **closure.**

group maintenance The arrangement of individuals in a group, with either a centralized or decentralized leader, in such a way that work flow and satisfactory performance are established and continued.

group process The process by which such intangible elements of a work group as morale, tone, participation, competition, and cooperation interact and coalesce into a working force of high motivation and productivity striving toward a common goal.

group structure An arrangement of individuals within a particular framework that varies in degree of openness and centralization in proportion to size.

group technology (*abbr* GT) The grouping of items into families with similar characteristics and manufacturing requirements and the arrangement of equipment into cells or work stations for efficient processing of these families.

growth fund 1. A mutual fund whose net asset value has been rising at a rate greater than that of business as a whole. 2. A mutual fund whose net asset value has been rising at a rate of 10 percent or more.

growth stock A stock that is expected to increase in value as its issuing corporation grows in size and earnings.

GTC (*abbr for* good *till* canceled) See **open order.**

guarantee An assurance, written or implied, that a product is as represented and will perform satisfactorily. See also **express warranty; full warranty; implied warranty; limited warranty.**

guaranteed annual wage (*abbr* GAW) Also called **gross annual wages.** A minimum income guaranteed to employees by agreement between union and management.

guaranteed position An assurance given by a publisher that an advertisement will be displayed in a specific location in each edition printed. See also **run-of-paper.**

guaranty 1. An agreement to pay a debt or perform a duty owed by another person if that person fails to do so. **2.** Something given or possessed as security for the fulfillment of some action.

H

half-life (*marketing*) The estimated time required for half of the total number of responses to a mailing to be received.

halo effect **1.** A tendency to permit a high rating on one aspect of an employee's performance or of a job applicant's personality or background to exert undue influence on one's overall evaluation of the individual. **2.** The high regard for one brand name that is shared by a new product marketed under the same brand.

hand-to-mouth buying The practice of maintaining only enough stock to meet short-term basic business needs.

hangup An unintentional stoppage or closing down of a computer, generally caused by miscoded information in the software.

hard copy Text material in printed form, as in a manuscript or a computer printout. See also **soft copy**.

hard currency Money that is backed by gold reserves and thus is easily convertible into the currency of another country. See also **soft currency**.

hard disk A rigid disk coated with magnetic material, for storing computer programs and relatively large amounts of data.

hard goods See **durable goods**.

hard sell Forceful, aggressive, high-pressure salesmanship. See also **soft sell**.

hardware The electronic, mechanical, electrical, and magnetic components of a computer system. See also **software**.

hash total A sum (as of serial numbers of products) that has no meaning except as a control that can ascertain if any item has been omitted, as from a list or inventory.

Hawthorne studies A series of motivational studies conducted at a Western Electric Company plant (the Hawthorne Works) in Illinois that revealed the extraordinary autonomous power of the informal group to motivate workers' behavior.

head An electronic device in a computer or an audiotape or videotape machine that is responsible for recording, reading, and erasing incoming and outgoing messages.

headhunter See **executive search firm; recruiter.**

health-maintenance organization (*abbr* HMO) An organization of physicians and other health-care professionals that offers a prepaid medical plan entitling its members to unlimited access to medical and other health-care services.

hedge 1. To protect oneself against a possible loss (in an investment, in financial position, etc.) by diversifying one's investments, buying or selling commodity futures, etc. **2.** An act or means of protecting oneself against loss on an investment with a partially counterbalancing one.

helping relationship A client-centered therapeutic relationship, introduced by Carl Rogers, in which the professional is supportive of the client's self-discovery and personal growth.

Herzberg two-factor theory A theory introduced by Frederick Herzberg that bases employee satisfaction and motivation on factors intrinsic to the work itself and on a work environment in which employees can be entrusted with responsibility and achieve recognition. See also **extrinsic reward; intrinsic reward.**

heuristic Something that serves as a guide (as a rule of thumb) or that stimulates thought or research in the absence of known facts or proof. Such a procedure can be used to generate satisfactory solutions to decision problems but cannot guarantee that such solutions are optimal.

hiatus A temporary suspension of a regularly broadcast television or radio program (usually in the summer) because of reduced audience interest or because the number of programs prepared is insufficient to fill a full year's schedule.

hidden reserves The amount of understated value on a balance sheet, resulting from overvaluation of liabilities or undervaluation of assets.

hidden tax A tax that is included in the price of goods or services but is not separately stated.

hierarchy A management structure that has graduated top, middle, and lower levels, with the majority of employees occupying the bottom level and each successive higher level occupied by progressively fewer employees. See also **management pyramid.**

hierarchy of needs A five-step system of human needs proposed by Abraham Maslow, ranging from basic survival needs upward through needs for security, social interaction, self-esteem, and self-actualization, such that each successive level of need becomes dominant as the need at the preceding level is satisfied.

high-tech Related to or making use of high technology.

high technology Scientific technology involving advanced, sophisticated electronic devices, particularly for use in computers and in machines controlled by computers.

hiring hall A union-operated placement office where members are referred to available jobs.

histogram A graph of a frequency distribution in which the widths of rectangles based on the horizontal axis are equal to class intervals and their heights are equal to the corresponding frequencies.

historical cost See **acquisition cost.**

historical summary A selected list, usually part of an annual report, itemizing such significant financial figures as net income, total revenues, assets, liabilities, and earnings per share in each of the past five or ten fiscal years, including the current year. See also **comparative financial statement.**

HMO See **health-maintenance organization.**

holder A person who owns and is entitled to payment of a negotiable instrument (e.g., a promissory note).

holder in due course A person other than the original owner who holds a negotiable instrument and is entitled to payment.

holder-of-record date The final date on which stockholders can register with a corporation in order to receive future dividends, vote at shareholders' meetings, and be entitled to certain other benefits and rights.

hold-harmless agreement A contractual agreement that provides that one party will not hold the other liable for any damages that may result from the performance of the contract.

holding company A corporation that controls or is in a position to control one or more other companies by virtue of ownership of stock in those companies, usually without direct participation in productive activities.

holding cost Those costs incurred as a result of carrying inventory, usually expressed as a percentage of dollar value.

holding gain (loss) The difference between the price or value of an asset at the beginning of a period in which it is held and its value at the end of that period.

holding power (*marketing*) The ability of a television program to hold an audience for a full season.

home-industry argument The argument that competition in the domestic markets of any industry is increased by foreign imports, to the detriment of domestic firms.

home office 1. The main office of a company; headquarters. **2.** A work or office space set up in a worker's home.

homeowner's policy Also called **homeowner's insurance.** A form of home insurance that provides compensation for damage, loss, or injury of property, personal belongings, or persons due to fire, theft, accidents, etc.

homeshopping The purchase, usually by a phone call to an 800 number, of products displayed on television.

horizontal buying The practice of purchasing advertising space in a wide variety of publications as a way of reaching many target audiences with a wide diversity of interests.

horizontal integration The acquisition of one company by another in the same line of business.

horizontal merger Absorption of a company by another in the same field for the purpose of achieving economies of scale and lessening competition. See also **conglomerate merger; vertical merger.**

hospitalization insurance Insurance covering a specified percentage of hospital costs related to covered illnesses and injuries.

hostile takeover The act of taking control of a

company by buying up, often surreptitiously, enough of its stock to gain a controlling interest.

house shop An advertising agency owned or controlled by an advertiser.

human assets accounting See **human resources accounting.**

human engineering See **ergonomics.**

human factors engineering Management of the work of industrial workers with a view to minimizing the physical actions required to perform a task and maximizing efficiency.

human relations A field of management study concerned with problems arising from the interactions of people in organizations, specifically the relationship of managers and subordinates and its contribution to productive efficiency and work satisfaction.

human resources accounting Also called **human assets accounting.** Evaluation of the productive capacity of a company's employees by consideration of such variables as aptitude and intellect, training, quality of leadership, morale, communications, and decision making.

human resources forecast Prediction of future personnel needs based on analysis of the numbers and skills of current employees and the numbers and skills required to meet anticipated levels of production under anticipated economic and technological conditions.

human resources management Also called **personnel administration.** The recruitment, assessment, hiring, training, and counseling of employees at all levels within a company, and administration of employee benefit programs, health and safety programs, and labor relations.

human resources planning Establishment of schedules designed to facilitate the provision and maintenance of an efficient work force capable of meeting current objectives and anticipated future production requirements.

hygiene factor See **dissatisfier.**

hyperinflation Extreme or excessive inflation.

hypothecation The securing of a loan by a pledge of property that does not involve the transfer of title or possession.

I

IC See **integrated circuit**.

ICC 1. See **International Chamber of Commerce**. 2. See **Interstate Commerce Commission**.

idea-development interview (*abbr* IDI) (*marketing research*) A technique for eliciting product and advertising ideas from groups of consumers through the use of questions skillfully designed to tap consumer attitudes and perceptions of new products and advertising concepts. See also **consumer advisory board; consumer panel**.

identified goods Existing products that are allocated for sale under contract, thereby meeting the legal requirement for transfer of title to goods under a sales contract.

IDP See **integrated data processing**.

i.e. (*abbr for id* est) That is; in other words.

image The impression of a product, service, or company held in the minds of consumers or conveyed by its physical and qualitative characteristics or by advertising and publicity. See also **brand image; product position**.

image building (*public relations*) The process by which an organization tries to influence the public's attitude toward the firm and its products or services.

IMF See **International Monetary Fund**.

immaterial Not substantive; not large enough to count, to record, to affect decisions, or to require adjustment.

implicit cost A cost that is involved in the conduct of business and that is the responsibility of the owner.

implied warranty A guarantee assumed to have been given in connection with a transaction, though not expressly stated, and arguable at law for reasons of public policy (as that an automobile sold is safe to drive). See also **express warranty**.

import 1. To purchase goods or raw materials in one country and bring them or cause them to be brought to another country. 2. A product brought into a country from another country.

import quota A limitation on the number of

products in a specific category that can be brought into a country from another country. See also **embargo**.

imprest fund Also called **imprest account**. An account or fund (such as a petty-cash account) that is constantly diminished but periodically replenished to an established amount.

impulse item A product that customers are likely to buy impulsively rather than as a result of advance planning.

imputed interest Estimated interest due and assumed to be included in a single repayment of a loan, as the difference between the face value of a note upon maturity and the price actually paid for it.

inactive stock A stock for which there is little demand.

in-basket exercise A training exercise in which participants simulate the handling of messages, reports, memos, and other communications that may come to their attention during the course of a business day.

in bond See **bond** (def. 3).

Inc. See **incorporated**.

incidental damages Any expenses incurred in the process of gaining redress for failure to fulfill the terms of a contract. See also **actual damages**.

incident pattern Also called **critical incidence**. A behavioral pattern that emerges in the course of observations of individuals as they perform various tasks, which serves to indicate areas of strength and weakness.

income from continuing operations All revenues less all expenses, exclusive of gains or losses on the sale of business segments and extraordinary items (including tax effects), cumulative accounting charges, and the results of operations that have been or soon will be discontinued.

income from discontinued operations Net income, after taxes, from business segments or lines that have been or soon will be sold or otherwise discontinued.

income fund A mutual fund that invests in stocks that have a good record of dividend payments and high likelihood of continued and increasing dividends.

income statement Also called **profit and loss statement; statement of operations.** A concise financial statement that reports a company's revenues, associated expenses and losses, and the resulting net income over a specified period, and that may also include earnings per share and a reconciliation of beginning and ending retained earnings balances.

income summary (*bookkeeping*) A temporary account representing an income statement, to which revenue closing entries are transferred as credits and expenses are closed as debits; after all other closing entries are made, the closing balance is transferred to the retained earnings account, where it represents net income for the period.

income-tax expense Also called **provision for income tax.** An estimated charge for a company's income tax, considered part of operating expense.

incorporated (*abbr* Inc.) Chartered by a state as a corporation and thus as an entity burdened with certain obligations and freed from certain liabilities. See also **corporation.**

incorporation The process of forming or being formed as a legally chartered corporation, with legal rights to make contracts, to own, buy, and sell property, and to sue and be sued. See also **corporation.**

incremental budgeting The practice, followed by most organizations, of basing each period's budget on that of the previous period, with increases to keep pace with inflation or to permit expansion. See also **zero-based budgeting.**

incremental cost **1.** A cost incurred by the exercise of one option rather than another. **2.** Also called **differential cost; marginal cost.** The cost of producing each additional unit.

incremental revenue Also called **marginal revenue.** The additional net or gross income (depending on context) that would come from the sale of one more unit.

indemnity **1.** Protection or security against loss or damage. **2.** Compensation for damage or loss. **3.** Protection (as by insurance for a private individual or by law for a public officer) against liabilities and penalties otherwise incurred by one's actions.

indenture A contract between a bond issuer and a bondholder specifying the form of the bond, any property that backs it, the authorized amount of bonds issued, restrictions on the issuer's indebtedness and dividend payments, provisions for a sinking fund and premature redemption, and other pertinent facts.

independent accountant An accountant temporarily employed by an organization to conduct public accounting, who is financially and familially detached from the audited organization and whose only nonremunerative interest in the task is impartial fairness, accuracy, and honesty.

independent auditor See **external auditor**.

independent contractor A person or firm hired to do a specific task or to provide a specific service but not as an employee under the control of an employer. See also **freelance**.

independent variable (*statistics*) A variable whose value is known and which can be used to predict the value of a dependent variable.

index See **index number**.

index arbitrage An attempt by stock traders, especially those representing large institutions, to lock in profits by selling off the more expensive futures and buying those that are less expensive.

indexation The practice of adjusting salaries or other payments to some index of inflation. See also **consumer price index**.

index fund A fund, as a mutual fund or pension fund, with a portfolio that contains many of the securities listed in a major stock index in order to match the performance of the stock market generally.

index number A quantity whose variation from one day to the next or over a period of time measures the change in relative value of prices or some other phenomenon. See also **Dow Jones average; Standard & Poor's 500**.

indirect action advertising Advertising activities designed to give a product or brand significant exposure for the purpose of generating favorable attitudes and long-term commitment to it.

indirect cost An expense that cannot readily be charged to a particular product or project. See also **factory overhead; overhead.**

indirect labor Factory labor that cannot readily be charged to the production of specific units, and whose costs are therefore recorded as part of factory overhead. See also **direct labor.**

indirect materials Raw materials that are consumed in the production process but that cannot readily be charged to the production of specific units, and whose costs are therefore recorded as part of factory overhead. See also **direct materials.**

indirect supervision Management characterized by adherence to guidelines and policies established at higher levels of the organizational hierarchy and significantly influenced by the overall climate of the organization.

individual retirement account See **IRA.**

industrial democracy A participative method of management that involves workers in company decision making, exemplified in the United States by cooperatives, in Israel by the kibbutz and moshav movements, in Peru by industrial communities, and in Yugoslavia and Jamaica by the self-management system.

industrial espionage The stealing of research data, blueprints, technological secrets, etc., especially by an employee in the hire of a competing company.

industrial goods Items, sometimes raw materials, used to make other goods and sold to manufacturers rather than consumers.

industrial humanism A philosophy of human resources management and related practices designed to alter the conventional complex structure of work relationships and the content of work itself by special attention to staffing and supervising.

industrial park Also called **business park.** An industrial complex of buildings and offices set in parklike surroundings, usually in a suburban or rural area.

industrial psychology A branch of psychology concerned with the behavior and motivation of individual workers in industrial organizations.

industrial-revenue bond A tax-exempt municipal bond sold to help finance local private industry, on which the interest rate is typically 3 percent lower than that of the average corporate bond.

industrial spy A person who engages in industrial espionage.

industrial union A labor union representing both skilled and unskilled workers in a particular industry. See also **Congress of Industrial Organizations.**

industry 1. The aggregate of manufacturing or technically productive enterprises in a particular field. **2.** Manufacture or trade in general. **3.** The ownership or management of factories.

inelastic demand A demand for a product or service that remains more or less constant despite changes in its price.

inelastic supply A supply of a product or service that remains more or less constant despite changes in its price.

in escrow See **escrow** (def. 2).

infant-industry argument The argument that in the absence of protective tariffs a new domestic industry can lose its market to foreign imports before it has time to develop sufficiently in technology, skill, and size to compete effectively with them.

inflation A general increase in consumer prices over time, usually expressed as an annual percentage rate.

Infomaster A computer service of Western Union consisting of translation of TWX messages into Telex and vice versa (so that the user needs only one dispatching teleprinter), the sending of messages to multiple addresses, storage of mailing lists, and the sending of collect messages.

infomercial A program-length television commercial that is cast in a standard format so as to disguise the fact that it is an advertisement.

informal group A group of people (in a business organization usually consisting of co-workers) who identify themselves as part of a system and create objectives and standards of behavior for themselves without the support of formal guidelines or leadership. See also **Hawthorne studies.**

informal leader Also called **peer leader.** A nonsupervisory employee who is recognized as a leader by members of his or her work group by reason of demonstrated influence, knowledge, or power. See also **formal leader.**

informal organization 1. An interconnection of managers and subordinates not specified by the formal structure of an organization. **2.** The personal and social level at which members of the organization interact. See also **grapevine.**

informal search An active effort to gather information from a limited and unstructured base of resources, as through discussion with co-workers or colleagues.

informal structure A set of objectives, duties, and behaviors that is not formally acknowledged but that influences and directs the actions of group members.

in good faith See **good faith.**

in-house 1. Employed on the staff of a company. **2.** Utilizing an organization's own staff or resources rather than external facilities.

in-house course Instruction offered by management to members of its staff.

initialize 1. To set variables, switches, etc., to their starting values at the beginning of a computer program. **2.** To prepare a computer or printer for reuse by clearing previous data from memory. **3.** To format a computer disk.

initial markup Also called **initial mark-on.** The amount by which the purchase price of a product is first raised to establish a selling price.

initial public offering, See **IPO.**

injunction A court order either directing someone to do something or prohibiting an activity or practice, often issued to restrain violence, restrict picketing, and prevent damage to property.

inner circle A small coalition of individuals within a larger dominant coalition formed to work out the plans and strategies of the organization. See also **dominant coalition.**

innovation 1. Introduction of something new; alteration of an existing situation; a change. **2.** A goal for organizational development that can be directed from outside or within the organization.

innovative design A formally designated framework of activities and relationships created for an organization and subdivided into project groups to meet the specific goals of the organization in a unique manner.

input 1. See also **output. a.** Data entered into a computer for processing. **b.** To enter data into a computer. **2.** An idea or suggestion made as part of the group process.

insert 1. An announcement usually printed by an advertiser and delivered to a publisher for insertion in a magazine or newspaper during the production process, either loose or bound into the publication. **2.** A clip added to a videotape program after the program has been assembled.

in-service training See **on-the-job training.**

inside out Proceeding from inside an organization to the outside, as when the publisher of a newspaper or magazine supplies demographic data about its readers to a potential advertiser. See also **outside in.**

insider trading The illegal practice of using inside information (e.g., merger agreements not yet made public) as a basis for trading stocks.

insolvency Inability to pay debts. See also **bankruptcy.**

installment sale A sales agreement allowing for periodic partial payments (installments) by the buyer, who receives conditional title or ownership of the goods purchased until all payments have been made.

Institute of Internal Auditors An organization of professional accounting auditors that maintains and develops standards of practice in the profession, and awards certification to practice professionally upon completion of examination requirements.

institutional advertising Advertising designed to establish a favorable image for an organization by emphasizing the quality of its products or services, its role in the community, etc.

institutional approach A method of studying marketing that focuses on the means by which middlemen can facilitate marketing functions.

institutional investor An organization that invests large sums of money in the securities market, such as a bank, mutual fund, insurance company, or pension fund.

institutional level The executive management level in an organization.

instrument A legal document (e.g., a bond, lease, note, check, ticket, agreement) giving evidence of rights and responsibilities between two parties.

insurable risk A loss that an insurance company will insure against, especially a common one (e.g., fire) beyond the control of the insured and of a major monetary value that can be calculated in such a way as to arrive at an economically acceptable premium.

insurance Protection purchased from an insurance company against losses of property or earning power or losses due to liability or to a disbarred or nonperforming employee.

insurance policy A written contract between an insured person and an insurance company specifying the exact losses to be covered and the costs to the insured person.

intaglio A printing process in which images etched or otherwise incised in a hard surface are transferred to paper by ink applied to the sunken design. See also **gravure.**

intangible asset Any nonphysical property (e.g., a patent, copyright, trademark, and such other nonphysical assets as goodwill and credit rating). See also **tangible asset.**

intangible property Property not physical in nature and usually consisting of legal rights. See also **intangible asset.**

integrated circuit (*abbr* IC) A network of many electronic circuits and transistors pressed into a small silicon chip that functions as the memory storage for a computer.

integrated data processing (*abbr* IDP) Coordination of all steps required to process data by computer.

integrated work team A group of workers whose jobs and tasks are interrelated and rotated among group members.

intensive marketing plan A marketing plan designed to offer a product in as many outlets as possible. See also **exclusive marketing plan.**

interactive Designating a computer system or program that allows users to enter commands or data, allowing immediate communication between computer and user.

interactive videodisk A videodisk system that permits the operator to branch off or access a pre-recorded program by means of a hand-operated device.

interdependency A relationship between an organization and its environment, two or more organizations, or two or more people, such that neither can survive without the help of the other.

interest 1. A sum paid or charged for the use of money or for borrowing money; such a sum expressed as a percentage of money borrowed to be paid over a given period, usually one year. 2. A business in which a person has a share, right, or title.

interface 1. A surface or general area regarded as the boundary between two diverse and independent systems, where certain aspects of those systems interconnect. 2. To connect with (another independent system). 3. Computer hardware or software designed to communicate information between hardware devices, between software programs, between devices and programs, or between computer and user.

interlocking directorate A board of directors one or more of whose members are simultaneously directors of one or more other corporations, especially those that are in direct competition.

intermerchant A specialist in foreign trade who arranges the payments for goods sold between a country with hard currency and a country with soft currency.

intermittent process Also called **job-order production.** A manufacturing operation involving frequent alterations in equipment setup and materials for the production of different products, as in the manufacture of clothing and in custom manufacturing.

internal accounting See **management accounting.**

internal administration The aggregate of procedures required for the proper functioning of an organization, including the keeping of records on losses and values, communications involving claims and loss-prevention techniques, preparation of manuals and administration of company policies, maintenance of paperwork dealing with insurance purchases, and distribution of risk costs among organizational units.

internal audit An analysis of records, reports, policies, and procedures that is regularly performed by the organization itself. See also **internal auditor.**

internal auditor A person permanently employed by a company to scrutinize its accounting data and financial statements in order to determine whether operations and managerial practices conform to company policy and the law, and to find opportunities to decrease costs and improve efficiency.

internal consultant An adviser permanently employed to determine by surveys, interviews, and observations practical means of improving the effectiveness of an organization's personnel and practices.

internal control Modification of the behavior of employees in order to increase willingness to accept company standards.

internal rate of return (*abbr* IRR) Also called **time-adjusted rate of return. 1.** The effective yield of an investment project, calculated annually over the life of the project. **2.** The discount rate used to evaluate a proposed long-term project, derived by equating the present value of the cash outlays needed to start and maintain the project and the expected cash receipts and payments. **3.** The interest rate on an amount to be invested in a project that, if it were paid on an equal amount otherwise invested, would be equal to the expected future cash-flow rate to be generated by that project.

internal reporting Also called **management reporting.** The reporting of a company's financial situation to management or any other audience inside the firm. See also **external reporting.**

Internal Revenue Service (*abbr* IRS) The agency of the U.S. Treasury Department charged with administering the Internal Revenue Code and collecting income, excise, and other federal taxes.

International Chamber of Commerce (*abbr* ICC) An international organization that seeks to improve trading conditions among nations by supporting free movement of people, goods, and services and by sponsoring a court of arbitration, a service to help standardize business practices and documents, and a publication.

international firm A company that produces goods in one country for distribution in other countries. See also **multinational firm.**

international law The body of rules developed to guide and control nations in their conduct toward each other.

International Monetary Fund (*abbr* IMF) A fund established by the U.S. government to promote international trade by making loans to countries that require assistance and by promoting stability in foreign exchange, orderly markets, and international liquidity.

international trade The profitable interchange of goods and raw materials between countries. See also **export; import.**

Internet A large computer network linking smaller computer networks worldwide.

interperiod income-tax allocation Also called **deferred income-tax liability.** Allocation of one year's income-tax liability to two or more years' operations so that those liabilities are deducted from the revenues of those years, sometimes used as a means of reconciling differences of timing in the recording of transactions and charges for purposes of financial reporting.

interpersonal relationship A social relationship characterized by distinctive styles of expression and behavior and by a pattern of shared expectations.

interrole conflict Disagreement between individuals based on a variance in their expectations and preconceived perceptions of each other's role or the procedures that each is to follow.

Interstate Commerce Commission (*abbr* ICC) The first independent regulatory agency established (1887) by the federal government, now authorized to regulate the rates charged for transporting goods by rail, ship, and motor vehicle across state lines and other matters concerning public transport.

interstate traffic The movement of goods across state lines.

intervening variable An incidental element (e.g., group loyalty, conflict, technological assistance, attitude) that influences performance.

intervention 1. A change in action or behavior from accepted ways of doing things with an anticipated new end result. **2.** The process of interceding in aspects of an organization's management operations for the purpose of increasing effectiveness and work output.

interview A consultative meeting between people in which information is gathered, shared, or evaluated. See also **directed interview; exit interview; nondirected interview; stress interview.**

intestate 1. Having made no valid will. **2.** Not disposed of by a valid will.

in toto (*Latin*) Totally; entirely.

intranet A computer network with restricted access, as within a corporation, that uses software and protocols developed for the Internet.

in-transit storage Temporary storage of cargo or goods at some point between producer and customer.

intrapreneur An employee of a large corporation who is given the freedom and financial support to create new products, services, systems, etc., free of the corporation's usual routines and restrictions.

intrasender role conflict Discomfort produced within a superior by the need to give directions that conflict with a personal concept of his or her proper role or behavior.

intrastate traffic Movement of goods within the boundaries of a state.

intrinsic reward Satisfaction derived from work itself or from the results of work accomplished. See also **extrinsic reward.**

invention An original or improved design of a process, product, or idea, for which the law provides ownership protection upon the filing and acceptance of an application for a patent.

inventory Goods on hand, particularly finished products that have not been sold or raw materials that have not gone through the manufacturing process.

inventory control Any system designed to determine the economic order quantity, the reorder point, and the proper quantity of safety stock that should be maintained in order to minimize the cost of ordering and carrying an inventory.

inventory equation Ending inventory equals beginning inventory plus net additions (usually net purchases) less withdrawals (cost of goods sold).

inventory profit The amount by which the current replacement cost or selling price of an inventory exceeds the amount carried in the company's accounting records.

inventory recession A slump in business caused by increased production and decreased consumer spending, resulting in a rapid buildup of inventories followed by employee layoffs. See also **final-goods recession; recession.**

inventory turnover The number of times an inventory as a whole has been sold or consumed during a period, as calculated by the inventory turnover ratio.

inventory turnover ratio Sales divided by average inventory for the period. See also **activity ratio.**

inverse demand pattern A pattern of consumer buying habits associated with some status goods and characterized by an increase in demand for a product as its price rises (but only to a certain point, after which demand drops).

inverted-U hypothesis The hypothesis that at low levels of stress, performance is low; with moderate stress (perceived as challenge), performance increases; at very high levels of stress, performance deteriorates.

investment bank An intermediary institution that underwrites (buys complete issues of) securities and then sells them in smaller units to individual investors.

investment company Also called **investment fund.** A company or trust (such as a mutual fund) that invests in other companies the capital contributed by investors, who buy shares that rise and fall in value with the average price of the company's investment. See also **closed-end investment company; Investment Company Act of 1940; open-end investment company.**

Investment Company Act of 1940 Federal legislation providing that an investment company cannot invest more than 5 percent of its capital in any one company or own more than 10 percent of any one company.

investment counsel One whose business is to advise investors and supervise their investments.

investment fund See **investment company**.

investment grade Designating bonds with ratings from AAA to BBB. See also **bond rating**.

investment tax credit A corporate tax credit obtainable through investments in certain categories of long-term assets, equal to a percentage of the value of the asset. See also **tax credit**.

invisible hand The underlying principle (in the economics of Adam Smith) that ensures the optimum level of economic welfare of a society when each person acts out of self-interest.

invoice A printed acknowledgment of a sale from the seller, usually accompanying a shipment of goods, giving a description of the merchandise supplied, the quantity, etc., as well as the terms of the sale, total charges, and amount due.

involuntary bankruptcy Bankruptcy initiated by a court action brought by a creditor. See also **voluntary bankruptcy**.

IPO (*abbr for i*nitial *p*ublic *o*ffering) A company's first stock offering to the public.

ipso facto (*Latin*) By the fact itself; by the very nature of the case.

IRA (*abbr for I*ndividual *R*etirement *A*ccount) A plan that permits individuals to set aside savings that are tax free until retirement. See also **Keogh account**.

IRS See **Internal Revenue Service**.

issue 1. To create or sell shares or bonds. 2. Shares or bonds created and offered for sale at one time. See also **primary offering**.

itemized deductions A list of allowable expenses (e.g., unreimbursed medical expenses) that can be deducted from gross income to determine taxable income. See also **standard deduction**.

itemized statement A detailed list specifying all

expenses and costs involved in an individual purchase.

item validity (*employment testing*) The extent to which an item (question) on a test measures what it is intended to measure.

J

Java (*trademark*) A computer programming language used to create interactive applications running over the Internet.

JCL See **job control language.**

J hook Also called **spindle.** A small shelf mount, usually shaped like the letter J, extending from a supermarket shelf for the display of impulse items.

j.i.t. See **just-in-time manufacturing.**

job 1. A task or group of tasks performed as part of one's occupation or for a specific price. **2.** Those operations and activities performed by the members of a work group, and an integral part of the design and structure of an organization.

job analysis A description of the standards for effective performance of a job and the responsibilities and necessary skills expected of the jobholder.

jobber A person who buys from manufacturers or importers and sells to retailers; a wholesaler.

job bidding A procedure that allows present workers to be considered for future job openings.

job control language (*abbr* JCL) A computer language used to construct statements that identify a particular job to be run and specify the job's requirements to the operating system under which it will run.

job cost sheet A record or schedule of accumulated costs incurred in the production of a single unit, batch, or job, such costs usually being divided into direct labor and direct materials with a special allocation for factory overhead.

job description A detailed written account of the tasks, responsibilities, skills, and environmental dynamics of a job.

job design Those aspects of a job that influence employee attitudes, satisfaction, and motivation.

job enlargement An increase in the horizontal scope of a job, with a concomitant increase in responsibility but not in authority.

job enrichment An increase in the vertical scope of a lower-level job, with a concomitant increase in the areas of responsibility, authority, and recognition: the employee is allowed to plan work schedules to fit overall deadlines. See also **autonomous work group.**

job evaluation Assessment of the specific tasks involved in the various jobs in an organization for the purpose of establishing a scale on which their relative worth may be measured.

job involvement The personal commitment of an individual to a job, including his or her involvement with the growth, importance, and value of the job.

job-order costing A cost accounting system in which costs are categorized, assigned, and accumulated in accordance with the units or batches that incurred them. See also **process costing.**

job-order production See **intermittent process.**

job rotation 1. Movement of employees into a variety of jobs in one organization for the purpose of filling vacancies or for acclimating and motivating new employees. See also **job enlargement.** 2. Movement within an organization which can lead to promotion. See also **job enrichment.**

job safety training (*abbr* JST) Instruction in safe work practices and in their importance.

job satisfaction 1. Gratification derived from one's job or from evaluation of work accomplished. 2. The difference between an individual's feeling about a particular job situation and the general purpose and goals of the organization. 3. The fit between an individual's qualifications and the requirements of a specific job.

job scope The number of measurable skills and tasks required by a specific job.

job security Protection of a worker's job, usually by a clause in a union contract.

job sharing The sharing of one full-time job by two persons, each working half time.

job specification A detailed description of the duties of a particular job, the skills and experience necessary, the salary range, etc.

job tension The degree of stress that an individual experiences in the performance of a task, such stress generally being related to the individual's ability to meet internal or external expectations in regard to performance.

joint and several liability Responsibility held

by two or more persons, both together and individually.

joint contract A written agreement by which two or more persons are responsible for fulfilling the terms specified.

joint cost Also called **common cost.** A cost that confers benefits on two or more departments, projects, or products (e.g., rent, utilities).

joint estate Property owned by two or more persons; the survivor or survivors receive the interest of the first to die, with full title going to the last survivor.

joint liability The responsibility of two or more persons (as partners) for the actions of any one of them taken in connection with a project or business in which all are contractually engaged.

joint tenancy A form of co-ownership of real property in which the owners agree that at the death of one of them, the interest of the deceased will pass to the survivors, full title finally passing to the last survivor. See also **tenancy in common.**

joint tenant A co-owner of an estate in joint tenancy.

joint venture A partnership entered into by two or more people or companies to accomplish a specific task or engage in a specific undertaking.

journal A book in which transactions not entered in specialized books are recorded.

journal voucher A document supporting the validity or accuracy of an accounting entry.

journeyman A union craftworker who has successfully completed an apprenticeship and is recognized as fully qualified to practice a particular specialty.

judgment sample A sample of a population selected at least in part on the basis of a personal judgment as to those persons who would constitute the best, fairest, most representative or equitable sample.

jumble basket A jumble display, such as a large basket, that holds an assortment of usually unrelated products. See also **dump bin.**

jumbo Referring to certificates of deposit having a denomination of $100,000 or more, traded by large institutional investors.

jumbo certificate A type of certificate of deposit issued in denominations of $100,000 or more; usually pays an interest rate above 10 percent.

junior security Also called **subordinate security.** A security (as common stock) that represents a claim to dividends or assets of lower priority than the claims of other securities (as preferred stock and bonds).

junk bond Slang term for a high-risk bond rated BB or lower. It offers a high return but is considered to have dubious backing; sometimes offered to shareholders in lieu of cash in takeover bids.

jurisdiction 1. The authority given to a court or judge to hear and decide a legal case. **2.** The limits within which authority (as of a labor union) may be exercised.

jurisdictional strike A strike caused by conflict between two or more labor unions over the right of one of them to organize the workers in an organization, trade, or industry, to control certain work, or to operate in a certain territory.

just-in-time The practice of manufacturing and shipping products only as they are required.

just-in-time inventory Inventory on hand to support just-in-time manufacturing

just-in-time manufacturing (*abbr* j.i.t.) A production control method that authorizes the manufacture of components, subassemblies, etc., or the receipt of raw materials, only when needed and in the quantities needed to support specific downstream activities.

just noticeable difference (*abbr* j.n.d.) Also called **differential threshold.** The smallest increase in the intensity of a stimulus that can be detected.

K

kanban A method of inventory control, similar to just-in-time procedures, originally developed by Japanese automobile manufacturers.

keiretsu A loose coalition of business groups, especially in Japan.

Keogh account A type of retirement account for self-employed persons, providing income-tax deductions and tax-deferred income.

key A code number or letter printed on coupons, orders, or consumer inquiries which when returned indicates to the advertiser the mailing list that generated the response.

key-executive insurance Also called **key-man insurance**. Insurance that protects a business against financial loss in the event of the death of an important executive.

Keynesian economics The economic concepts advanced by John Maynard Keynes in the 1930s, emphasizing the role of expectations in investment decisions and advocating governmental fiscal and monetary programs to increase employment. See also **classical economics**.

keynote idea The most important idea presented in an advertisement or in any document.

keystone To set the retail price of an item at double the manufacturer's price.

kickback A rebate given (usually secretively) by a seller to a buyer, a supplier to a contractor, etc.: usually considered an unethical practice.

kite To create a false bank balance by depositing a check for nonexistent funds, which may then be covered by another check written against an overdrawn account.

knockoff An unlicensed copy of something, especially fashion clothing, intended to be sold at a lower price than the original.

L

label A piece of paper or other material affixed to a product, especially food or medicine, and stating its contents, the name of the manufacturer, and other information as required by law.

labor 1. Physical or mental work done for pay. **2.** The body of people who perform work for wages, as distinguished from entrepreneurs and managers.

labor arbitration See arbitration.

laboratory training Training in which participants are helped to experience and diagnose their own behavior and relationships in a specially designed environment and are both experimenters and subjects in joint learning. See also **sensitivity training.**

labor-efficiency variance See labor-rate variance.

labor-intensive Requiring a greater expenditure for labor per unit of production than for capital assets. See also **capital-intensive.**

Labor-Management Reporting and Disclosure Act Also called **Landrum-Griffin Act.** An act of Congress passed in 1959 in response to evidence of collusion between some employers and union officials and misuse of funds by certain union officials: provides for the regulation of internal union affairs, restricts secondary boycotts and organizational and recognition picketing, and protects union members against abuses by a bill of rights that guarantees freedom of speech and periodic secret elections. See also **National Labor Relations Act; Taft-Hartley Act.**

labor-rate variance In a standard cost accounting system, the difference between the standard or normal labor cost of producing a certain number of units and the actual cost of producing those units, attributable to a difference in the average hourly wages paid: arrived at by multiplying the difference in wage rates by the number of hours worked.

labor relations Relations between management and labor, especially as conducted by a business organization in regard to collective bargaining and fulfillment of the terms of a union contract.

labor union An organization of workers that bargains with management on the part of its members over wages, hours, working conditions, etc.

lagging indicator An economic factor that is considered to respond to an economic trend after the aggregate of economic activity, as measured by the National Association of Business Research. See also **business cycle; leading indicator; roughly coincident indicator.**

laissez faire (*French*) Allow to act; the economic theory that government should intervene as little as possible in the direction of economic affairs. See also **classical economics; invisible hand.**

laissez-faire style A management style found mainly in organizations that emphasize high levels of creativity, whereby the manager permits subordinates to exercise a high degree of autonomy and acts largely as a consultant.

LAN See **local-area network.**

landlord A person who owns and leases apartments, buildings, land, etc. See also **lease.**

Landrum-Griffin Act See **Labor-Management Reporting and Disclosure Act.**

lapping (*accounting*) Embezzlement carried out by an employee who steals payments made to accounts receivable, covering the theft by using a second customer's payment to pay the account of the first, a third customer's payment to cover the account of the second, and so on until the thefts are repaid or discovered or the accounts are thoroughly muddled.

laptop A type of microcomputer that is portable and so compact that it can be operated while resting on the user's lap.

large-cap Designating a stock with a market capitalization of $1 billion or more.

large-scale integration Location on a single computer chip of many thousands of electronic circuits, each having a distinct function.

last in, first out See **LIFO.**

late charge A penalty charge in addition to the regularly scheduled payment, as of a loan, if such payment has not been made when due.

latent demand (*marketing*) Desire for or willingness to buy a certain type of product that has not yet been manufactured, often increased by offering discount coupons for such products.

lateral leadership Interaction of formal leaders with their peers outside their specific work groups, occasioned by a need to influence other members of an organization in order to complete a work assignment.

lateral reasoning Thought processes that permit a person to adapt the procedures used in the creation of one product or service as tools for the creation of a second, unrelated product or service.

launder To disguise the source of illegal or secret funds or profits, usually by transmittal through a foreign bank or a complex network of intermediaries.

lawful purpose Legally acceptable intent (an element necessary for the validity of a contract).

law of demand The assumption that the quantity of a good demanded at any particular time increases as its price falls and decreases as the price rises. See also **law of supply and demand.**

law of diminishing returns The assumption that at any given stage of technology, there is a point at which additional inputs of capital or labor fail to yield a proportional increase in production.

law of effect The assumption that feelings associated with a situation have a powerful effect on the recurrence or nonrecurrence of that situation.

law of supply and demand The assumption that the competitive price that prevails in a market is determined by the interaction of the supply of products and services for sale and consumers' willingness to buy.

layaway plan See **will-call.**

layoff A temporary or permanent involuntary termination of work, usually resulting from a cutback in production.

layout A composition or arrangement of elements in an advertisement (text, headlines, trademark, illustrations) designed to communicate a message effectively.

LBO See **leveraged buyout.**

LDC less developed country.

leader An individual who by virtue of his or her superior ideas, forceful personality, etc., is able to direct and control the attitudes and actions of others.

leadership 1. The capacity to inspire in others a willingness to accept one's direction. **2.** Influence acquired by a person above and beyond that which is bestowed by the position he or she occupies. See also **achievement-oriented leadership; authoritative leadership; benevolent leadership; democratic leadership; exploitive leadership; lateral leadership; multiple-influence approach; participative leadership; situational approach; trait approach.**

leadership contingency model See **Fiedler's leadership contingency model.**

leading indicator An economic factor, such as interest rates or housing starts, that is considered to signal the general direction of economic activity. See also **business cycle; lagging indicator; roughly coincident indicator.**

lead system One's primary representational system, or the form one uses for storing and recalling experiences (e.g., a visual orientation to experience).

lead time 1. The time between the placement of a purchase order and the receipt of materials from a supplier. **2.** The time between the beginning of a production run and the completion of either the first product or the entire run.

learning curve Also called **experience curve. 1.** A graphic representation of the sharp increase in proficiency demonstrated by an individual, group, or organization in the course of learning a new task or procedure, followed by a leveling off. **2.** The relationship between production labor or cost per unit and cumulative production volume, often resulting in a constant proportional decline in effort per unit for each doubling of cumulative volume.

lease A document evidencing an agreement allowing one party (a tenant or lessee) to rent real estate, equipment, or some other asset from a second party (a landlord or lessor) for a specified time in exchange for specified periodic payments. See also **financial lease; leaseback; operating lease.**

leaseback The sale of property to a buyer who then leases it back to the seller. The seller often becomes the principal tenant, and both benefit from tax savings.

lease-based arrangement An arrangement whereby a franchisor maintains primary control on property to be used by a franchisee by signing the primary lease on the property and subleasing it to the franchisee.

leasehold Property used, rented, or otherwise held under a lease.

leasehold improvement An improvement made to leased property by the lessee (e.g., a new parking lot, building, landscaping), which is considered a long-term asset that depreciates over the term of the lease or the life of the improvement, whichever is shorter.

leave Permission to be absent from work, as to care for a new baby; leave of absence.

ledger (*bookkeeping*) A book containing accounts of a specialized nature (e.g., sales, overhead), usually posted from a journal of chronological transactions.

legal capital Also called **stated capital.** The par value of a corporation's outstanding stock, an amount usually required by state law to be retained for the protection of creditors, and thus unavailable for return to stockholders as dividends, the repurchase of outstanding stock, or other uses as long as the corporation has outstanding debts.

legal list A document drawn up by a state listing corporations, funds, and other investment possibilities in which fiduciaries, banks, insurance companies, and certain other organizations are allowed to invest for the reason that they meet certain high standards and are unlikely to breach the responsibilities of those entrusted with other people's money. See also **prudent man rule.**

legal tender The amount of currency that may be lawfully tendered or offered in payment of a debt and that a creditor may not lawfully refuse.

legitimate power Authority attached to a position, office, or rank and recognized by others as conferring upon its holder the right to command. See also **charismatic power; expert power.**

lessee A person who rents property owned by another. See also **lease.**

lessor A person who permits another the use of property under a lease. See also **lease.**

less than carload lot (*abbr* LCL lot) A shipment of goods that does not completely fill a freightcar, and therefore requires a scheduler (freight forwarder) to combine lots in order to complete a shipment to a destination.

letter of credit 1. A document issued by a banker allowing the person named to draw money to a specified amount. **2.** A letter from a bank notifying a person that drafts on the issuer have been authorized up to a specified amount.

level playing field A state of equality, as between business competitors; an equal opportunity to achieve or succeed.

leverage The increased strength an investor musters by using borrowed funds to finance a portion of an investment (as in a margin transaction). See also **financial leverage.**

leveraged buyout (*abbr* LBO) A procedure by which an investor or group of investors borrows money to purchase enough of a company's assets to gain a controlling interest, using the assets of the targeted firm as collateral, with the expectation of increasing the firm's profits sufficiently to repay the debt plus high interest charges quickly and realize a profit (often by liquidating the company).

leveraged marketing The process of expanding a manufacturing business by diversifying a product's use, as from an industrial use to a consumer use.

levy 1. To seize or attach property by judicial order. **2.** An assessment (as of taxes or contributions).

liability Anything that is owed, whether money, a product or commodity, or a service. See also **asset.**

liability insurance Insurance that protects the insured against losses arising from injury to or death of another or from damage to another's property.

libel A false written or printed statement that causes injury to another's reputation. See also **slander.**

licensee A person, company, etc., to whom a license is granted.

lien 1. A claim made on property as security for a debt owed. See also **artisan's lien; carrier's lien. 2.** A contracted claim to a piece of property that has been specified as collateral for a loan. See also **blanket lien; specific lien.**

life estate An interest in property held only during the lifetime of the holder, who must maintain the property, make mortgage and tax payments, and use the property's natural resources only for its maintenance, and who may sell or mortgage the interest in the property only under the same terms as those under which he or she holds it.

life insurance Insurance providing for payment of a specified sum to a beneficiary upon the death of the insured. See also **employee life insurance.**

life interest Interest on property that is payable during the owner's lifetime but cannot be passed on to another or others after his or her death.

life planning Also called **career development.** An organic approach to organizational renewal by which employees can review, evaluate, and examine their organizational roles and determine the congruence of those roles with their life plans and career goals.

LIFO (*acronym for* last in, first out) A method of costing inventory that assumes that the stock acquired most recently will be sold first. Goods sold are therefore costed at the price of the latest stock, and ending inventory is costed at the price of the earliest purchases (opposite of FIFO). See also **weighted average cost.**

limited company A company (usually British) whose owners are liable for its debts only to the extent of the par value of their stock.

limited liability The responsibility of shareholders in a corporation for the corporation's debts only up to the amount invested by each. See also **unlimited liability.**

limited-line store A relatively small retail store that carries a narrow line of goods (e.g., women's apparel, men's haberdashery).

limited partner An investor whose liability is limited to the amount of his or her investment and who makes no management decisions. See also **silent partner.**

limited partnership A partnership in which the

liability of at least one of the partners for the debts of the firm is limited to the extent of that partner's capital contribution, and in which at least one partner does not enjoy such limited liability.

limited warranty A written statement accompanying a product specifying what the manufacturer will do in the event of a defect or malfunction, for what period of time, and other pertinent information, but not guaranteeing free repair, replacement, or refund of the purchase price. See also **full warranty; Magnuson-Moss Act.**

limit order A market order to a broker that specifies the highest buying price or lowest selling price (exercise price) the investor is willing to accept for a given stock, and which normally expires if not executed by the end of the day.

Lincoln incentive management plan An incentive plan, developed by J. F. Lincoln, by which exempt as well as nonexempt employees share in the firm's profits on the basis of their merit ratings, and which provides a guaranteed 32-hour workweek and three weeks of vacation each year.

line 1. Collectively, those employees who are directly responsible for the company's profit and loss. See also **staff. 2.** A stock of commercial goods of the same general class but including a variety of styles, colors, sizes, etc.

linear programming A method used to solve decision problems, usually involving resource allocation, that can be represented by linear relationships among the objective, the decision variables, and the constraints.

line authority The power vested in management personnel to make decisions and give orders to subordinates in the chain of command.

line balancing Design of a production line so that work flows evenly and without delay from one work station to the next, accomplished by assigning approximately equal tasks to each and allowing adequate time for each to meet the desired production rate.

line of balance (*abbr* LOB) A charting device, containing elements of the PERT method, for planning and monitoring the progress of an order, project, or program to be completed by a specific date.

line of credit The maximum amount that a bank

or other lending institution is willing to lend a given customer or the extent to which he or she may make charges over a specified period.

line organization An organizational system in which the line of authority is clearly defined from the top positions down to the lower management positions (e.g., shop foremen). See also **chain of command.**

linking-pin concept A concept developed by Rensis Likert that holds that every manager is a subordinate to the person or group to whom he or she is responsible, and that effective supervision of one's work group depends to a great extent on one's ability to exert influence upward, and thus on the skill with which one plays the subordinate role.

links and role indicators Elements of a method of information retrieval designed to eliminate false drops, in which groups of words or ideas that are linked in the original material are linked in the computer, which is also programmed to show the role that each term plays in the concept of the original material.

liquid asset See **quick asset.**

liquidation 1. The general conversion of a firm's assets into cash (often as a result of bankruptcy). 2. Conversion of a (usually short-term) asset into cash.

liquidation damages An amount that parties to a contract agree in advance will be payable by any party who breaches the contract.

liquidation value 1. The price an asset can bring if it is liquidated (i.e., converted into cash). 2. The value of a share of a mutual fund when it is redeemed (normally equal to the net asset value).

liquidity The extent to and ease with which a given asset can be converted into cash.

liquidity ratio Any of several ratios taken to indicate a company's ability to meet its obligations if it should be subjected to stress. See also **acid-test ratio; current ratio.**

list broker A person or firm that buys mailing lists from companies and sells them to other organizations.

listed stock A stock that is traded at a regional or national stock exchange, and thus one that has been shown to meet the standards of the exchange and is subject to certain government regulations.

list price The advertised retail price of an item, usually suggested or determined by the manufacturer.

lithography A printing process by which ink impressions of a picture or design are taken from a stone or metallic surface prepared with a greasy or oily substance.

load fund A mutual fund sold by a broker or other salesman that carries a sales charge or commission deducted from the amount invested or the net asset value.

local advertising Advertising intended to reach only a defined regional area and designed to attract customers to a local retail store, restaurant, or other place of business.

local-area network Also called **LAN.** A computer network confined to a limited area, linking personal computers so that programs, data, peripheral devices, and processing tasks can be shared.

local private line (*abbr* LPL) A line connecting two telephones in such a way that one phone rings as soon as the receiver of the other is picked up, without the need for dialing or operator assistance.

location habit (*marketing*) A customer's tendency to shop at a certain store, usually because of special treatment or service or some other appeal that the establishment has over other local stores.

lock-box plan The use by a company of a post-office box to which remittances are sent and collected by a bank for immediate deposit: expedites collection and availability of funds.

locked in 1. Obligated, contracted, finalized, or otherwise beyond the possibility of change. **2.** Unable or unwilling to sell a security that could render profit because of the wish to avoid payment of tax on capital gains.

lockout The closing of a plant or other means taken to prevent workers from entering a workplace in an effort to force a union to accept management's last contract proposal.

locus sigilli (*Latin; abbr* LS) The place of the seal; the place on a legal document where a seal required by law is to be affixed.

logical task A task requiring logical reasoning, such as comparing one item with another or categorizing items according to a predetermined set of characteristics, which a computer is programmed to perform.

logo (*abbr for logo*type) A design incorporating words, letters, and/or symbols and used as an identifying mark. See also **brand; trademark.**

logotype See **logo.**

long 1. Referring to a bond that matures in more than ten years. 2. Holding or accumulating stocks, futures, commodities, etc., with the expectation of a rise in prices.

long-form report An external audit report that includes explanations in addition to a basic financial statement and audit opinion, specifying whether the audit opinion covers the explanations as well as the financial statement.

longitudinal study A series of observations of a subject or subjects over a long period of time and under a variety of conditions, used to supplement survey research.

long-range plan A plan setting forth an organization's goals, objectives, and policies to be pursued over an extended period of time, usually two to five years and sometimes longer.

long-term asset See **fixed asset.**

long-term capital gains Capital gains resulting from the sale of assets held more than six months, formerly subject to special tax breaks, but now taxed as ordinary income. See also **short-term capital gains.**

long-term liability See **fixed liability.**

long-term performance bonus A bonus in the form of stock offered to an executive, its dollar value hinging on the attainment of a designated long-term performance objective.

long-term variation A pattern of increased or decreased activity in a specific industry over a long period of time, usually 20 or 30 years.

loss 1. The amount by which expenses exceed revenues for a given transaction, project, investment, period, etc. 2. A consumption of assets that does not generate minimal income. 3. The assessed damages caused by a disaster, accident, etc.

loss control The deterrent means taken, under the supervision of a risk manager, to curb or minimize all accidental losses (as by fire protection, a security program, regulation of claims adjusting). See also **risk management.**

loss leader An item offered for sale by a retail store at or below cost as a means of attracting customers, many of whom will presumably make impulse purchases while in the store.

loss ratio The total amount of claims paid by an insurance company divided by the total amount of premiums received.

Lotus 1-2-3 A computer program developed by the Lotus Development Corporation, combining spreadsheet, data management, and graphics capabilities.

lower of cost or market The valuation of an asset (usually an inventory) in accordance with either its original cost or its current market value (replacement cost or quoted selling price), whichever is lower.

low-margin retailing The selling of merchandise at low prices (and presumably in large quantities).

low-pressure selling See **soft sell.**

lump-sum purchase See **basket purchase.**

luxury tax A tax levied on items that are not considered essential for daily living.

M

ma-and-pa store See **mom-and-pop store.**

machine language Instructions encoded in a form that can be understood and used by a computer. See also **programming language.**

macroeconomics The study of an entire economic system, with focus on such broad issues as money flow, growth in gross national product, national inflation rate, and general factors of production rather than on individual components of the system. See also **microeconomics.**

MAD See **mean absolute deviation.**

Madison Avenue A street in New York City that was once a center of the advertising and public relations industries and remains a symbol of their attitudes, methods, and practices.

magazine concept A strategy by which commercial sponsors select television advertising time on the basis of the known buying habits of the audiences that watch particular shows.

magnetic disk A floppy disk or hard disk.

magnetic tape Magnetized plastic tape on which data and programs are stored for use in a computer but can be retrieved only sequentially.

Magnuson-Moss Act Also called **Consumer Products Warranties Act.** An act of Congress that became law in 1975 and that, while not requiring manufacturers to give any warranties on their products, requires that all warranties that are given must set forth 13 specific pieces of information (among them the products or parts covered, the steps the warrantor will take in the event of defect or malfunction, and the steps the consumer must take) and distinguishes between full and limited warranties. See also **full warranty; limited warranty.**

mailgram A telegraph-type message sent overnight by Telex or TWX teleprinter for delivery with the first mail distribution the following day, through a joint venture of the U.S. Postal Service and Western Union.

mailing list A list of names and addresses of actual and potential buyers of a product or service, available for purchase, often from the company itself or from companies that compile and deal in such lists, or sometimes created by in-house research.

mail merge A word-processing feature that allows the user to create a form letter by storing lists of names and addresses in one file and the text of the letter in another file. The merge command is used to generate the personalized letter.

mail-order sales Generation of mail or telephone orders for products to be sent directly to consumers by means of catalogs, brochures, fliers, sales letters, and other forms of advertising.

mainframe 1. The largest category of computer on the market, to which terminals in distant locations may be linked. **2.** Historically, the physical casing around a central processing unit.

main memory Also called **primary storage**. See **RAM**. See also **auxiliary memory**.

maintained mark-on The difference between the amount paid for goods and the amount actually received when they are sold.

maintenance factor A characteristic of a job (e.g., salary, job security) that must be present in order to prevent employee dissatisfaction and that serves as a strong motivator when it is present in an adequate amount.

maintenance management Regulation and adjustment of the organizational system to ensure its survival through disciplinary measures, advertising and public relations, and lobbying.

maintenance requirement Reimbursement required by a broker from an investor who has bought stock on margin or sold short and seems to be losing money.

major medical insurance Insurance that pays for a percentage of medical costs not covered by either hospitalization or surgical/medical plans, usually subject to a deductible clause.

make-or-buy A decision to make an item or buy it from some other organization.

maker A person who signs a promissory note and thus incurs the debt that the note represents.

make-to-order Customized manufacturing, in

which products are built to meet unique customer specifications.

make-to-stock Manufacture of standardized products for inventory in anticipation of future customer demands.

mall 1. A large retail complex containing stores and restaurants in adjacent buildings or in a single large building. **2.** An urban street lined with shops and closed off to motor vehicles.

malpractice insurance Insurance protecting a professional person against liability claims arising from alleged negligence or improper performance of professional activities.

Malthusian Referring to the theories of T. R. Malthus, an English economist, which state that population tends to increase faster than the means of subsistence, and that this will result in an inadequate supply of the goods supporting life unless war, famine, or disease intervenes or the increase of population is checked.

managed care Comprehensive health care provided by a health maintenance organization or similar system.

management 1. The process of setting an organization's goals and directing the activities by which they may be achieved. **2.** The functions of planning, organizing, directing, and controlling an organization's resources. See also **five m's.**

management accounting Also called **internal accounting.** Accumulation of financial data needed for use by managers, for financial control reports, and for accounting reports intended for external audiences (e.g., stockholders, Securities and Exchange Commission) by the tracing of all costs and revenues to the specific managers responsible for them.

management audit A review, evaluation, and/or financial audit, internal or external, of management performance and its proper execution of company policies, procedures, and objectives, usually taking into account such qualitative factors as decisions made, results obtained, and physical and psychological work environment.

management by exception A type of management control system in which measured results of performance and productivity are compared with the expected outputs in order to establish a balance between them, and only exceptions from the expected outputs are brought to the attention of higher levels of management.

management by objectives (*abbr* MBO) A process whereby the manager and the subordinates of an enterprise jointly identify common goals, define each individual's major areas of responsibility as well as the results expected of him or her, and use these measures as guides for operating the unit and assessing the contributions of its members.

management consultant A professional in any area of management activity who for a fee lends his or her experience, expertise, and objectivity to client organizations to aid in analyzing management problems, propose solutions, and if necessary carry out the activities suggested.

management control system A system by which managers determine the organization's objectives, measure performance in light of those objectives, and take any corrective steps found to be necessary.

management development The organization, direction, and control of an organization's tangible resources and the provision of opportunities for training, education, experience, and growth for its employees.

management fee An annual fee charged to a mutual fund (about 0.5 percent of the fund's net asset value) for the service of maintaining the fund's portfolio.

management information system (*abbr* MIS) A computer-based system that links the divisions within a company and can furnish any information needed for decision making.

management pyramid The structure formed by the various levels of management, generally divided into three categories: top, middle, and supervisory management.

management reporting See **internal reporting**.

management science A technique for developing and using computer-based mathematical aids for decision making.

managerial grid A technique for assessing a manager's leadership style, by which the degrees of the individual's concern for production and concern for interpersonal relationships are plotted on a grid measuring nine squares both horizontally and vertically.

M & A Mergers and acquisitions.

mandatory subject A topic (e.g., wages, hours) that the National Labor Relations Board rules must be discussed during the negotiation of a labor contract. See also **permissive subject.**

manifest 1. A shipping document that itemizes the contents, value, point of origin, destination, and other important information concerning a shipment of goods. **2.** A list of passengers and cargo carried on an airplane.

manipulation An illegal attempt to generate an erroneous and general impression of a trend in securities prices by buying or selling large numbers of securities and thus deceptively inducing other investors to follow suit, thereby altering prices in a way beneficial to oneself.

manufacturer's agent Also called **manufacturer's representative.** A person who acts as a broker between wholesaler and retailer, offering no credit or storage services to clients.

manufacturer's brand Also called **name brand.** A trade name owned by the maker of a particular item.

manufacturing cell A grouping of equipment organized specifically to perform a sequence of operations common to a family of parts.

manufacturing cost Any cost incurred in the production of goods, normally within the categories of direct materials, factory overhead, and sometimes indirect costs.

manufacturing overhead See **factory overhead.**

margin 1. The amount of an investor's equity in an investment made in part with money borrowed from a broker. See also **margin transaction. 2.** The difference between cost and selling price.

marginal analysis Decision analysis that determines the best trade-off between two marginal costs.

marginal cost See **incremental cost** (def. 2).

marginal costing See **direct costing.**

marginal customer A customer who is on the borderline between being profitable and unprofitable to a seller.

marginal revenue See **incremental revenue.**

marginal tax rate The change in total personal income tax divided by the change in total taxable income.

marginal utility The extra utility or satisfaction derived by a consumer from the consumption of the last unit of a commodity.

margin call Notification that the price of stock bought on margin has dropped to a value below which the buyer's equity in the investment fails to equal a specified minimum percentage, and that the buyer must therefore invest further or accept the loss by allowing the broker to sell the stock and to keep the part of the proceeds that represents the money borrowed from the broker plus interest.

margin of safety The amount by which sales exceed the break-even point.

margin rate Also called **margin requirement.** The minimum percentage an investor must personally invest in a stock transaction (a figure that can vary from 50 to 100 percent), as established by the Federal Reserve Board.

margin transaction A purchase of stock in which the investor uses a broker's capital, in effect borrowing it, as part of the investment. See also **margin call; margin rate.**

markdown A reduction in the originally established selling price of an item.

market 1. A specific place where things are bought and sold. **2.** A region (e.g., Latin America, United Kingdom) where things are traded. **3.** The stock market. **4.** The sphere of commercial activity in general.

marketable securities 1. Corporate stocks and government, municipal, and corporate bonds that can be readily converted into cash. **2.** Short-term investments in such securities intended to provide cash as needed without disruption of normal business operations, considered as current assets and part of working capital.

market analysis Systematic gathering and processing of data related to consumer needs for the purpose of designing a product to meet those needs and developing market strategies to minimize the impact of competing products on a target audience.

market atomization A market segmentation strategy that addresses the needs of consumers individually rather than grouping them into segments.

market capitalization The total market value of a company, computed by multiplying the number of outstanding shares of its common stock by the current share price.

market development The process of reaching new target markets with existing products by placing stock in new territories or redesigning advertising to attract a new audience. See also **market share; product development.**

market economy See free-market system.

marketing The aggregate of strategies developed and activities performed before the actual selling of goods, including market research, product positioning, packaging, pricing, selling, distribution, publicity, and advertising and sales promotion.

marketing mix The elements of product, price, distribution, and promotion considered in relation to ongoing market conditions and the company's market position.

marketing research Also called **market research.** The gathering of data on consumer needs through needs assessment, economic forecasts, and motivation studies for the purpose of developing product ideas and marketing strategies.

marketing risk A factor that produces a loss in anticipated profit from the production of goods (e.g., damage, waste, theft, declining demand, obsolescence).

Marketing Science Institute (*abbr* MSI) A nonprofit marketing research organization made up of academics, professionals, and companies that conducts research projects, workshops, and conferences, publishes newsletters and marketing reports, and issues statement papers.

market-minus pricing The practice of estimating the maximum cost-to-produce allowance for a product by subtracting middleman fees from the anticipated retail price. Also called **demand-backward pricing.**

market order An investor's instruction to a broker to execute a transaction at the best price possible at the moment.

market penetration See **market share.**

market-plus pricing The practice of setting the prices of some goods (e.g., gourmet foods) higher than those commanded by similar products.

market power Ability to control trade channels (i.e., suppliers, delivery services, outlets) so that one's products have a competitive advantage.

market price 1. The price or value of a product or service determined by the operation of an uncontrolled open market, in which price varies directly with demand and inversely with supply. **2.** The price at which supply and demand are in a state of equilibrium.

market profile An analysis of present or potential customers for a particular good or service in terms of age, sex, income level, and other characteristics.

market research See **marketing research.**

market segmentation Division of the total market into consumer subgroups on the basis of age, income, and/or other characteristics for the purpose of identifying and matching particular consumer groups with potential products or services.

market share Also called **market penetration.** The percentage of total sales in a particular market segment represented by the sales of a particular product.

market timing An investment strategy in which decisions to buy or sell securities are made by analyzing economic indicators such as the direction of interest rates or stock prices.

market value. The price at which a seller is willing to sell and a buyer is willing to buy.

Markov chain analysis A technique developed by Andrei A. Markov for studying the movement of individuals within an organization from one job to another in a specified time frame, used to determine probable positions available at various levels of an organization, numbers of people in other positions available to fill vacancies, career planning contingencies, and turnover rates.

markup 1. An amount, stated either in dollars or as a percentage, added to the estimated cost of an item in order to determine its selling price. **2.** The difference between the cost of an item and the manufacturer's suggested retail price.

Maslow's hierarchy of needs See hierarchy of needs.

master agreement A union agreement that covers several companies or multiple locations of a single firm.

master budget A plan projecting the financial statements for an entire organization and its individual components, often including details of component budgets (e.g., cash, factory overhead, finished goods).

master production schedule (*abbr* MPS) A schedule of all items to be produced by manufacturing, indicating both the quantity and timing of production.

materiality 1. The quality of being significant enough to affect decisions and require adjustment. **2.** The principle that requires or allows only important financial events (i.e., material events) to be disclosed in accounting records.

material price variance In a standard cost system of accounting, the difference between prices actually paid for materials and the current prices of those materials, calculated by multiplying the per-unit differences by the number of units used or purchased.

materials budget A budget based on the cost of materials needed to fulfill a production plan.

materials flow The pattern of materials movement from one operation to the next throughout a manufacturing facility.

materials handling Methods and equipment (e.g., conveyors, fork lifts, cranes) for physically moving materials from one location to another.

materials management The organizational unit that oversees purchasing, production control, and physical distribution of materials.

materials requirements planning (*abbr* MRP) A computerized manufacturing planning-

and-control system used to schedule production, determine when to order materials from suppliers, and prioritize work on the shop floor.

mathetics The study of techniques for reinforcing and programming behavior responses by which the concepts of behavioral science are adapted to the practices and procedures of organizational personnel.

matrix design Also called **matrix structure**. A rectangular grid used to plot the interaction of a function manager and a program manager.

maturity The date stated on a bond, bill, note, or other instrument as that on which it must be or can be redeemed by its issuer, after which no further interest is payable.

maturity yield See **yield to maturity**.

M.B.A. Master of Business Administration.

MBO See **management by objectives**.

mean Average; having a value midway between extremes. See also **median; mode**.

mean absolute deviation (*abbr* MAD) A common measure of forecast error, computed by determining the average error without regard to whether the error was positive or negative.

means-end chain A linkage of organizational subgoals such that each is seen as a means toward the accomplishment of another and the entire series as a means toward the achievement of the organization's major goals.

mean square error (*abbr* MSE) A measure of forecast error, computed by averaging the square of the errors.

Mechanic's lien See **artisan's lien**.

mechanistic system A corporate management system that relies heavily on the strict hierarchical structure of obedience to authority, narrow specialization, and internal communications that take the form of rules and directions. See also **organic system**.

media buying service An independent firm that buys broadcast time on television and space in publications as a service to advertisers, and sometimes also advises them on the selection of media, the presentation of messages, and the frequency of their appearance.

median Having a value that is midway between the extremes of high and low. See also **mean; mode.**

media support The aggregate of media advertising and publicity that occurs in the course of the launching of a new product or service.

media survey A series of interviews or written questionnaires administered for the purpose of measuring the effectiveness of a medium in selling and promoting a product.

mediation See **arbitration.**

megaselling Also called **big-ticket sales.** The selling of items that command very high prices (big-ticket items).

meltdown (*stock market*) A sudden and catastrophic collapse in stock prices (as on Oct. 19, 1987), causing large losses to most investors.

memory The capacity of a computer to store and process data. See also **RAM; ROM.**

mental health insurance Insurance that covers a percentage (generally 50 percent) of the costs of psychiatric counseling and hospitalization in excess of an amount specified in a deductible clause.

mercantile Of or relating to merchants or trade; commercial.

merchandise inventory The aggregate of finished products in a manufacturer's warehouses and stockrooms.

merchandise mart A building devoted to the display of merchandise to retailers (not to the general public).

merchandiser A product display unit provided (usually at no charge) by a manufacturer to a retailer.

merchandising The totality of activities designed to stimulate and encourage interest in a product or service. See also **promotion.**

merchandising group A group of people who join together to take advantage of the benefits of cooperative advertising.

merchant wholesaler A distributor of products who carries both full lines and specialty lines of merchandise, extends credit to clients, provides transportation and storage services, and takes title to the products carried.

mergee The object of a merger; a company acquired by merger.

merger A consolidation of two or more companies, effected by the sale of one company's assets and liabilities to another, with the result that the identity of only one of the companies remains or an entirely new company is created. See also **amalgamation; conglomerate merger; horizontal merger; vertical merger.**

merit rating See **performance rating.**

method analysis Study of existing operations so as to improve them through simplification, specialization, mechanization, etc.

me-too See **congruent innovation.**

Michigan Four-Factor Scale A method of measuring (on an ascending scale of 1 to 5) a leader's (a) support (use of ego motives), (b) interaction facilitation (encouragement of close relationships among group members), (c) goal emphasis (maintenance of high standards of performance), and (d) work facilitation (provision of resources to employees and coordination of activities).

microchip See **chip.**

microcomputer A computer smaller than a minicomputer and with less capacity to store and process data.

microeconomics The study of economics in terms of individual components (e.g., the family, consumers, industries, retailers, local employment). See also **macroeconomics.**

microfiche Also called **micropublisher.** A film bearing a photographic image, greatly reduced in size, of printed material (e.g., documents, books), for storage in a file, archive, or library.

micromanage To manage or control with excessive attention to minor details.

microprocessor An integrated computer circuit that performs all the functions of a CPU.

micropublisher See **microfiche.**

mid-cap Designating a stock with a market capitalization of between $500 million and $5 billion.

middleman A person who plays an economic role intermediate between producer and retailer or consumer.

middle management Collectively the people

(middle managers) who manage particular operations within an organization, developing detailed plans and procedures to carry out the directives of top management.

military-preparedness argument The argument that imports of certain goods should be restricted for the protection of industries that are critical to national defense.

minicomputer A computer with processing and storage capabilities smaller than those of a mainframe but larger than those of a microcomputer.

minimum-maximum inventory system An inventory control method that reviews items at fixed intervals and places a replenishment order if the on-hand inventory is below the minimum, the quantity ordered being sufficient to increase inventory to the maximum level.

minimum planning horizon The cumulative time needed to manufacture a product, including the time required for procurement of needed materials and for all steps to be completed in the manufacturing process.

minimum wage the lowest hourly wage that may be paid to an employee, as fixed by law or by union contract.

minority group A segment of a population consisting of people who share a cultural or racial background, physical handicap, or other characteristic that historically has deprived them of economic advancement.

minority interest The number or percentage of shares in a subsidiary company not owned by that company, its parent company, or related subsidiaries, and reported in a balance sheet account or a consolidated statement reporting the owners' equity of a subsidiary.

MIS See **management information system.**

mixed cost Also called **semivariable cost.** A cost that includes both variable and fixed costs (e.g., the part of a utility bill not attributable to an increase in production).

mixed economy Also called **modified capitalism.** An economy based on the private enterprise system but influenced by nonmarket (chiefly governmental) forces.

MNE multinational enterprise.

mockup **1.** A life-size facsimile or model of a product or an environment used to simulate reality for television or filming. **2.** See **dummy.**

mode The value that occurs with greatest frequency in a series of observations. See also **mean; median.**

model stock An ideal inventory expected to be maintained when a wide variety of goods is sold rapidly, in order to keep inventory and sales in relative balance.

modem (*acronym for mo*dulator/*dem*odulator) An electronic device that makes possible the transmission of data to or from a computer via telephone or other communication lines.

modified capitalism See **mixed economy.**

mom-and-pop store Also called **ma-and-pa store. 1.** A small retail business, as a grocery or candy store, usually owned and operated by members of a family. **2.** Any small, independent modestly financed business.

mommy track A path of career advancement for women who are willing to forgo some promotions and pay increases so that they can spend more time with their children.

M-1B The total supply of money in circulation in the United States, defined as the total of all cash, demand deposits, NOW accounts, checks, and other drafts that entitle the bearer to a designated sum.

monetarism A theory that the direction of a nation's economy is determined by changes in its money supply. Monetarists believe that steady economic growth is achieved only when the increase in the money supply is commensurate with the increase in a nation's ability to produce.

Monetary Control Act of 1980 Federal legislation providing for the phasing out, over a six-year period, of the ceilings on bank interest rates required by Regulation Q, permitting savings and loans associations and savings banks to perform many of the services previously reserved for commercial banks, and extending the federal government's control of nonbanking financial institutions.

money Currency plus demand deposits. See also **M-1B.**

money market The aggregate of financial institutions that buy, sell, and transfer the short-term, higher-interest securities and other credit instruments.

money-market fund A mutual fund that invests in short-term corporate and government securities, including bonds, stocks, Treasury bills, and commercial paper, permitting small investors access to high-interest securities that would otherwise require an investment of more than $10,000.

money order An order for the payment of money, as one issued by one bank or post office and payable at another.

money-purchase plan A type of pension plan to which the employer contributes a specified sum each year, the total benefits depending upon the amount such invested sums have earned.

money supply The sum of demand or checking-account deposits and currency in circulation.

monopoly Exclusive control of a market for a product or service, or sufficient control to permit manipulation of prices.

monopsony The market condition that exists when there is only one buyer for a product or service from a large number of sellers.

mooch A slang term in telephone sales for the name of a prospect, who is given a sales pitch, often for a phony investment scheme.

moonlight To work at an additional job after one's regular, full-time employment, as at night.

moratorium 1. Legal authorization to defer payment of a debt or performance of an obligation. **2.** The period during which such deferment is in effect.

mortgage 1. A long-term loan backed by real estate or valuable equipment (often the item bought with the money borrowed), which the creditor can seize if the borrower fails to make all payments when they are due; listed under long-term liabilities on a balance sheet, with the possible exception of payments due within the next year. **2.** To pledge property as security for a loan.

mortgage bond A corporate bond backed by real estate, machinery, equipment, or other property to which the holder is entitled in whole or in part should the issuer of the bond fail to pay the principal and interest to which the bond entitles the bondholder. See also **closed-end mortgage bond; debenture; open-end mortgage bond.**

mortgagee A person who holds a mortgage.

mortgage real estate investment trust (*abbr* mortgage REIT) A mutual fund that makes loans secured by real estate and distributes at least 90 percent of its income as dividends. See also **equity real estate investment trust.**

mortgagor A person who mortgages his or her property.

motivation See **classical theory of motivation.**

motivational research A multiphase investigation that seeks to discover why consumers choose one product rather than another.

motivator Also called **motivating factor.** A factor, such as the likelihood of advancement or the prospect of a wage increase, that motivates an employee to produce more work or work of higher quality.

moving-average method 1. An inventory costing method in which an average is computed over time by periodically adding the value of purchased items, subtracting the value of goods sold, and dividing the running total by the number of units currently in inventory. 2. A forecasting procedure that uses either a weighted or unweighted average of a limited set of past observations.

MPS See **master production schedule.**

MSE See **mean square error.**

multiemployer bargaining Collective bargaining between a union and two or more employers negotiating jointly.

multinational firm A business that has both production and distribution facilities in more than one country. See also **international firm.**

multiple-influence approach A contingency approach to leadership in which the leadership role is seen as directly or indirectly influenced by the environment and structure of the group and by the leader's own behavior, which in combination affect the leader's ability to balance the requirements and outcomes of performance on the one hand and employees' desires and present level of satisfaction on the other.

multiple listing The listing of a home for sale

with a number of real-estate brokers who participate in a shared listing service.

multiple management plan A plan whereby employee advisory boards pass on new ideas and proposed policy changes and thus develop management potential by taking part in decision making.

multiplier The multiple by which an initial change in spending will alter aggregate demand after an infinite number of spending cycles.

multiplier effect A sequence of adjustments initiated by a reduction in total income, which leads to cutbacks in consumer spending, which cause a further decrease in income, leading to additional spending reductions, and so on, until an increase in income causes the process to reverse direction.

municipal bond Also called **municipal note.** A promissory note issued by a state or local government or by an authority established by such a government and yielding interest at a rate determined by current interest rates at the time of issuance, the credit rating of the issuer, and relevant tax laws. See also **corporate bond; government bond.**

mutual fund See **open-end investment company.**

mutual insurance company An insurance company cooperatively owned by its policyholders, who usually receive dividends or reductions in premiums.

mutual savings bank A noncapitalized bank that distributes its available net earnings to its depositors.

N

NAFTA North American Free Trade Agreement.

name brand See **manufacturer's brand; national brand**.

NARB See **National Advertising Review Board**.

NASDAQ (*acronym for* National Association of Securities Dealers Automated Quotations) A computerized communication system that transmits over-the-counter price quotations to terminals in dealers' offices.

National Advertising Review Board (*abbr* NARB) A national organization whose purpose is to help regulate advertisers by reviewing problems of disclosure, deception, truth, and accuracy brought to its attention and to encourage advertisers' compliance with FTC rules.

National Alliance of Businessmen A federally financed organization of businessmen offering job training and placement assistance to the unemployed.

National Association of Accountants (*abbr* NAA) A national society of managerial and cost accountants that oversees the CMA examinations and publishes the periodical *Management Accounting.*

National Association of Securities Dealers (*abbr* NASD) A private organization created by and reporting to the Securities and Exchange Commission that establishes self-regulatory rules for brokers and enables the SEC to exercise some authority regarding over-the-counter transactions.

National Association of Securities Dealers Automated Quotations See NASDAQ.

National Association of Wholesaler-Distributors (*abbr* NAW) An association of wholesalers that publishes newsletters and research findings affecting the wholesaling industry, represents the industry in legislative matters, and works with other groups to solve mutual problems.

national brand Also called **name brand**. A brand that is privately owned and advertised and distributed throughout the country.

National Bureau of Economic Research

(*abbr* NBER) A nonprofit organization that reports on economic indicators.

National Industrial Conference Board (*abbr* NICB) An organization founded in 1916 for the purpose of collecting and disseminating information of importance to business and industry.

National Labor Relations Act Also called **Wagner Act.** An act of Congress passed in 1935 requiring employers to negotiate in good faith with any union chosen by a majority of their employees and prohibiting blacklisting, yellow-dog contracts, and other tactics directed against the formation of unions.

National Labor Relations Board (*abbr* NLRB) A five-member board appointed by the president of the United States to enforce the provisions of the National Labor Relations Act and to investigate complaints of violations.

National Training Laboratory Former name of **NTL / Institute of Applied Behavioral Sciences.**

natural monopoly A business that provides services thought to be too expensive to duplicate locally (e.g., utilities).

NC See **network computer.**

near money Any asset that is easily converted into cash, such as government bonds or savings deposits.

need for acceptance The desire to be liked and approved by peers, subordinates, and authority figures.

need for achievement The desire to perform work successfully and to receive recognition for it.

needle trades Businesses involved in the production of wearing apparel.

needs assessment Also called **needs analysis. 1.** An analysis of a company's strengths and weaknesses regarding skilled workers in order to determine whether present workers can be retrained or new workers must be hired. **2.** The use of marketing research to determine potential markets for a new product. **3.** A marketing analysis of a community to determine which kinds of stores, as in a shopping mall, would best serve the area.

need satisfaction Fulfillment of a want or desire, such that a new need arises to serve as motivation for behavior. See also **blocked need satisfaction; hierarchy of needs.**

needs hierarchy See hierarchy of needs.

negative amortization An increase in the principal of a loan by the amount by which the regular payment falls short of the interest due, usually the result of an adjustable rate loan whose interest rate increases after the loan is taken out.

negative assurance An auditor's report that nothing emerged in the course of an audit to indicate any irregularities or noncompliance with acceptable policies, principles, standards, or contractual conditions.

negative confirmation (*accounting*) A customer's failure to respond to a letter requesting that he or she notify the designated auditor if the account balance stated in the letter is incorrect. See also **positive confirmation.**

negative float A reduction of cash flow attributable to payments by check that have been received and deposited but have not yet been cleared by a bank. See also **lock-box plan.**

negative income Invested income that has produced a loss and may be used as a tax deduction.

negative income tax A system of income subsidy through which persons having less than a certain annual income receive money from the government rather than pay taxes to it.

negative option A clause in a sales contract, as for books or recordings, stating that merchandise will be sent periodically to the subscriber unless the company is notified in writing that the item or items are not wanted.

negotiable Capable of being converted into cash or transferred to a new owner.

negotiable instrument A written document signed by the maker representing an unconditional promise to pay a stated amount of money to the bearer either on demand or at a specified time.

negotiate To bring about (a labor agreement, etc.) by discussion and settlement of terms, usually by means of mutual compromise.

net A value reduced by all applicable deductions (e.g., net income is total or gross income reduced by the expenses incurred in the generation or earning of that income).

net asset value The price of a share in a mutual fund, equal to the total value of the fund's securities divided by the number of shares outstanding.

net capital gains Capital gains less capital losses.

net change 1. The difference between the closing price of a security on one day and its closing price on the following day. **2.** A change in price after all other factors have been accounted for (e.g., a dividend included one day but not the next is computed as part of the net change).

net current assets See **working capital**.

net income Also called **net earnings; profit.** The amount by which revenues exceed expenses or the amount of earnings remaining after all operating expenses, interest on debt, and taxes are deducted from gross income.

net operating income (*abbr* NOI) Also called **earnings before interest and taxes.** A company's earnings before payment of taxes and interest on debt.

net present value (*abbr* NPV) The present value of foreseen returns from an investment less the initial outlay for the investment.

net realizable value Estimated selling price less estimated costs of completion and disposal.

net sales Gross sales less all discounts, exchanges, and returns effected in the course of normal business transactions.

net weight The weight of an item shipped exclusive of packing material and container.

network 1. A group of television or radio stations physically linked by lines, coaxial cables, or microwave relays so that they may simultaneously broadcast the same programs. **2.** A series of planned activities organized in the order in which they must occur. **3.** A group of college alumni or professional people from diverse organizations who meet regularly to pool job tips, business contacts, and other knowledge for the benefit of the individual members. **4.** A computer or telecommunications system linked to permit exchange of information.

network computer (*abbr* NC) A relatively inexpensive computer with minimal processing power, designed primarily to provide access to computer networks, as corporate intranets or the Internet.

network promo (*abbr for* network *promo*tion) A series of announcements provided by a network, without cost to advertisers, to promote a program.

network time A guarantee that a sponsor's advertisement will be broadcast at a particular time on a very large number of network-affiliated television stations.

net worth The excess of the book value of all assets over liabilities.

news release Also called **press release.** A news or publicity story or announcement sent to publications or to radio and television stations for dissemination to the public for the purpose of publicizing an event, an individual, a company, or a product.

New York Stock Exchange (*abbr* NYSE) The largest stock exchange in the U.S., located in New York City.

New York Stock Exchange Index (*abbr* NYSE Index) A continuously computed index reported by the New York Stock Exchange every half hour during the working day, indicating the average price per share of a large number of stocks considered to be representative of the market.

niche A distinct segment of a market.

Nielsen rating Also called **program rating; rating.** A rating of a television program made by the A. C. Nielsen Company indicating the percentage of television homes in which the program was viewed. See also **share** (def. 2).

night differential An addition to the regular pay rate offered for work during evening and early-morning hours.

Nikkei An index showing the average closing prices of 225 stocks on the Tokyo Stock Exchange.

NLRB See **National Labor Relations Board.**

no-fault insurance A type of auto insurance in which the insurer of each car involved in an accident pays for damages and injuries up to a specified amount regardless of who is at fault.

no-frills See **plain-vanilla.**

NOI See **net operating income.**

no-load fund A mutual fund not sold by a broker or other salesperson and therefore free of any sales charge.

nolo contendere (*Latin*) No contest; a defendant's pleading that does not admit guilt but subjects the individual to punishment as though he or she had pleaded guilty.

nominal Referring to money or income measured in an amount rather than in real value.

nominal account Also called **temporary proprietorship account.** A temporary account (e.g., income statement account, dividends account, special closing account) opened for use during one accounting period and then closed to owners' equity.

nominal capital The total par value of a company's issued stock: of little practical significance, since a stock's par value has no exact or permanent relationship to its book value or market value.

nominal group technique A group decision-making technique whereby participants write their ideas and potential solutions to problems on a sheet of paper and all ideas contributed are then listed on a chart pad. The listed contributions are discussed and ideas clarified or modified, after which participants rank the ideas in order of preference, and the results are mathematically evaluated to arrive at a group decision.

noncontributory pension plan A company pension plan financed entirely by the employer.

noncumulative preferred stock Preferred stock on which dividends unpaid in any year are not carried over to be paid in a subsequent year.

noncurrent asset See fixed asset.

noncurrent liability See fixed liability.

nondirected interview A free-flowing interview in which the interviewer's questions and the interviewee's comments are unstructured, conducted for the purpose of ascertaining the interviewee's work methods, attitudes, and ambitions.

nonnotification plan A method of pledging accounts receivable, often as collateral, to a bank or other creditor, whereby the creditor has the right to receive and keep, without notification to the company's customers, the payments made on those accounts, which are sent to the company as usual and forwarded to the creditor institution. See also **notification plan.**

nonoperating expenses/revenues 1. (*income statement*) Those revenues or expenses generated by transactions not related to the company's normal line of business. **2.** (*statement of changes in financial position*) All uses of working capital other than operations.

nonprofit corporation An organization whose prime reason for operating is not to make economic gain but rather to provide a needed public service (e.g., a hospital, church, school).

nonprogrammed decision A decision concerning an unstructured problem that involves no specific objective, only general elements difficult to measure; a decision arrived at through personal judgment, intuition, and creativity.

nonqualified pension plan A deferred compensation plan whereby each year an executive can increase his or her retirement benefits by additional contributions to the company's basic plan (so called because such plans exceed the maximum amount imposed by ERISA on qualified pension plans). See also **qualified pension plan.**

nonqualified stock option A stock-option plan that does not qualify for tax treatment as capital gains, permitting an executive to buy stock during a period of up to ten years at the market price or lower. See also **qualified stock option.**

nonrecurring charge A cost or expense that is not likely to occur again.

normal spoilage The level or extent of deterioration of inventories or materials that is expected even under efficient business operations and optimum sales (usually allocated to product cost rather than to expenses).

normative reward and punishment system A system for regulating an individual's behavior that involves rewards for acceptable performance and punishment for unacceptable performance.

note See **instrument; negotiable instrument.**

notebook A small, lightweight laptop computer.

notes receivable Promissory notes that must be paid on or before a specified date, often with accumulated interest (considered current assets, as they are routinely collected before that date by being discounted at a bank).

notification plan A method of factoring accounts receivable whereby a company's customers are notified that their accounts have been sold to a financial institution (a factor), and that payment on those accounts should be made directly to that institution. See also **nonnotification plan.**

novation The substitution of a new agreement or contract for an old one, usually following the substitution of a new debtor or a new creditor.

NOW account (*acronym for* **n***egotiable* **o***rder of* **w***ithdrawal account*) An interest-paying savings account offered by savings banks and savings and loan associations, on which the depositor may write checks as on a checking account.

NSF check (*abbr for* **n***ot-sufficient-***f***unds check*) A check written against a bank account that has insufficient funds to cover the amount named. See also **bad check.**

NTL/Institute of Applied Behavioral Sciences A private, academically oriented consulting organization that provides nationally known speakers and training activities for business groups.

numbered account A confidential bank account whose owner is identified only by a serial number.

NYSE See **New York Stock Exchange.**

NYSE Index See **New York Stock Exchange Index.**

O

O & O (*abbr for* **o**wned *and* **o**perated) A designation for a facility that is owned and operated by another company.

oath A sworn statement signed before a notary public affirming that all information given in a document is true to the best knowledge of the signer. See also **declaration** (def. 2).

objection (*sales training*) A statement made by a prospective customer or client in opposition to some aspect of a salesperson's presentation, which the salesperson tries to turn into a reason for buying.

objectives Broad, long-range organizational goals that provide direction in the areas of profitability, customer service, and social responsibility.

obligee A person to whom a bond is given. See also **bond** (def. 2); **surety bond**.

obligor A person who gives a bond. See also **bond** (def. 2); **surety bond**.

Occupational Safety and Health Administration (*acronym* OSHA) An agency of the U.S. Department of Labor established by Congress in 1970 to set and enforce health and safety standards for the protection of workers, to train workers and employers in proper health and safety practices, and also to conduct field investigations of alleged violations.

OD See **organization development**.

odd-even pricing Also called **psychological pricing**. The setting of prices slightly below a full dollar value (e.g., $5.95 rather than $6.00).

odd lot Also called **broken lot**. A number of shares of stock smaller than the standard 100-share unit normally exchanged in a single transaction (fewer than 10 if the stock is inactive), costing a premium of $1/8$ of a point above the market price to buy.

OEM See **original equipment manufacturer**.

offering price The price quoted when something is offered for sale, especially the price per share, as of an investment security or mutual fund available for purchase by the public.

office park Also called **business park; executive park.** An office building containing commercial offices and set in parklike surroundings, usually in a suburban area.

officers of the board The chairman of the board, assistant chairman of the board, chairpersons of various committees, and secretary.

off-line Also, **offline.** Operating independently of, or disconnected from, an associated computer.

off-peak Of or relating to a period of less than maximum frequency, demand, intensity, or use, such as the off-peak travel season or off-peak train fares.

off-price Offering or dealing in goods, esp. brand-name apparel, at prices lower than those at regular retail stores or discount stores.

off-shore Registered, located, conducted, or operated in a foreign country, such as an off-shore investment company.

off-the-books Not recorded in account books or not reported as taxable income.

Old Age and Survivors Insurance (*abbr* OASI) The part of the federal social security program that provides income for retired people and for surviving dependents of deceased covered workers.

oligopoly A market condition that exists when a few large companies dominate an industry.

oligopsony The market condition that exists when there are few buyers, who can thereby greatly influence price and other market factors.

ombudsman An individual who hears and investigates complaints and problems and assists in their resolution.

one-time rate The highest rate charged for the running of an advertisement, because the advertiser is buying insufficient space or air time to qualify for a volume discount.

on-line Also, **online. 1.** Operating under the direct control of, or connected to, a main computer. **2.** Connected by computer to one or more other computers or networks, as through a commercial electronic information service or the Internet. **3.** Using a computer.

on spec (*abbr for* on *spec*ulation) Executed (as a

creative effort) with the hope that the work will be accepted and paid for by a client, but with no actual commission to do the work.

on-the-job training (*abbr* OJT) Also called **in-service training**. Instruction in skills required to perform a job by a supervisor or experienced worker in the actual work environment rather than in a simulated work site.

open account A mutual fund account that allows the investor to buy or redeem shares at will, to receive dividends in cash, or to have them automatically reinvested.

open-book credit An informal agreement whereby a customer may obtain goods with a promise to pay later, usually within 30 to 120 days.

open corporation A large corporation whose stock is owned by many stockholders, so that it is usually possible to buy shares from existing shareholders.

open-date labeling The practice of printing the last date on which a product should be sold on the package of a perishable product. See also **shelf life**.

open display A merchandising display case that permits access to goods by customers. See also **closed display**.

open-end credit Also called **revolving credit**. A credit agreement that permits the incurrence of additional debt, as for goods purchased, up to a specified limit before the original debt is canceled. See also **closed-end credit**.

open-end investment company Also called **mutual fund**. An investment company that is capitalized by the continuous sale of its stock, which it may eventually buy back at the current value. See also **closed-end investment company**.

open-end mortgage bond A corporate bond backed by property that may be used to back other bond issues or may otherwise be used as collateral. See also **closed-end mortgage bond**.

open-end order See **blanket order**.

open-market operations Buying and selling of government securities by the Federal Reserve system to control the money supply and thus the availability of credit.

open order 1. Also called **good-till-canceled (GTC) order.** An instruction to a broker to buy or sell securities until the investor issues contrary instructions. **2.** An order placed with a supplier for items that have not yet been delivered.

open shop A workplace where a union represents all employees in negotiations with the employer but where membership in the union is not a condition of employment.

open-systems planning Study of an organization by an outside consultant who identifies its objectives and analyzes all relevant variables outside as well as within the organization.

open-to-buy The amount of money or goods to which a retailer's purchases from suppliers are limited, or the amount of money allocated for such purchases remaining to be spent.

operating expenses Either (broadly) those expenses incurred in normal business activities or (more narrowly) selling, general, and administrative expenses only, exclusive in either case of the cost of goods sold, interest, income tax, and the costs of financing the organization.

operating income The amount by which revenues exceed operating expenses, i.e., income from normal operations before the addition or subtraction of income and expenses not associated with normal operations.

operating lease Also called **service lease.** A rental agreement that obliges the lessor to maintain and service the leased property (usually equipment) and may allow the lessee to return the property and terminate the lease at any time.

operating leverage The extent to which fixed costs affect net income in a company's expense structure: the greater the revenues and net income in relation to variable costs, the greater the leverage.

operating period The time between the purchase of materials or merchandise and the collection of payment from the sale of the finished products.

operating system The software that directs a computer's operations, as by controlling and scheduling the execution of other programs and managing storage and input/output.

operational auditing Extension of the internal auditing function into the areas of finance, production, marketing, and personnel management, undertaken by either a task force composed of people within the company or by external independent analysts.

operational goals 1. The significant goals and behavioral objectives that actually direct and modify the conduct of employees. **2.** Organizational standards of performance for marketing, sales, manufacturing, finance, research and development, and other operations.

opportunity fund An investment fund specializing in buying distressed companies at bargain prices and applying more skillful methods of management to make them profitable.

optical coincidence system Also called **peek-a-boo.** A filing system in which holes punched in large cards correspond to documents in which a particular word or term is used or concept discussed; when several cards are juxtaposed it is easy to see which documents contain the terms or words.

optical scanner See **scanner.**

option 1. The right to buy or sell a security at a specified price within a specified period of time. See also **call** (def. 1a); **put** (def. 1). **2.** The right, as granted in a contract or upon an initial payment, to buy or sell a property or a service at a stated price within a specified time.

order bill of lading A receipt for goods shipped which provides that the shipped articles can be delivered only upon presentation to the transportation company of the original bill of lading. See also **straight bill of lading.**

order cycle Also called **lead time.** The time interval between the placement of an order with a vendor and the order's delivery to a customer.

ordinary income Income generated by a firm's normal business operations, exclusive of capital gains realized through the sale of capital assets that are not normally sold by that business; revenue.

ordinary life insurance Life insurance with premiums paid throughout the lifetime of the insured. Also called **straight life insurance; whole life insurance.**

organic system A corporate management system that emphasizes decisions based on group interaction, individual choice of methods, group goals, etc., and has the flexibility to adjust to changes inside and outside the organization. See also **mechanistic system.**

organizational analysis and planning A long-range design for an organization's structure that takes into account such variables as turnover and anticipated environmental changes.

organizational development specialist A change agent, consultant, or behavioral science professional who employs behavioral theory and technology as well as action research to instruct trainees in effective functioning within the context of the organization.

organizational picketing The picketing of an employer in order to encourage union membership.

organization chart A formal plan in graphic form indicating the formal chain of command in an organization and identifying major departments, staff and line relationships, and permanent committees.

organization cost The cost of planning, incorporating, and setting up an organization, including legal and incorporation fees and the costs of issuing stock.

organization development (*abbr* OD) A process for improvement of an organization that involves philosophies, concepts, techniques, and procedures that influence the progress and betterment of individuals performing within the system.

original cost See **acquisition cost.**

original entry An entry in a journal, as opposed to an entry posted to a ledger.

original equipment manufacturer (*abbr* OEM) A company that produces items that are products in themselves and are also used as components of larger products (e.g., batteries, carburetors).

OSHA See **Occupational Safety and Health Administration.**

ostensible partner An individual who is represented as a business partner with his or her knowledge and consent and who therefore may be held liable for company loans (and for whose actions the firm may be held liable) although he or she has no real business function in the company.

OTC stock See **over-the-counter stock.**

OTO (*abbr for* one *time only*) A designation for a commercial that runs only once.

outlet See **factory outlet.**

outplacement The process of aiding a newly separated executive in finding a new job (as through the company-paid services of a counselor or placement agency).

output 1. a. Production; amount manufactured. **b.** The amount produced by one person in a specified time period. **2. a.** The information fed out by a computer, either as hard copy (a printout) or soft copy (an image on a screen). **b.** To produce by a computer. See also **input** (def. 1).

outside consultant See **external consultant.**

outside director A member of the board of directors of a corporation who takes an active part in the company's affairs but who is not an employee of the corporation.

outside in Proceeding (as information about magazine readers' tastes and habits) from persons outside the organization (as subscribers) to a person inside the organization (as an advertising director who asks readers to reply with that information). See also **inside out.**

outsource To buy or hire from an outside supplier (e.g., a car manufacturer may outsource a substantial percentage of its parts).

outstanding check A check that has been written, signed, and released by a maker but not yet cleared (paid) by the bank holding the account.

outstanding shares Shares of stock that have been issued and are still in the open market or in the possession of individuals or organizations not of the issuing corporation; does not include treasury stock or stock that has been authorized and registered but not issued.

over and short Any expense account used to reconcile or account for differences between book balances and actual balances of receipts and remaining cash in petty cash or change funds.

overapplied overhead An amount of factory overhead charged to a particular product in excess of the actual overhead incurred during the period; the amount of the credit balance of an overhead account at the end of the period.

overbought 1. (*stock trading*) Having an artificially and temporarily high price as a result of unusually active trading, most of which has consisted of more offers to buy than to sell. 2. (*retailing*) Having stocked more goods than can be sold by normal methods.

overdraft 1. The overdrawing of a checking account. 2. A check overdrawn on an account. 3. The amount overdrawn.

overdraw To draw upon an account, allowance, etc., in excess of the balance standing to one's credit or at one's disposal.

overhead Charges that cannot be assigned exclusively to any particular product or project (e.g., rent, taxes, office expenses). See also **fixed overhead.**

overhead rate A predetermined rate at which overhead costs are charged or applied to units of production.

overtapping See **telescoping.**

over-the-counter stock (*abbr* OTC stock) Stock issued by a company that has insufficient earnings or shares outstanding to be listed by a stock exchange, or by a bank or insurance company, and which is traded between brokers acting either as principals or as agents for customers.

overtime Time worked in excess of the hours stipulated by union contract or by agreement and for which a worker may receive additional payment (usually $1\frac{1}{2}$ to 2 times the normal wage). See also **straight time.**

owners' equity Also called **shareholders' equity.** The portion of a company's assets that represents shareholders' investments, after all liabilities have been settled.

P

PA See public accountant.

package 1. (*television*) **a.** A program or other production ready for broadcast or publication, exclusive of commercials or advertising. **b.** A group of such productions sold as a unit. **c.** To produce such programs or other productions. **2.** To design or produce a protective container for a product.

package-consolidating agency See **freight forwarder.**

packager 1. A person or firm that packages a product or merchandise for commercial sale. **2.** A person or firm that creates and assembles a television show, book, or other product and offers it for sale, use, exhibition, etc., in a completed form.

Pac-Man defense A tactic, named after the video game, in which a targeted company tries to avert a hostile takeover by taking over the acquirer.

paid-in capital Also called **contributed capital.** The capital that a corporation has raised through the issuance of common and preferred stock; that part of owners' equity which does not include retained earnings. See also **capital surplus.**

paid-in surplus See **capital surplus.**

paired comparison questions Duplicative multiple-choice questions on a questionnaire designed to reveal respondents' overall rankings of subjective items.

palmtop A battery-powered microcomputer small enough to fit in the palm.

P. & L. profit and loss. See **profit and loss statement.**

panel See **consumer panel.**

panic A sudden widespread fear concerning financial affairs leading to credit contraction and widespread sale of securities at depressed prices in an effort to acquire cash.

paper profit A profit that one has in theory because a stock or other investment has increased in price but remains unrealized until the holding is sold.

par See **par value.**

pareto analysis An approach that determines the

relative frequency of various problems or causes for problems so that primary attention can be focused on the most important ones. See also **80-20 rule.**

parking An accommodation employed especially in covert takeover attempts, whereby an agent buys shares of stock for the client for future delivery, usually at purchase price plus a commission; allows a client to accumulate shares without having to report them.

Parkinson's law Any of various facetious statements about business and office management expressed as if a law of physics, such as the statement that work expands to fill the time allotted for its completion. These rules were proposed by the English historian C. Northcote Parkinson.

parliamentary procedure The procedure followed in conducting a meeting or conference, conforming to the rules, usages, and precedents that govern proceedings of legislative and deliberative assemblies.

parol evidence rule A legal rule stating that parties to a written contract are bound by its terms and are debarred from offering proof of an oral agreement that contradicts or is not specified by those terms.

participant observer An investigator who studies a group engaged in work-related problem solving by taking part in its activities.

participating preferred stock Stock that carries with it the right not only to its fixed dividend but to additional dividends on a specified basis after payment of dividends on common stock.

participation show A television show with many sponsors, whose commercials appear before, during, and after the program. See also **magazine concept.**

participative leadership See **democratic leadership.**

partner A person associated with one or more others as a contributor of capital in a joint enterprise who shares in its risks and profits. See **dormant partner; general partner; limited partner; ostensible partner; secret partner; silent partner.**

partnership A legal association of two or more

persons who share in the risks of financing and managing a business and in its profits.

party plan Also called **party selling.** An arrangement whereby a consumer, in exchange for either a gift or a discount on items purchased, gives a party at which a salesperson demonstrates and sells a line of products to the guests.

par value The face value of a stock or bond (e.g., a $100 savings bond that sells for $75 is selling *below par:* a bond that sells at its face value is selling *at par*).

passbook savings account A type of savings account in which transactions are entered into a passbook in the possession of the account holder. Cf. **statement savings account.**

passive income Income from an activity in which one does not actively participate (e.g., limited partnerships, research and experimentation projects).

pass-through Also called **passalong.** The additional amount charged in a price increase.

patent An exclusive right granted by a government to an inventor to make, use, license, or sell a new device, process, material, or other innovation for a specified period of time (currently 17 years in the United States).

path-goal approach The technique of motivating a subordinate by indicating the relationship between work goals and the employee's personal goals.

patronage discount See **quantity discount.**

payable A liability; a debt. See also **accounts payable.**

payback period The time until the net cash flow from a project equals the amount invested in it, calculated as the net operating income less taxes and depreciation, exclusive of potential salvage value of assets and the present value of cash to be received after the termination date of the project. See also **bailout period.**

payee A person to whom money is paid or is to be paid.

payer The person named in a bill or note as obligated to pay.

payout The amount of dividend paid by a company on each share of common stock.

pay-per-view A pay television service in which a subscriber pays for each program viewed.

payroll costs Wages, salaries, and payroll taxes.

payroll taxes Also called **employment taxes.** Federal, state, and local taxes levied on salaries and wages paid to employees, the employers' share of social security taxes, and unemployment compensation insurance taxes.

PC 1. See **personal computer. 2.** See **professional corporation.**

PDA See **personal digital assistant.**

p/e See **price-earnings ratio.**

peek-a-boo See **optical coincidence system.**

peer leader See **informal leader.**

penetration pricing A strategic pricing approach by which a company prices a new product below its anticipated normal price during its introduction to the marketplace in order to discourage competition and in the hope of recouping its initial investment quickly. See also **skimming.**

penny stock A low-priced stock of a small company, sold on a local stock exchange but usually not traded on the major exchanges and not officially indexed: so named because the price of such shares was formerly (especially in the 1930s) less than $1.

pension A fixed amount paid at regular intervals to a retired person in consideration of past services.

pension plan A benefit plan by which an employer, alone or jointly with employees, makes regular contributions to a fund that will provide income to employees after their retirement. See **contributory pension plan; noncontributory pension plan.**

per capita output The output by or for each person; the value of a nation's output divided by its population: a commonly used measure of a country's standard of living.

percentage depletion Depletion of a natural resource calculated as a percentage of the gross income earned from the resource during a certain period: often used as a tax-deductible expense. See also **cost depletion**.

percentage-of-completion method A method of accounting used for a long-term project by which revenues and expenses are entered in proportion to either (*a*) the costs incurred during the period divided by the total estimated costs or (*b*) an estimate of the percentage of job completion.

percentage-of-last-year's-sales method A budgeting technique applicable to any aspect of business by which the current year's budget for a specific area (e.g., advertising, marketing) is based on a percentage of the previous year's sales.

percentage-of-next-year's-sales method A budgeting technique applicable to any aspect of business by which the current year's budget in a specific area (e.g., advertising, marketing) is based on a percentage of the expected sales for the following year.

perceptions (*marketing*) Those features and benefits recognized by a prospective customer as critical to a purchase.

perceptual defense The mind's ability to block out certain stimuli that, if acknowledged, could be threatening to one's deepest values or ideas.

perceptual distortion The tendency to interpret reality in a subjective way consistent with one's personal value system.

perceptual map (*marketing*) A graph or visual diagram used to demonstrate how consumers perceive each attribute of a product in terms of its relevance and importance to them, or to measure the relative importance of a product's benefits to a consumer.

per diem (*Latin*) By the day; for each day.

perfect competition A hypothetical market condition in which a large number of small businesses produce the same products. Since none can independently influence prices, buyers and sellers are well informed about prices and resources, and all are free to enter and leave the market as they wish, with little effect on the general economy.

perfected Brought to a state of completion by the fulfillment of all conditions stipulated by the Uniform Commercial Code: said of a security interest in goods pledged by a debtor as security for a loan. The secured party (the lender) has greater legal rights to the goods than any other party.

performance plan A bonus arrangement whereby executives are paid extra compensation on the basis of the growth of the company, measured by increases in capital spending, earnings per share of stock, return on assets, and other figures.

performance rating Also called **merit rating.** A systematized evaluation of an employee's performance as to quantity and quality, usually used as a basis for promotions, salary increases, and the like.

performance shares Shares of common stock given to executives when a designated corporate performance objective is attained.

per inquiry advertising A form of television advertising in which the price the advertiser pays to the station for air time is based on the number of inquiries about the advertised product received as a result of the advertising.

period An accounting period; a fiscal year or portion thereof.

periodic expense Also called **periodic cost.** An expense normally incurred in order to stay in business during a period of time (e.g., rent and insurance); a fixed cost: charged to the operating expenses of that period.

periodic inventory A system that records changes in inventory that have occurred over a period of time, noting the total purchases and uses during that period (and sometimes during previous periods) rather than noting each transaction as it occurs: frequently used by companies that sell large numbers of small items. See also **perpetual inventory.**

perk (*abbr for perq*uisite) An extra benefit, often not taxable, that forms part of a job and is often used to entice a coveted executive into accepting a company's job offer. Perks may consist of chauffeured limousines, all-expense vacations, luxury living accommodations, and club memberships.

permissive subject A topic (e.g., retirees' benefits) that may arise during negotiation of a labor contract but that one side prefers not to discuss, and that the National Labor Relations Board rules may be omitted from consideration. See also **mandatory subject**.

perpetual inventory Also called **continuous inventory**. A system that accounts for every purchase or use of raw materials or goods as it occurs, often on a perpetual stock record: frequently used by manufacturing firms that sell limited numbers of expensive items or wholesale shipments. See also **periodic inventory**.

perpetual stock record A list of materials on hand that is changed daily as items are received or issued.

personal computer (*abbr* PC) A type of microcomputer designed for individual use, as at home or in an office.

personal digital assistant (*abbr* PDA) A handheld computer that provides organizational software, such as an appointment calendar, and communications hardware, such as a fax modem. Most of these devices use a stylus rather than a keyboard for input, so that they can recognize handwriting.

personal information manager (*acronym* PIM) A type of computer program that allows the user to enter reminders, lists, appointments, etc., and link the information in useful ways. Most of these programs offer scheduling and calculating capabilities.

personal property Anything owned other than land.

personnel administration See **human resources management**.

PERT (*acronym for* program *e*valuation and *r*eview *t*echnique) A technique for project scheduling and cost control, originally developed for the U.S. Navy, that incorporates uncertainty concerning activity times and costs.

PERT cost method A technique for controlling the cost of a large project that uses the critical path method to compute the estimated completion time and costs associated with scheduling an early start or a late start.

Peter Principle A principle set forth by Laurence J. Peter to explain humorously "why things always go wrong": "In a hierarchy every employee tends to rise to his level of incompetence."

petrodollars Surplus revenues in dollars accumulated by petroleum-exporting countries, such as those of the Middle East, especially when used for foreign investments.

petty cash 1. A small amount of cash kept on hand for minor expenditures. **2.** (*accounting*) An imprest fund that is continually depleted and periodically replenished to an established level; a current asset account with a normal debit balance.

phantom diagram A cutaway diagram or drawing of a product, showing its internal construction or composition.

phantom freight A freight cost not paid by the seller but charged to the buyer, calculated by the addition of a base-point charge to the unit price. See also **base-point pricing.**

phantom stock Units of company stock to be granted as part of an incentive program to executives, who may be told that, should business conditions continue to improve, they will receive a bonus equal to the value of a specified number of shares on a certain date.

physical distribution The movement of goods from the point of origin to the consumer.

physical inventory The procedure of physically counting the number of items in an inventory.

pictogram A chart in which figures, such as simple line drawings, are used to indicate the relative values of the variables being compared.

piecemeal opinion An auditor's opinion on certain identified individual items on a financial statement rather than on the statement as a whole, submitted when a disclaimer or adverse opinion has been rendered on the financial statement (not a generally accepted auditing practice).

piecework system An incentive procedure whereby each employee's pay is based on the number of units he or she produces.

pie chart A circle diagram that is divided into sectors, each representing the relative value of a variable to the whole.

piggyback Also called **trailer-on-flatcar.** Transportation of goods in a truck that is then driven onto a railroad flatcar for delivery to the destination.

PIM See **personal information manager.**

pioneering stage (*marketing*) The first stage in the life cycle of a product, when the marketer places emphasis on building demand for the product.

pirate To appropriate and reproduce (a videotape, phonograph record, etc.) without legal authorization.

pit The physical area of a commodities market where traders conduct their business. See also **ring.**

place utility (*marketing*) A value added to a product by a consumer on the basis of its convenience and accessibility.

plaintiff 1. A person who brings a lawsuit against another person in an effort to recover the value of injury to his or her rights. See also **defendant. 2.** The complaining party in any litigation.

plain-vanilla Also called **no-frills.** A product or service whose features are limited to those considered basic or standard.

planned obsolescence (of a manufactured product) The condition of becoming unusable or outmoded by the deliberate design of the manufacturer, so that every few years consumers will be — or will feel themselves to be — obliged to buy a new model of the product.

planning horizon An arbitrary time frame specified for the achievement of a goal or the accomplishment of a course of action.

plug An unsubstantiated amount added to or subtracted from a verified total to obtain agreement with a target amount.

PM See **push money.**

PO See **purchase order.**

point A unit of price change: (*stocks*) $1, usually expressed as a fraction of a dollar (e.g., $+\frac{1}{8}$ or $-\frac{1}{8}$, a gain or loss of 12.5 cents); (*bonds, real estate*) 1 percent of $1000, or $10 per $1000.

point of origin The location at which goods are received into the physical distribution system.

point-of-purchase advertising (*abbr* POP advertising) Also called **point-of-sale advertising.** A display, usually provided by a product manufacturer to promote the sale of a new or specialty item, placed strategically in a store, usually near a sales counter, as a means of influencing consumers to buy.

poison pill Any of various methods devised by a company to thwart a hostile takeover attempt, as by issuing new stock or instituting a generous package of employee bonuses, any of which would prove costly to a potential acquirer.

pollution-control bonds Bonds authorized by Congress (and exempted from taxes) in 1968 to help companies finance activities or devices to control the emission of pollutants.

Ponzi scheme A type of swindle in which new investors are lured by quick profit on small sums invested and are soon enticed into investing large sums, which are not returned.

pooling-of-interest method An accounting method for combining the assets, liabilities, and owners' equity of two or more previously distinct companies. See also **purchase method.**

POP (*abbr for p*oint of *p*urchase) See **point-of-purchase advertising.**

population An aggregate of people or items of any sort from which a sample is to be taken for statistical measurement.

portability Capable of being transferred, as pension benefits, from one company plan to another employer's plan, to an individual IRA, or from an IRA to a company pension plan.

portfolio 1. A collection of securities and other investments (e.g., real estate, precious metals, collectibles) held by or managed for a company or individual. **2.** A collection of samples of a freelancer's work (e.g., writing, artwork) for presentation to a prospective employer.

POS (*abbr for p*oint of *s*ale) See **point-of-purchase advertising.**

positioning The technique of influencing the way a product is perceived by consumers through the effective use of advertising, promotion, and selling techniques.

positive confirmation A customer's written response to a letter requesting confirmation of an account balance, indicating to the institution that the stated balance is correct. See also **negative confirmation.**

post 1. To transfer accounting information from a journal to a ledger. **2.** A place in the stock exchange where a particular stock is traded.

postage-stamp pricing Also called **freight allowed.** The practice of including delivery costs in the prices of goods quoted to customers, such costs not being based on the destination of the goods.

potential-competition doctrine The principle that one company may not legally acquire another company in order to eliminate a potential competitor but may do so for other reasons, such as to expand its business base.

potential demand The anticipated market for a particular item predicted on the basis of economic and demographic projections.

power of attorney A notarized document specifying the manner in which an agent may act for a principal.

PPI (*abbr for producer price index*) See **wholesale price index.**

preapproach The totality of strategic planning and development work done before a client is approached for a sales presentation.

predatory pricing The practice of reducing prices so as to lure customers from one's competitors.

predictive behavior sample A selection of job-related events involving an individual, used to predict the individual's future actions and conduct.

preemptive pricing The practice of setting prices so low that potential competitors are kept out of the market. See also **predatory pricing.**

preemptive right The right of current shareholders to have a first option on the purchase of new issues of the same stock, such that corporate management is prevented from issuing new shares at below-market value for the purpose of either diluting the value of issued shares or of immediately buying them up and thus acquiring the voting control they could represent.

preferred stock Also called **preferred issue.** A share of the ownership of a corporation that entitles the holder to a fixed dividend that must be paid before any dividend is paid on common stock. See **convertible preferred stock; cumulative preferred stock; noncumulative preferred stock.**

premium 1. The difference between par value and the market value of a preferred stock. **2.** The periodic fee paid to an insurance company for coverage of risks. **3.** A free or reduced-price product offered to consumers as a means of stimulating interest in a company's products or services.

premium pay A rate of pay that is higher than the amount paid for work performed during normal hours or under normal conditions.

prepaid expense A stock of supplies on hand or a service paid for but not yet used or expired (e.g., an insurance policy, prepaid utilities), included among current assets because it will not reduce cash in the future.

preretailing The affixing of retail prices to merchandise by its manufacturer or wholesaler.

presentation graphics A kind of computer software that allows users to create charts, graphs, and other graphic images for business presentations and reports.

present value Also called **present discounted value; present worth.** The amount of money that must be invested at a specified rate of interest for a specified length of time to yield a specified sum (e.g., the present value of $100, invested for 5 years at 6 percent interest, is $75).

press release See **news release.**

prestige pricing The marketing strategy of increasing the price of an item for the purpose of establishing an image of high quality for the product or for the firm that sells it.

pretest (*marketing*) A procedure by which prospective customers are asked detailed questions about a new product's strengths and weaknesses for the purpose of fashioning selling strategies.

preventive maintenance Those maintenance activities performed before equipment breaks down, intended to increase operating performance and reduce the likelihood of breakdown. See also **remedial maintenance.**

price-earnings ratio (*abbr* p/e) The price of a share of stock divided by earnings per share for a 12-month period (e.g., a stock selling for $10 a share and earning $1 has a price-earnings ratio of 10).

price elasticity of demand The responsiveness of demand to a change in price, measured by the formula

$$\text{elasticity} = \frac{\text{\% change in quantity demanded}}{\text{\% change in price per unit}}$$

price elasticity of supply The responsiveness of price to a change in demand, measured by the formula

$$\text{elasticity} = \frac{\text{\% change in quantity supplied}}{\text{\% change in price per unit}}$$

price guarantee Also called **price protection.** A seller's guarantee that if a product's price is reduced within a specified period of time, a buyer of a large amount of that product will be refunded the difference between the price paid and the new (lower) price.

price leader A company whose pricing strategy influences the prices set by competing companies.

price lining (*marketing*) The practice of varying the features of a basic product slightly in order to offer high-, medium-, and low-priced versions of the product for different target audiences.

price point The price for which something is sold on the retail market, especially in contrast to competitive prices.

price protection See **price guarantee.**

price war A market characterized by repeated price cutting by competitors for the purpose of capturing each other's customers.

prima facie (*Latin*) At first view; based on first impression; self-evident.

primary boycott Refusal by union members to purchase goods or services from a company against which their union is conducting a strike.

primary data Information gathered directly from the original source, as from original documents or research. See also **secondary data.**

primary distribution See **primary offering.**

primary earnings per share (*abbr* primary

EPS) Total corporate earnings available to holders of common stock divided by the number of outstanding shares: so called because the value does not reflect unexercised warrants and unconverted convertible bonds and preferred stock.

primary liability An absolute obligation to pay, with no conditions.

primary offering Also called **primary distribution.** An issue of shares or bonds. See also **issue** (def. 2).

primary storage See main memory.

prime rate Also called **prime interest rate.** The interest rate that banks charge for loans to their biggest and highest rated customers, which fluctuates in accordance with the corporate demand for money and with the discount rate that the Federal Reserve Bank charges for loans to banks: used as a major economic indicator.

prime time The hours, generally between 7 and 11 P.M., considered to have the largest television audience of the day.

principal 1. An original amount of money, without accumulated interest. **2.** A person who acts for himself or herself, or who is represented by an agent.

printer A computer output device that produces a paper copy of data or graphics. Dot-matrix printers form characters by dot configurations. Laser printers use lasers to form dot-matrix patterns and an electrostatic process to produce a page at a time. Ink-jet printers spray droplets of ink through nozzles. Line printers print an entire line at one time.

private brand Also called **dealer brand; private label.** A brand owned by a retailer or wholesaler.

private carrier A transportation company that carries goods exclusively for the owner or leaser of the transportation equipment, providing no service to the public.

private enterprise See free enterprise.

private label The label of a product, or the product itself, sold under the name of a wholesaler or retailer, by special arrangement with the manufacturer or producer.

private sector Economic activities that do not directly involve the government, including those of nonprofit corporations, private firms, and individuals. See also **public sector.**

proact To take active measures to influence future events rather than simply to react to events as they occur.

proactive Tending to initiate change and to influence events rather than reacting passively; enterprising.

probability assessment method The forecasting of sales volume and market size on the basis of the subjective opinions of experts.

problem clinic A training session at which groups of employees discuss various alternative solutions to common problems, thereby revealing any needs for further training.

procedural audit A planned evaluation or inspection that involves subjective analysis of a process for the purpose of quality control.

procedure The precise sequence of steps to be taken to accomplish a given end (e.g., to move raw materials from a receiving platform to an assembly line).

procedure flow chart A chart that shows the precise sequence of steps for a procedure, including the routing of all documents involved.

process approach An effort to increase productivity by the imposition of fixed conditions and job standards by which performance may be measured.

process audit Chemical analysis of fluids or substances used in the production process for the purpose of quality control.

process consumable Any material that must be bought for and is subsequently consumed in the manufacturing process.

process costing A cost accounting method in which costs are categorized, assigned, and accumulated in accordance with the departments, processes, or products that incurred them (used for assembly-line processes that produce continuously). See also **job-order costing.**

process layout A method of production in which personnel and equipment are grouped by function or process. See also **product layout.**

producer goods Such goods as raw materials

and machinery that are used in the making of consumer goods.

producer price index (*abbr* PPI) See **wholesale price index.**

producer's risk The risk run by a producer that an acceptable lot will be accidentally rejected due to a sampling error. See also **consumer's risk.**

product Something made to be sold; a good or service that is or can be marketed.

product audit Measurement of individual components and parts of a product for the purpose of quality control.

product cost A cost associated with the manufacture of a product. See also **period cost.**

product development The process of improving existing products and creating new products, product lines, and product applications.

production The process of converting raw materials into finished goods by human labor and machinery.

production budget A budget based on forecasts of sales and production costs.

production control The function of coordinating people, materials, and machinery to provide maximum efficiency during the assembly of products, generally involving five basic steps: planning, routing, scheduling, dispatching, and follow-up.

production era In the United States, the early twentieth century, when business managers focused mainly on production rather than marketing: an era characterized by specialization and the introduction of assembly lines.

production management Control of quality, the setting of completion and delivery dates, and the making of decisions in regard to the most economical way of carrying out the production process.

production method 1. Also called **service basis.** A method of depreciation whereby the cost of an asset is depreciated over its useful life in accordance with units of production consumed or created by the asset. **2.** The technological steps used to manufacture a product.

production planning Estimating how much goods and services must be produced in order to meet anticipated demand and determining the most efficient way to accomplish this in order to maximize profits while maintaining quality.

production schedule A detailed chart showing the manufacturing procedures to be carried out on a product, the time required for each, the expected completion date, etc.

productivity Economic output per unit of labor, expressed as revenue per employee, units produced per labor hour, etc. It is a measure of the amount and quality of the finished product against the amount of resources required to accomplish this, and can be regarded as measuring the efficiency of a company, a worker or workstaff, or production methods.

product layout A method of production in which personnel and equipment are arranged in a manner consistent with the sequence of steps necessary to manufacture a specific product. See also **process layout.**

product liability A manufacturer's legal responsibility for injuries suffered by consumers as a result of defective, dangerous, or unhealthful products, whether or not the manufacturer was aware of the defect or danger.

product life cycle The commercial life of a product from introduction, maturity, and peak through decline and disappearance from the market.

product line A group of related products (e.g., cosmetics) produced by a manufacturer.

product manager The company executive responsible for developing new products, from the idea stage through marketing.

product market A market in which finished goods are bought and sold.

product mix The variety of products offered by a company to consumers.

product-oriented marketing Marketing efforts that do not rely on feedback from consumers.

product planning The aggregate of activities engaged in before the actual production of a new product, which may include an assessment of the original product idea, an analysis of market conditions, the creation of a prototype, and product testing.

product position Also called **product space.** The relative standing of a product with regard to its competition, as perceived by consumers.

product protection Also called **commercial protection.** A television network's guarantee to an advertiser that no other commercial advertising a similar product will be scheduled during the program on which the advertiser has bought time.

product research 1. In general, scientific or market research into ways of perfecting or popularizing a manufactured product; also, determining the feasibility of manufacturing new products. **2.** Systematic gathering and analysis of consumers' responses to polls, panel discussions, and questionnaires as a means of directing product design and packaging; also, test-marketing of new products in selected areas prior to general distribution.

product safety The professional area dealing with the continuous inspection of products for the purpose of identifying and eliminating features that may cause harm to the user and with the recall of products so identified that have already been sold.

product space See **product position.**

professional corporation (*abbr* PC) A corporation formed by one or more licensed practitioners, especially medical or legal, to operate their practices on a corporate plan.

profile A list of the distinguishing characteristics of a human population or a segment of it, a new product, etc. See also **demographics.**

profit See **net income.**

profitability ratio A measure of the extent to which a company is making a profit.

profit and loss statement See **income statement.**

profit center A self-contained unit within a business organization that has or may develop a profitable base independent of the larger system.

profit corporation A private organization operated for gain.

profit margin on sales Net income as a percent of total sales.

profit sharing 1. A compensation plan whereby employees receive a fixed share of any profits made by the employer. **2.** An incentive plan whereby each employee receives as a bonus the portion of the company's profits that represents his or her productivity.

profit squeeze A decline in profit resulting from declining prices, intense competition, or increasing costs.

profit taking The selling of stocks or other securities for the purpose of gaining the additional value that has resulted from rising prices.

pro forma (*Latin*) For the sake of form.

pro forma financial statement A statement that projects the financial position of a company under certain hypothetical conditions or assumptions (e.g., a possible merger, expansion, retrenchment).

pro forma invoice An invoice sent to a customer before shipment of goods as a memorandum specifying goods to be shipped, means of shipment, and terms.

programmed instruction Presentation of information in a structured format such that each step of the learning process is mastered before advancing to the next.

programmer 1. A person who programs a computer. **2.** A person who schedules radio and television programs. **3.** A person who inculcates new behavior in another person.

programming language The artificial language in which computer programs are written, such as COBOL or BASIC. See also **machine language.**

program rating See **Nielsen rating; share** (def. 2).

program trader A specialist in program trading.

program trading The often computerized trading by large institutions of vast quantities of stocks, sometimes blamed for the instability of the stock market.

progressive tax Also called **graduated tax.** A tax structured so that the rate increases as taxable income increases.

project management Direction by a team brought together to carry out research on and development of a specific project within a specified time limit.

promissory note A borrower's written promise

to pay a specified amount plus interest at a specified rate on a designated date in the future.

promotion 1. An advancement to a position with higher status and greater responsibility, usually with an increase in salary. **2.** The totality of communications designed to sell a product, service, or idea, including personal selling, advertising, publicity, and public relations.

property Anything of value that is owned. See also **personal property; real estate.**

property dividend A dividend paid in resources, assets, goods, etc., rather than cash.

property insurance Insurance that protects the insured against losses resulting from damage to or destruction of property as a result of unavoidable risks.

proprietary information Information about a company or about an aspect of its business that should be known only to a limited number of people involved in the relevant activities.

proprietorship An ownership interest in a company, equal to assets less liabilities or contributed capital plus retained earnings.

pro rata (*Latin*) In proportion; proportionately determined.

prorate To calculate on a proportionate basis; to divide or distribute proportionately.

pro se (*Latin*) For himself/herself/oneself/themselves.

prospect A potential customer.

prospecting (*sales*) Also called **farming.** The totality of activities designed to identify legitimate prospects and eliminate those unlikely to become customers.

prospective planning Planning to meet the needs of an organization's employees that takes into account their long-range expectations as well as their present needs.

prospectus A published summary of a corporation's earnings, financial condition, product lines, and the qualifications and salaries of its officers, required by the Securities Exchange Act of 1934 to be provided to all potential investors in the corporation's securities.

protectionism The protection of domestic industries against foreign competition by enacting high tariffs and/or restrictions on imports. Advocates of such procedures are called *protectionists*.

protective tariff A tariff imposed on a class of imports for the purpose of protecting a domestic industry against foreign competition.

prototype A model of a product prepared for testing, evaluation, and possible modification before the product is mass-produced.

provision for income tax See **income-tax expense.**

proxy Written authorization for one person to act for another, as to vote one's shares of stock.

proxy fight A competition between management and disagreeing shareholders for control of the company, each group attempting to secure the major portion of shareholders' proxies.

prudent man rule A rule adopted by states that lack a legal list, indicating that a fiduciary has wide discretion in investment decisions, provided only that they be such as would conceivably be made by any prudent investor.

psychographics Also called **psychographic segmentation.** A market-segmentation strategy by which consumers are grouped according to their behavior patterns and lifestyles, as indicated by responses to questionnaires.

psychological pricing See **odd-even pricing.**

public accountant (*abbr* PA) An independent accountant who offers his or her professional services to the public for a fee. See also **certified public accountant.**

public corporation A corporation owned and operated by a government, established to administer a designated governmental program and managed in accordance with business principles.

public domain The rights belonging to the public at large; the status of properties (as writings, music, or inventions) on which copyright or patent protection has expired or which have been issued without such protection, and which may be used by any person.

public good A product or service whose consumption by one person does not exclude consumption by others (e.g., fire and police protection).

publicity Information designed to appear in any medium of communication for the purpose of keeping the name of a person or company before the public or of creating public interest in their activities.

public law A law enacted by a legislative body, applicable throughout the geographical area over which the legislature has jurisdiction. See also **common law.**

public-liability insurance Insurance that provides coverage against claims by the public for damages arising from negligence.

public offering An issuance of a security for sale to the public.

public relations Promotion of a favorable image for a company through particular attention to how, when, why, and what information is given to customers, employees, stockholders, and the general public.

public sector That part of the economy which is considered to be the government's domain, involving such activities and decisions as have an effect on the society at large. See also **private sector.**

public warehouse A warehouse in which storage space is rented to any person.

puffery 1. Undue or extravagantly flattering praise issued for promotional purposes. **2.** Also called **puff piece.** An example of this in the form of a newspaper or magazine article, usually commissioned and placed by a hired public-relations specialist.

pull distribution strategy A marketing strategy based on efforts to induce consumers to ask retailers for a product they have seen advertised, so that retailers will then order the product. See also **push distribution strategy.**

pulsing See **flighting.**

pump priming Government spending designed to stimulate the economy.

purchase journal An accounting journal used to record purchases of merchandise, the total being posted as a credit to accounts payable and a debit to the purchases account.

purchase method An accounting method whereby two previously distinct companies are combined by adding the value of one company's assets to the total assets of the other. See also **pooling-of-interest method.**

purchase order (*abbr* PO) A printed agreement to buy a product, indicating the quantity of goods desired, delivery dates, order number, and other relevant information.

purchasing agent A person who has the authority to select and buy supplies for a company.

purchasing power See **buying power.**.

push distribution strategy A marketing strategy based on efforts to place a product with wholesalers, who will then make an effort to place it with retailers, who will make an effort to sell it to customers. See also **pull distribution strategy.**

push money (*abbr* PM) Commissions, bonuses, etc., paid to retail sales personnel for selling specified items.

put 1. Also called **put option.** An option to sell a stock or commodity at a specified (put) price within a specified period, purchased from a broker for a premium based on a percentage of the current market price of the stock or commodity; if the price falls during the option period, the owner of the option can sell the shares or commodity at the (higher) price specified. See also **call. 2.** To exercise such an option.

pyramid selling An illegal marketing scheme whereby an initial investor recruits and establishes subordinate distributors, each of whom recruits additional distributors, and so on, each distributor to receive a commission on the sales of all subordinate distributors recruited by him or her and by those recruited by subordinates.

Q

qualified endorsement An endorsement that limits the liability of the endorser by specific words added above the signature (e.g., "Without recourse").

qualified opinion Also called **qualified report.** An auditor's report that includes a statement to the effect that the auditor has been unable to examine all relevant documents or has some doubts about the impact of some information on the financial report.

qualified pension plan A pension plan that conforms to the provisions of the Employee Retirement Income Security Act and so qualifies the employee to receive tax benefits for tax-deducted contributions and tax-free investment growth (e.g., a profit-sharing plan or a money-purchase plan).

qualified prospect A prospective buyer who has the financial ability and authority to buy the product being offered.

qualified report See **qualified opinion.**

qualified stock option A once popular but now rarely used plan by which executives could buy stock during a five-year period at the market price, with appreciation in value being taxed as capital gains. See also **nonqualified stock option.**

quality assurance Any steps taken to improve and maintain the quality performance of an organization.

quality circle A group of workers (typically 5 to 12) who meet regularly to identify, analyze, and solve work-related problems, such as quality improvement.

quality control Spot checking of goods after manufacture, before assembly, or through laboratory testing, for the purpose of eliminating defective products or improving performance standards and practices.

quality of work life (*abbr* QWL) Employee involvement in the making of decisions involving the organization as a whole, instituted to increase morale and individual productivity. See also **quality circle.**

quant A slang term for a specialist in quantitative analysis (quantitative analyst).

quantitative analysis Also called **quantitative research.** The use of statistical data, usually computerized, to support management decision making, make business forecasts or recommendations to investors, etc.

quantity discount Also called **patronage discount.** A price reduction offered for purchases of large quantities of a product.

quasi contract An obligation imposed by law in the absence of a contract in order to prevent one person from being unjustly enriched at the expense of another.

quasi-public corporation A corporation created jointly by public and private funds.

quasi reorganization A reorganization of a company effected by court intervention following bankruptcy or near bankruptcy in which no new company has been formed. See also **Chapter 11.**

QUBE (*trademark*) A device that enables television viewers to answer questions, order merchandise, or otherwise respond to information projected on their television screens.

queuing theory Analytical models used to describe customer service systems with waiting lines, or queues, and to provide various performance measures, such as average waiting time and expected line length.

quick asset Also called **liquid asset.** An asset that can be quickly converted to cash (e.g., a marketable security, current accounts receivable).

quick ratio See acid-test ratio.

quitclaim deed A legal instrument transferring any interest, claim, or title that a person may have in real property, normally with no warranty in regard to rights others may have in the property.

quorum The minimum number of people whose presence is considered necessary before business may be conducted.

quota 1. The quantity of goods that an employee is expected to produce or sell within a given time span. **2.** A government-imposed restriction on imports of a specified product or on the amount or number imported from a particular country, often on a par with exports. **3.** A percentage of minority or handicapped workers hired by a company.

quotation (*abbr* quote) The highest bid price a dealer offers for a given stock and the lowest asked price that a seller is willing to accept for that stock.

quoted bid See **bid price.**

QWL See **quality of work life.**

R

rabble hypothesis The hypothesis that employees are motivated by self-interest: a principle of early management theorists who believed that no employee could be expected to cooperate with management for any reason other than monetary reward.

rack jobber A wholesaler (usually in the food business) who provides goods and then stacks, arranges, and displays them in retail stores.

RACORNOS (*acronym for* race, color, religion, national origin, sex) A term that first appeared in the Civil Rights Act of 1964 as part of the text defining and outlawing discrimination in employment.

raider Also called **corporate raider.** A person, company, etc., that attempts to take over another company, especially by surreptitiously buying up the target company's stock.

rail average The average price per share of 30 transportation stocks as calculated by the Dow Jones transportation index. See also **Dow Jones average.**

rainmaker An employee who generates money for a firm, such as an account executive who brings in lucrative clients.

rainmaking The action or process of generating revenue for a firm, especially by bringing in new clients with large accounts, as in a law firm or advertising agency.

rally A sudden reversal of a downward trend in the prices of all stocks or in the price of a particular stock.

RAM (*acronym for* random access memory) Also called **main memory.** Computer memory used for creating, running, and loading programs and for manipulating and temporarily storing data. See also **ROM.**

R & D (*abbr for* research and development) See **development; research.**

random sampling Selection of a small portion of a population, group of products, etc., in such a way that the response, quality, etc., of the sampling can be considered typical of the whole.

rate Charge per unit (e.g., a price for advertising time or space based on the average number of viewers or readers or a premium cost per $1000 of insurance).

rate base An amount of circulation guaranteed to advertisers by a publisher and used as the basis for the charge per unit of advertising space.

rate card A printed statement distributed to purchasers of media space indicating advertising rates and technical requirements for use of each medium.

rate cutting An employer-initiated reduction in employee wage rates.

rate of exchange See **exchange rate.**

rate of return The profit shown by an investment, expressed as a percentage of the total money invested in it.

rate protection A guarantee that advertising rates will not be increased during a specified time period.

rate stop See **freeze rate.**

rating See **Nielsen rating; share** (def. 2).

ratio analysis An analysis of the various elements that make up a financial statement, with their relationships expressed either as percentages of the whole or as ratios.

reacquired stock See **treasury stock.**

real account A permanent balance-sheet account, as opposed to a nominal account.

real earnings The actual value of earnings after adjustment for inflation, deflation, or devaluation of the currency.

real estate Also called **real property.** Land and anything permanently attached to it.

real estate investment trust (*abbr* REIT) A mutual fund that invests only in real estate and must distribute at least 90 percent of its income as dividends. See also **equity real estate investment trust; mortgage real estate investment trust.**

real GNP (*abbr for* real *gross* national *product*) The value of the output of a nation's goods and services in a given period measured in the prices of a previous period.

real income The total purchasing power of an individual or a nation.

realizable value Market value; the amount that can be obtained on the open market for a given asset.

realization The final earning of revenues and subsequent recognition of them in bookkeeping accounts.

real property See real estate.

real-time Of or relating to computer programs or processes that respond immediately to user input.

rearrangement costs Costs incurred in the reinstallation of an asset either after maintenance work or for the purpose of relocating it.

reasonable value A value placed on an asset that accurately reflects its worth on the open market.

reassessment An official reevaluation of the value of real property.

rebate A return of part of the original payment for some service or merchandise.

recall 1. To summon laid-off employees back to work. **2.** To cause defective or unsafe products to be returned to the manufacturer for repair, replacement, or refund.

receipt-of-goods dating See ROG dating.

receivable A claim against a customer or debtor, listed as an asset on a balance sheet. See also **accounts receivable.**

receiver A person with the legal authority to receive and to hold in trust property that is or could be involved in a lawsuit.

receiving apron A document used by retailers to account for incoming shipments of merchandise.

recession 1. A period when business production, employment, and earnings fall below normal levels. **2.** A period when real GNP declines for two consecutive quarters. See also **final-goods recession; inventory recession.**

reciprocity Mutual exchange of trade between two parties, such that trade with nonparticipating parties is virtually eliminated.

recognition 1. The entering of the amount of a transaction into a bookkeeping account. **2.** Formal acknowledgment of the right of a union to act as bargaining agent for employees.

recognition picketing Picketing by union members of a company where a rival union is already recognized in an effort to replace that union as bargaining agent for the employees of the company.

reconciliation 1. The act of calculating or analyzing how the balance of one account was derived from another. **2.** Also called **reconcilement.** The act of accounting for differences between two financial balances. **3.** See **bank reconciliation.**

record The documents that must be processed during the filing of a patent and that remain a permanent part of the application.

record date See **holder-of-record date.**

recovery A turnaround in economic conditions following a recession or depression.

recruiter A staffing specialist employed by a company or by an outside agency to find qualified persons, especially executives, for specific positions. See also **executive search firm.**

redeemable bond See **callable bond.**

redemption price 1. The price a corporation must pay to redeem (buy back) its preferred stock or a bond before its maturity date. **2.** The price a mutual fund must pay to redeem an outstanding share, usually the fluctuating net asset value.

red herring An unofficial prospectus distributed to potential investors for the purpose of ascertaining the extent of their interest in a new issue of stock.

red rush See **crash time.**

reentry An employee's return to work after time spent in a training program, a leave of absence, or any other interruption of work.

reference column Also called **ref.** The column in an accounting journal in which is recorded the account number of the ledger to which the journal data were posted, or the column in a ledger in which is recorded the page number of the journal from which the ledger data were posted.

reference group A group with which an individual identifies and whose opinions, attitudes, and values strongly influence the individual's decisions.

referral scheme A sales technique whereby the seller promises to give the purchaser a monetary rebate or free products if a certain number of the buyer's friends buy the item also.

refinance **1.** To finance again. **2.** To satisfy a mortgage or other debt by making another loan on new terms. **3.** To increase or change the financing of, as by selling stock or obtaining additional credit.

refinancing **1.** Satisfying a mortgage or other debt by making another loan on new terms. **2.** Changing the financing of a debt, as by selling stock or obtaining additional credit.

reflective listening An interpersonal problem-solving technique that requires those individuals involved in conflict to restate the assertions of the other party before answering them.

reframing A training technique whereby a person is encouraged to view a commonplace event from a new vantage point that is useful or enjoyable, with the expectation that when the frame of reference of the event changes, the person's responses and behavior will likewise change.

refreeze To strengthen, support, and routinize newly established behavior patterns within a work group, usually as the final phase of a planned intervention program. See also **intervention** (def. 2).

refusal to deal A refusal to do business with a particular company; a right recognized by the Supreme Court so long as there is no indication of conspiracy, price fixing, restraint of trade, or racial or religious discrimination. See also **Colgate doctrine.**

registered representative (*abbr* RR) See **broker** (def. 1).

registrar An outside agent, usually a bank or trust company, that approves the issuance of stock, authenticates stock certificates, keeps track of registered stockholders and dividend distributions, and sometimes also serves as a transfer agent.

registration The formal recording of a stock issue by the Securities and Exchange Commission, required by the Securities Act of 1933 for all public offerings of more than $1.5 million within 20 days of issuance, with financial, legal, and technical information about the company, which is condensed in the prospectus.

regression analysis A statistical technique used

to describe the relationship between two variables, so that if the value of one variable is known, the value of the other can be predicted.

regressive tax A tax structured so that the tax rate decreases as taxable income increases. An example is the Social Security tax.

Regulation B A regulation of the Federal Reserve Board issued to carry out the provisions of the Equal Credit Opportunity Act of 1975, limiting the kind of information that an applicant for credit may be required to supply, in particular a woman of childbearing age or one who is widowed or divorced.

Regulation S-X A regulation of the Securities and Exchange Commission specifying the form and content of reports that must be filed with the Commission.

Regulation T A regulation of the Federal Reserve Board that sets the maximum amount of credit that a broker or dealer can extend to customers for the purchase of securities.

Regulation U A regulation of the Federal Reserve Board that sets the maximum amount a bank may loan a customer for the purchase of listed securities when such a loan is to be secured by listed securities.

Regulation Z A regulation of the Federal Reserve Board issued to carry out the provisions of the Truth-in-Lending Act, requiring that borrowers be informed of the exact costs of credit offered up to $25,000 for personal, family, household, or farming purposes.

Rehabilitation Act An act of Congress passed in 1973 requiring that any employer who has a government contract take affirmative action to employ and promote the handicapped.

reinvestment rate The rate at which the cash generated by a project before its completion is reinvested.

REIT See **real estate investment trust.**

relative advantage (*marketing*) The advantage that one product has over another or over competing products, as viewed by consumers.

release A signed authorization for the use of a photo, name, property, film or tape clip, or testimonial for commercial purposes.

relevant costs Differing future costs of alternative courses of action.

relevant environment The individuals outside an organization who directly affect its operations and sales (e.g., suppliers, customers, competitors, regulatory agencies).

reliability The degree to which an experiment, test, or survey will repeatedly yield the same results. See also **validity.**

remainder A future estate that takes effect at the termination of another estate, as when property is conveyed to one person for life and thereafter to another.

remedial maintenance Those maintenance activities performed to restore equipment to an acceptable operating condition after a breakdown has occurred. See also **preventive maintenance.**

remedy A legal means of correcting a wrong or recovering a legal right or privilege.

remittance Money forwarded from one person or firm to another as payment for purchased goods or services.

renegotiable-rate mortgage Also called **flexible rate mortgage; rollover mortgage.** A federally sponsored loan that requires the holder to renegotiate its terms every three to five years, when interest rates are subject to increase or decrease, depending upon market conditions. See also **adjustable-rate mortgage; variable-rate mortgage.**

rent 1. A periodic payment made by a tenant to a landlord in return for the use of property. **2.** A series of payments made by a lessee to an owner in return for the use of equipment, machinery, etc. **3.** Profit or return derived from land or from any differential advantage in use.

reopener clause A contractual provision that allows a current contract to be renegotiated for specified reasons.

reorder point The quantity of materials or merchandise on hand that signals the need to reorder.

reorganization A reconstruction of a business corporation, including a marked change in capital structure and reporting structure.

replacement cost The actual cost to a company to replace an item or piece of machinery.

repo See **repurchase agreement.**

report form The standard form of a balance-sheet presentation, in which assets less liabilities are shown as one total in the top portion, often with a subtotal for current assets and current liabilities and a subtotal for noncurrent assets and liabilities, followed by the components of owners' equity. See also **account form.**

repossession The reclaiming of items that were sold on an installment sales contract but not paid for in accordance with the contractual terms.

representation election An election conducted by the National Labor Relations Board to determine whether a particular labor union is to represent workers in a designated bargaining unit.

repressive tax A government levy that discourages production and productivity.

reproduction cost The cost of acquiring an asset with physical characteristics similar to those of an asset already owned and for which a current value must be determined.

repurchase agreement Also called **repo. 1.** A contract between a dealer, such as a bank, and an investor, whereby the investor purchases securities with the promise that they will be bought back by the dealer on a designated date, for which the investor receives a fixed return. **2.** A contract between a buyer and a seller whereby the seller agrees to repurchase the item sold after a specified length of time or amount of use.

requisition A written authorization issued by one department of a company to another (e.g., supply department) for the release of goods.

rescission Revocation or abrogation of a contract, either by consent of the parties involved or by court order, as when one party has breached the contract or has signed it under fraudulent terms.

research Purposeful and methodical investigation or experimentation. See also **applied research; basic research.**

research and development (*abbr* R&D) See **development; research.**

reserve A special account (e.g., reserve for contingencies, reserve for warranty claims, reserve for income taxes) that appropriates retained earnings and limits dividend distributions in anticipation of likely future costs.

reserve for bad debts See **allowance for doubtful accounts.**

reserve requirement A percentage of the total amount of a bank's demand deposits that the Federal Reserve Board requires to be kept on hand as cash or on deposit with a federal bank.

resident buyer An individual located in a particular geographical area who provides services and assistance to retail buyers who wish to buy merchandise in that location.

residual income Income to be distributed to holders of common stock after the senior claims of bonds and preferred stock are paid.

residual value The net realizable value of a depreciable asset: the market or salvage value less the cost of removing and/or delivering the asset.

resource decision A euphemism often employed when a company is forced to scrap a project, close down one of its plants, and lay off a number of employees.

restraining order A court order that prohibits certain actions until all parties in a dispute can be officially heard.

restraint of trade Illegal restriction or impeding of competition or unfair imposition of limits on the right to do business.

restricted stock Company stock granted to an executive, often subject to forfeiture and with the right to sell limited.

restrictive covenant 1. An agreement accompanying a conveyance of land and restricting the use to which the land may be put. **2.** An agreement accompanying an employment contract whereby the employee promises not to work for anyone else in the same business or to form a competing business in a specified area for a specified number of years.

restrictive endorsement An endorsement that transfers an instrument for a particular purpose only (e.g., ''Pay to the order of...,'' ''For deposit only''), after which the instrument is no longer negotiable.

résumé Also, **resume.** A descriptive listing of one's job experience, education, and training, used in seeking employment: usually sent to a prospective employer prior to a job interview.

retailing The activities involved in selling goods or services directly to people for their own use.

retail inventory method A method commonly used by large retail stores to determine inventory cost for interim statements, in which total sales are subtracted from the total retail value of the goods available for sale during the specified period in order to determine the retail value of the inventory, the result being reduced by an estimated (or average) markup rate.

retained earnings 1. (*income statement*) The portion of a corporation's recent net profit that is reinvested in the business rather than distributed as dividends. **2.** (*balance sheet*) A corporation's total earnings in the current and previous periods reduced by the amounts distributed as dividends.

retainer A fee paid to secure the services of an individual with a particular skill or knowledge (e.g., lawyer, auditor).

retentive stage The point in the life cycle of a product where the brand has so much consumer acceptance that promotional activities can be kept to a minimum without loss of consumer loyalty.

retirement 1. (*accounting*) The disposal of an asset at the end of its useful life. **2.** Voluntary or involuntary withdrawal from active employment.

retroactive pay Delayed payment for services rendered in the past.

retrospective planning Organizational planning by which past errors in judgment are assessed and rectified before new objectives are set.

return 1. See **yield. 2.** See **tax return.**

return on investments (*abbr* ROI) Net income divided by total assets: expressed as a percentage.

revaluation surplus Part of owners' equity created by the upward revaluation of fixed assets.

revenue Incoming assets in the form of cash and other receivables resulting from sales of products or services and returns on investments, exclusive of borrowed assets and income from sales of capital stock.

revenue bond A municipal bond backed by the income-producing project it finances, as a toll road or bridge.

revenue tariff A tax levied on imported products for the sole or primary purpose of raising revenue.

reversal entry A journal entry usually made to reverse or undo the effects of an adjusting entry of a previous period.

reverse-annuity mortgage An income plan whereby homeowners may borrow against their equity in a house or other property, the loan providing them with a monthly income that is deducted from the amount of their equity.

reverse split Also called reverse stock split. The recalling of shares of stock by the issuer and the subsequent issuance of one new share for two or more old shares.

reversion The return of an estate to the original owner or to that owner's successor after the interest granted expires.

revolving charge account A type of retail charge account by whose terms no service charge is imposed if the customer pays the full amount owed within a given period of time after the billing date, usually 30 days; otherwise a specified percentage of the amount owed will be added as a service charge.

revolving credit See open-end credit.

revolving loan A loan expected to be renewed upon maturity.

reward See extrinsic reward; intrinsic reward.

reward/punishment system See utilitarian reward/punishment system.

rider An addition to a standard insurance policy offering further coverage.

rights See ex-rights; preemptive right.

rights on With the right to purchase a new issue of stock at a special subscription price offered to current shareholders; applied to shares of stock traded before the ex-rights date.

right-to-work law A state law that prohibits the practice of requiring a worker to join a union as a condition of employment.

ring The area of a commodities market, usually

ring-shaped, where traders conduct their business. See also **pit.**

risk The possibility or probability of an unfavorable occurrence. See also **absorbable risk; financial risk; insurable risk; pure risk; systematic risk; unsystematic risk.**

risk analysis Analysis of the possible outcomes of a management decision and the probability that such outcomes will occur.

risk arbitrage A high-risk type of trading in which the investor buys up large blocks of stock in a company rumored to be on the verge of expanding its operations, targeted for takeover, etc.

risk capital See **venture capital.**

risk finance The totality of procedures (e.g., insurance, bank lines of credit, pooling of risks among members of a particular industry) used to fund known or anticipated losses.

risk management The reduction of the risk of financial loss caused by unpredictable events by (1) avoidance of risk, (2) preparation to accept or absorb it without permanent financial injury, (3) minimization of the threat of risk or the extent of damages, or (4) purchase of insurance to guarantee full or partial recovery.

risk premium The difference in interest rates between a low- or no-risk security (e.g., a short-term government security) and a security of high risk (e.g., a corporate bond or stock).

risky-shift phenomenon A tendency to venture a more hazardous solution to a problem when the responsibility for its consequences is shared with others.

road warrior (*slang*) A person who travels extensively on business.

Robinson-Patman Act An act of Congress passed in 1936 to amend the Clayton Act by reducing the amount of proof needed to show anticompetitive effects of price discrimination. See also **Colgate doctrine.**

robotics The use of computer-controlled robots to perform mechanical tasks previously done by humans, as on an assembly line.

ROG dating (*abbr for* receipt-of-goods dating) The setting of the due date and the calculation of any discount in accordance with the date goods are actually received by the buyer.

role conflict Conflict experienced by a person as a result of incompatible behaviors expected in the carrying out of two or more contradictory functions or of expected behaviors incongruent with one's perception of oneself.

role indicators See **links and role indicators.**

role playing A training technique whereby individuals behave realistically in simulated situations, thus experimenting with new behaviors and new attitudes in a low-risk situation.

roll-in A film or tape commercial inserted into a television program for broadcast.

rollout 1. The inauguration of a new service, product, production method, etc. **2.** Specification of the most economical sequence of operations for work to be done during the manufacturing process.

rollover The reinvestment of funds, as from one stock or bond into another.

rollover mortgage See **renegotiable-rate mortgage.**

ROM (*acronym for* read-only memory) A form of computer memory in which operating procedures and programmed instructions to the system are permanently stored, usually imprinted on electronic chips during manufacture and which generally cannot be changed. See also **RAM.**

rough cut 1. A preliminary (rough) edited version of a film or videotape prepared for approval by a client or producer before the final transitions, titles, and audio effects are inserted. **2.** A method of capacity planning that roughly estimates the feasibility of a proposed production schedule, especially in determining the ability of the known bottlenecks to fulfill their part of the requirements.

round lot An even 100 shares of an active stock or a multiple thereof.

route sheet A document that specifies for a part, component, or product the sequence of operations in the production process, the amount of time each operation should take, and the work center or machine that will accomplish each task.

routing Determination of the path that work will take through the production process.

royalty Compensation in the form of a percentage of revenues payable for the use of property protected by a patent or copyright or of a natural resource.

RR (*abbr for* registered representative) See **broker** (def. 1).

rubber check See **NSF check.**

rule of 69 A formula used to calculate the number of periods it will take an amount invested to double in value at a particular compound interest rate, accurate to $\frac{1}{10}$ of a period. In the following formula, X is the percentage of compound interest per period:

$$69/X + 0.35 = \text{Number of periods}$$

rule of 72 A formula used to calculate the approximate number of periods it will take an amount invested to double at a given compound interest rate. In the following formula, X is the compound interest rate per period:

$$72/X = \text{Number of periods}$$

rule of 78 A method used by finance companies to allocate earnings on loans among the 12 months of the year when all monthly payments are equal, based on the sum-of-the-years'-digits concept: the sum of the digits 1 through 12 (for the 12 months) equals 78; $\frac{12}{78}$ of annual earnings are allocated to the first month, $\frac{11}{78}$ to the second month, and so on to the end of the year.

runoff election A second election conducted by the National Labor Relations Board when the first does not determine a clear majority of votes in favor of one of two labor unions.

run of paper (*abbr* ROP) An arrangement whereby an advertiser leaves the position of an ad to the discretion of the publisher. See also **guaranteed position.**

Russell Index One of several U.S. stock indexes maintained by the Frank Russell Company. The Russell 3000 is comprised of the largest U.S. companies, and the Russell 2000 is comprised of small companies. Each stock is weighted according to its market capitalization.

S

safety engineering Examination and analysis of potentially hazardous conditions in a plant or other industrial environment so that measures can be taken to prevent accidents.

safety stock Also called **buffer stock**. An extra supply of materials kept on hand to complete a production run or for use in the event that above-normal needs occur during the time required to receive new materials.

salary Payment to an employee for work done, based on a weekly, monthly, or annual rate rather than on an hourly rate.

sale 1. The delivery of goods in exchange for some resource, most commonly cash or a promise to pay cash. **2.** An agreement or contract to transfer title or ownership of property or movable goods from one individual, the seller, to another, the buyer, for a specified price.

sale and leaseback See **leaseback**.

sales (*accounting*) A revenue account with a normal credit balance that reflects revenues from the sale of goods for the period to date.

sales agent A marketing agent who handles all of the production of a manufacturer and acts as the firm's marketing department.

sales forecast A prediction of the sales of a product in an area, based on knowledge of past buying habits of the target audience plus identified and calculated environmental influences.

sales journal A special accounting journal used to record sales on credit, the total being posted as a credit to sales and a debit to accounts receivable.

sales promotion The aggregate of carefully and persuasively designed events, activities, and products (e.g., contests, coupons, direct mail, point-of-purchase displays, sales meetings, samples, sweepstakes, trade shows) used by an advertiser to encourage sales.

sales quota The amount of sales expected to be made by a salesperson, based on the number of stores in the territory and factors influencing buying patterns.

sales returns and allowances An account with a normal debit balance in which are recorded refunds and credit given to customers who have returned goods and the cost of goods damaged in shipment, which can be a contra account deducted from gross sales or can be treated as a selling expense.

sales tax A tax on a purchase, added to the total sale.

sales-type lease See **capital lease.**

salvage value Also called **scrap value.** The value of an asset that has been fully depreciated, i.e., the market price of an asset that is to be replaced.

sample A section or part of a larger group of people or items selected for statistical measurement. See also **random sampling.**

S & L See **savings and loan association.**

S & P 500 See **Standard & Poor's 500.**

satisfaction Execution of an accord; settlement of a claim or discharge of a legal obligation.

saturation 1. Frequent repetition of an advertising message. **2.** A stage of marketing at which a product or line of products has achieved as great a share of the market as can be expected.

Saturday-night special A buyout offer made directly to the shareholders of a company and which expires in one week.

savings account A bank account on which interest is paid, traditionally one for which a bankbook is used to record deposits, withdrawals, and interest payments. Cf. **checking account.**

savings and loan association (*abbr* S & L) An institution, organized either as a cooperative or a corporation, that uses deposits to finance loans, primarily those to homebuyers.

savings bond A U.S. government bond, sold in two forms: (1) **Series EE,** available in denominations of $50 up to $10,000 and sold at half the face value, to mature in 8 years, and (2) **Series HH,** sold at face value in denominations beginning at $500 and usually paying 6 to 8 percent interest.

scab 1. A union member who refuses to strike or goes back to work before a strike is ended. **2.** A person who is hired to replace a striking worker.

scalar chain of command A graduated or step-like pattern of authority and responsibility.

Scanlon plan A group incentive program in which an entire work group is rewarded for a suggestion by any member that, when implemented, increases productivity.

scanner Also called **optical scanner.** A device that scans and identifies data in printed, handwritten, bar-code, or other visual form. A type of handheld scanner is commonly used at retail checkout counters.

scanning The process of examining the elements of a problem in a patterned way, which varies from individual to individual. See also **conservative focus; focus gambling; simultaneous scanning; successive scanning.**

scenario 1. The plans made for dealing with an upcoming event. **2.** An imagined sequence of events, especially those resulting from an intended or possible course of action, as a *best-case scenario* or a *worst-case scenario.*

schedule (*accounting*) A display of the calculations used to arrive at the figures in a tax report or financial statement.

scheduling The phase of production control in which timetables for production operations are developed.

scientific management A concept popularized by Frederick Taylor, who developed the systematic use of time-and-motion studies to maximize efficiency.

scientific method See **effective interest method.**

scorched earth A tactic in which a targeted company divests itself of its most attractive assets, in an attempt to avert a hostile takeover.

SCORE See **Service Corps of Retired Executives.**

S corporation See **Subchapter S corporation.**

scrambled merchandising A profit-seeking strategy by which retailers add lines of goods unrelated to their basic categories of merchandise (e.g., children's underwear in a supermarket) as a way of stimulating sales.

scrap allowance The amount by which a second or subsequent batch must be increased to compensate for rejects considered unavoidable in the processing.

scrap value See **salvage value.**

search 1. A researched analysis of existing and filed patents conducted for the purpose of determining the position and validity of a new patent. **2.** Also called **title search.** A search of recorded deeds to a property, as by a lawyer, to make certain there are no encumbrances against it and that the present owner is free to transfer title.

search and recruitment executive A personnel specialist, usually the vice president of personnel, who is responsible for selecting the strategies for finding and hiring new employees.

search firm See **executive search firm.**

seasonal employment pool The aggregate of workers who do seasonal work and are let go when they are no longer needed (e.g., migrant farm workers, construction workers, store clerks employed for the Christmas season).

seasonal unemployment Unemployment due to seasonal changes in the number of workers required (as at Cape Cod resorts in winter) or in the number looking for jobs (as in summer, when students seek temporary work).

seasonal variation A regularly occurring annual change, such as the increase in sales that occurs before Christmas.

seat A paid membership on a stock exchange and the accompanying right to buy and sell securities there.

SEC See **Securities and Exchange Commission.**

secondary boycott A boycott of an employer by unionized employees for the purpose of inducing the employer to bring pressure to bear on another employer involved in a labor dispute with the union.

secondary data Information collected from a source other than original documents or research, as from a book. See also **primary data.**

secondary distribution Also called **secondary offering.** The sale by a stockholder of a large block of shares previously issued, usually offered at a fixed price.

secondary market Also called **aftermarket.** The

market, as a stock exchange or over-the-counter sales, for trading securities after they have been issued.

secondary stock A relatively inexpensive stock issued by a small company; regarded as somewhat less risky than a penny stock and traded on the major exchanges.

secondary storage See **auxiliary memory.**

secret partner A partner who is not publicly known to be a partner but who is active in management decision making and is equally liable with other partners for the company's financial obligations.

sector A distinct part of a nation's economy.

secured loan A loan whose repayment is guaranteed by a pledge of something of value. See also **unsecured loan.**

secured party A lender who is assured of payment by a pledge of or a mortgage on property.

Securities Act of 1933 An act of Congress passed in response to the collapse of the stock market in 1929, regulating the interstate sale of newly issued investment securities valued at more than $1.5 million by requiring them to be registered 20 days before they can be offered to the public. See also **registration.**

Securities and Exchange Commission (*abbr* SEC) A five-member board appointed by the president of the United States to regulate and oversee all trading in stocks, oversee proxy voting, analyze market aberrations and the financial reports of corporations listed on American stock exchanges, and enforce the provisions of the Securities Exchange Act of 1934 and later legislation bearing on securities, corporate reorganizations, and holding companies.

Securities Exchange Act of 1934 Federal legislation enacted to regulate the sale of previously issued securities by establishing the Securities and Exchange Commission to analyze financial and other information in regard to the issuing corporations and their officers.

Securities Investor Protection Corporation (*abbr* SIPC) A public corporation created by Congress to insure investors against the loss of cash and securities held by a brokerage house that goes bankrupt or engages in fraudulent practices.

securitization The packaging by banks of traditional loans (e.g., mortgages, car loans) into bond-like securities for resale to other investors: benefits consumer by lower interest rates and frees institutional capital for other investments.

security 1. Any evidence of debt or ownership (e.g., stock certificate, bond, promissory note). **2.** Property pledged as collateral to guarantee payment of a debt or of a potential debt.

security agreement An agreement by which a borrower guarantees payment to a creditor by pledging or mortgaging property.

security analyst Also called **securities analyst.** A financial expert, often employed by a brokerage firm, who specializes in evaluating information regarding stocks and bonds, as by measuring the ratio of their prices to their dividends and earnings.

security interest A right or share in the ownership of property pledged as security for a debt.

seed money Capital for the first stages of a new business or other enterprise, especially for the initial setup and operating costs.

segment A component part of a business organization whose activities can be financially and operationally distinguished from the organization's other activities, owing to a difference in assets, products, geographical location, or type of customers.

segment margin The amount that a segment of a business contributes to the profits of the entire organization; the amount by which that segment's revenues exceed its expenses.

segment reporting Financial reporting of the income and assets of an identified segment of a business.

selective marketing system A marketing plan whereby a manufacturer chooses retail dealers who will, in the manufacturer's estimation, best represent the manufacturer's products in a particular area.

selective retention (*marketing*) A tendency to recall information and events that are consistent with one's value system, feelings, and beliefs and to forget the rest.

self-actualization process An approach to employee development by which individuals are encouraged to analyze their needs and assume responsibility for the direction and extent of personal development.

self-employed Earning one's living directly from one's own profession or business, as a freelance writer or artist, rather than as an employee earning salary or commission from another.

self-insurance Money set aside to cover potential losses and permitted to accumulate interest; in time the maintenance of such a fund may cost less than a conventional insurance company.

self-liquidating 1. (of an asset) Capable of being converted into cash quickly. 2. (of an investment, project, loan, etc.) Generating enough cash to repay the funds invested.

self-mailer A direct-mail piece that can be sent without an envelope.

seller's market A market in which goods are scarce and variety is limited, so that prices tend to rise as buyers compete for the available supply. See also **buyer's market.**

sell-in Strategies used by a manufacturer to improve retail sales of its products, as by offering trade discounts.

sell-off 1. A sudden and marked decline in stock or bond prices resulting from widespread selling. 2. Liquidating of assets or subsidiaries, as by divestiture.

sell short See **short selling.**

sell-through 1. The characteristic of a product to continue selling in different media (e.g., a motion picture with sell-through is released in theaters, then repackaged as a videocassette, and finally shown on television). 2. The process through which a product is sold, from manufacturer to wholesaler to retailer and ultimately to consumer.

semifixed cost See **stepped cost.**

semivariable cost See **mixed cost.**

senior security A security whose claims on dividends or assets have priority over those of another security (e.g., bonds are senior to preferred stock, which is senior to common stock).

sensitivity analysis Testing of a decision to determine the impact of changes or potential errors in the data on which that decision was based.

sensitivity training A series of training sessions, usually in the form of discussion groups, in which trainees are encouraged to develop sensitivity not only to their own needs and emotions but to those of the other participants. See also **laboratory training.**

SEP Also called **SEP-IRA.** Simplified Employee Pension: A tax-deferred pension plan in which an IRA is funded by employer and employee contributions. SEPs are for companies with 25 or fewer employees, or for self-employed persons.

separation Termination of employment. See also **discharge** (def. 1); **layoff; retirement** (def. 2).

sequencer See **sorter.**

sequential processing Processing of data in a computer in sequence, such as alphabetical.

sequential sampling Testing of randomly selected units from a lot, one by one, until the proportion of defects found is either below an acceptance limit (in which case the lot is accepted) or above a rejection limit (in which case the lot is rejected) or until the entire lot has been tested.

serial bond One of an issue of bonds that have progressive or otherwise differing maturity dates, such that the issuing corporation has several years in which to redeem the bonds.

service A useful labor (e.g., dry cleaner, car wash, watch repair) performed directly for others, usually on demand and for a specified fee. See also **good.**

service basis See **production method.**

service business Also called **service establishment.** A company that provides useful work on behalf of the public, such as a barbershop, exterminator, or taxi service.

service center A company that makes repairs, usually on its own products or those of a particular manufacturer.

Service Corps of Retired Executives (*acronym* SCORE) A group of volunteer retired men and women, sponsored by the Small Business Administration, who offer free management advice to those managing small businesses and to people interested in starting a small business: supplemented in 1969 by Active Corps of Executives.

service lease See **operating lease.**

service level A performance measure for an activity showing the proportion of output meeting a target criterion, such as the proportion of customers served in two minutes or less or the proportion of demand satisfied from inventory.

service mark (*abbr* SM) A proprietary term, such as American Express, that is registered with the Patent and Trademark Office.

service potential The future benefits to be derived from an asset.

service rate The capacity of a service operation stated in terms of customers per unit of time (e.g., customers per hour).

service wholesaler See **distributor.**

settlement option Any of several alternative methods by which the benefits of an insurance policy, annuity contract, or pension plan may be paid to the person entitled to receive them, as described in the policy or contract.

setup costs The labor costs involved in setting up machines for a production run, either at the start of a workday or at the inauguration of a new product, machine, or method.

setup time The time necessary to prepare for a manufacturing operation and to clean up after it is completed.

severance pay Money, exclusive of wages, back pay, etc., paid to an employee who has tenure and who is dismissed because of lack of work or other reasons beyond the employee's control.

severance tax A tax levied by a state on the extraction of a natural product (e.g., oil, coal) sold outside the state.

sexual harassment Unwelcome sexual advances, especially when made by an employer or superior, usually with compliance as a condition of continued employment or promotion.

shadow price The value per unit of a specific resource based on the increased profit generated by one additional unit of the resource: used in decisions affecting resource allocation.

shakeout A mild recession or other decline or setback within an industry that forces out the weaker competitors.

share **1.** One of the equal fractional parts into which the capital stock of a corporation is divided. **2.** Also called **program rating; share rating.** The percentage of television homes with sets turned on that were tuned to a particular program. See also **Nielsen rating. 3.** See **market share.**

shared-appreciation mortgage A type of mortgage, usually extended for 10 years, that carries a lower down payment or lower interest rate than customary in return for the lender's sharing in the appreciation of the property when sold or when the loan comes due, whichever occurs first.

shareholder Also called **stockholder.** A person who owns shares of stock in a corporation.

shareholders' equity See **owners' equity.**

share of market See **market share.**

share rating See **share** (def. 2).

shark repellent Any methods used by a company to prevent a hostile takeover, as by changing bylaws to require approval by 75 percent of the company's shareholders before a merger can take effect.

shelf life The length of time that a product can hold its chemical stability and therefore can be sold without fear of decomposition or harm to a consumer.

shelf talker A cardboard, paper, or plastic advertisement of a product designed to be attached to a shelf on which the product is exhibited for sale.

Sherman Antitrust Act An act of Congress passed in 1890 to discourage the formation of monopolies, subsequently strengthened by the Clayton Act, the Federal Trade Commission Act, and the Robinson-Patman Act.

shift differential Additional compensation provided to employees who work during hours not considered part of the normal workday.

shop committee A group of union members who are authorized to speak for the entire membership of a particular bargaining unit.

shop floor control Procedures or systems used to establish priorities for tasks assigned to production work centers.

shopping goods Items (e.g., furniture, major appliances) that are purchased infrequently and usually only after comparison of features and prices offered by various manufacturers and stores.

shop steward Also called **union steward.** A union member who is elected by other union members to discuss grievances with the foreman or employer.

short-form opinion See **standard opinion.**

short-range planning Identification and implementation of specific strategies to influence an organization's daily, weekly, or monthly performance (e.g., budgeting procedures for action in a given situation, rules and detailed methods for handling problems).

short selling A transaction whereby a speculator, expecting a given stock to decline in price, borrows some shares from a broker, sells them at the current high price, waits for the price to fall, then buys new shares at the lower price and returns them to the broker, keeping the price difference (less interest to the broker) as profit. The transaction, though regulated, is extremely risky, since the speculator must return the shares at the stipulated time, regardless of their price.

short-term capital gains Capital gains resulting from the sale of assets held less than six months, formerly subject to special tax breaks, but now taxed as ordinary income. See also **long-term capital gains.**

short-term debt Indebtedness incurred to cover operating expenses, meet payrolls, etc., and scheduled to be repaid within a year.

shotgun approach An advertiser's attempt to reach a great many people with a message by placing a large number of untargeted advertisements in various media, especially mass-circulation magazines.

shrinkage Reduction in inventory value caused by theft, waste, breakage, water damage, etc.

shrink-wrap A flexible film of plastic used to wrap and seal a book, food product, etc. The plastic film is exposed to a heating process and shrinks to the contour of the merchandise.

SIC See **standard industrial classification system.**

sight draft A trade draft that is payable on demand.

signature loan A loan requiring no collateral.

silent partner A partner who is publicly known to be a partner and who is liable for the partnership's financial obligations but who takes no management role. See also **dormant partner.**

simple interest An amount or rate of interest calculated as a percentage of the principal only, exclusive of interest earned in past periods.

simplification A reduction without specific cause in the number of items offered for sale by a company.

simplified employee pension See **SEP.**

simulation 1. A re-creation or model of a real-world situation or event (e.g., a problem in queuing theory to be solved by computer). **2.** A training technique whereby individuals act out scenarios in artificial settings simulating the work environment, where they can safely practice skills and behaviors demanded of them on the job.

simultaneous scanning An orientation to problem solving characterized by a tendency to take an overall view of the situation rather than to focus on any one element. See also **scanning.**

single-entry bookkeeping A simple accounting system in which each transaction is recorded in a single entry in a single account, as in a checkbook or simple list of accounts receivable, with no balancing of debits and credits.

single-line retailer A retail store that concentrates on one type of goods or line of merchandise.

single-step statement An income statement that shows first the total of all ordinary revenues and gains and then the total of all ordinary expenses and losses, with the difference between the two, adjusted for income from discontinued operations and extraordinary items, shown as net income.

sinking fund A quantity of money that is set aside, usually in annual installments, for the purpose of satisfying a debt, replacing equipment, etc.

sinking-fund depreciation A method of depreciating an asset whereby periodic allocations of money to a hypothetical sinking fund are considered to be an annuity whose value at the end of the depreciation life is equal to the replacement cost of the asset, each periodic charge including the imputed interest on the accumulated depreciation.

sin tax A tax levied against liquor, cigarettes, racetrack betting, and other items or activities considered by some to be sinful.

SIPC See **Securities Investor Protection Corporation.**

situational approach A hypothetical approach to leadership based on the supposition that in a given situation a variety of individuals would be equally effective in the leadership role.

situational management Also called **contingency management.** A style of management whereby the theories and general practices of management are adapted to the needs of the company.

skeleton account See **T-account.**

skills inventory A list of qualifications and aptitudes necessary for the successful completion of a job.

skimming **1.** A strategic pricing approach by which a company prices a new product above its expected normal level during its introduction to the marketplace, hoping to appeal to the consumers who are the least price conscious, then reducing the price when the market competition appears to be growing. See also **penetration pricing. 2.** The removing of profits from a business and concealing the evidence from shareholders, tax authorities, or partners.

skip loss A cash loss resulting when a credit customer permanently leaves an unpaid balance in an account.

SKU (*pronounced* "skyōō") (*acronym for st*ock*keeping unit*) A retailer-defined coding system used to distinguish individual items within a retailer's accounting, warehousing, and POS systems.

slack See **float** (def. 4).

slander A false oral statement that causes injury to the reputation of another. See also **libel.**

slide A bookkeeping error in which all the digits of an entry are correct and in order but rendered incorrect by a misplaced decimal point.

sliding scale 1. A variable scale, especially of industrial costs, as wages, that may be adapted to changes in demand. **2.** A wage scale varying with the selling price of goods produced, the cost of living, or profits. **3.** A price scale, as of medical fees, in which prices vary according to the ability of individuals to pay. **4.** A tariff scale varying according to changing prices.

slowdown A planned lessening of effort in performance by workers for the purpose of securing concessions from management.

slump Any mild recession in the economy as a whole or in a particular industry.

SM See **service mark.**

small business Typically, a business that is independently owned and managed, operates in a local area (often a neighborhood), and does not dominate its field.

Small Business Administration (*abbr* SBA) A federal agency created in 1953 to help, counsel, and protect the interests of small business operations; to make and guarantee loans to small businesses; to conduct courses in management and special programs for minority-owned small businesses; and to assist small businesses in securing government contracts.

Small Business Institute An independent organization established in 1953 to help small businesses by issuing surety bonds and loans, by offering management assistance, and by counseling small businesses that wish to secure SBA loans and government contracts.

small-cap Designating a stock with a market capitalization of under $500 million: these small companies are considered to have more growth potential and higher investment risk.

small office/home office (*acronym* SOHO) Referring to small offices or home offices that have limited space. Some manufacturers design space-saving office equipment for this market.

smart money 1. Money invested or wagered by experienced investors or bettors. **2.** Such knowledgeable investors or bettors.

smoothing See **exponential smoothing.**

snapper An incentive (e.g., a discount coupon)

used to encourage customers to buy a product that is the subject of a big advertising campaign.

sniffer An advertising display in which fragrance is used to draw attention to the product.

snob effect Evidence of the desirability of a unique product in the form of less expensive imitations marketed by other manufacturers, so that the unique product has proportionately less appeal to the elite shopper.

Social Security Act See **Federal Insurance Contributions Act.**

sociotechnical   systems   Manufacturing operations that combine the technology required to perform tasks and the social organization in which the tasks are performed.

soft copy Readable material in the form of images created electronically on a computer screen. See also **hard copy.**

soft currency Currency that is subject to sharp fluctuations in value. See also **hard currency.**

soft goods Goods made of textiles, such as clothing, linens, and towels. See also **durable goods.**

soft sell Also called **low-pressure selling.** A selling technique that is low-keyed, persuasive, and indirect. See also **hard sell.**

software Any computer program or set of instructions for a computer. See also **hardware.**

SOHO See **small office/home office.**

sole proprietorship An unincorporated business owned and usually operated by one individual.

S-1 A standardized statement that a company must file with the Securities and Exchange Commission before it may list and trade securities on a national exchange, including such information as the company's business, its capital structure, financial statements, major contracts, the salaries of its directors and officers, and details regarding the stock it will trade.

sort A process that arranges items in accordance with a set of given rules.

sorter Also called **sequencer.** An automatic data-processing machine that can order data or items as directed.

source marketing The practice of setting a retail price for an item before it is shipped, generally accompanied by a price label for the retailer to apply to the product before displaying it.

space buyer A media consultant whose services to clients include recommendations concerning where, how, and when to advertise as well as the placement of ads.

space sales The business of selling advertising in either print or broadcast media.

span of management The number of people, departments, etc., that report to one manager.

span of recall (*marketing research*) The number of items, especially brand items, that a person can recall when asked to do so. See also **evoked set.**

spec See on spec.

special endorsement See full endorsement.

special identification method A method of evaluating cost of goods sold and ending inventory by which the costs of specifically identified individual items sold or in inventory (usually large or expensive items not sold in great quantities or lots, such as jewelry or cars) are added together.

special journal An accounting journal in which frequently occurring transactions of a similar nature are recorded (e.g., sales, cash disbursements).

special-revenue debt (*government accounting*) The debt of a specific governmental unit or agency that is paid by the revenues of a specific source, such as a bridge toll.

specialty goods Products whose distinctive qualities make consumers reluctant to accept substitutes (e.g., designer jeans, French champagne).

specification A detailed explanation of an invention, either with or without a claim. See also **claim** (def. 2).

specific lien A claim against a specific piece of property that has been pledged as security for an unpaid loan. See also **blanket lien; lien** (def. 2).

specific performance The carrying out of the terms of a contract exactly as they are specified: used chiefly in regard to the fulfillment of a contract ordered by a court in cases where damages would be inadequate compensation to the complaining party.

specific price changes Changes in the market

prices of specific goods or services, either individually or on average.

speculative presentation A formal, no-fee demonstration sometimes made by an individual or company to a prospective client showing how a job would be approached.

speculative risk See **financial risk**.

speedup An effort by management to increase production by increasing the speed of an assembly line, often without a simultaneous increase in wages or other employee benefits.

spindle See **J hook**.

spin-off 1. A process of reorganizing a corporate structure whereby the capital stock of a division or subsidiary of a corporation or of a newly affiliated company is transferred to the stockholders of the parent corporation without an exchange of any part of the stock of the latter. **2.** A product that is an adaptation, outgrowth, or development of another similar product.

spiral The evolution of a product's acceptance in the marketplace, often marked by three stages: pioneering, competitive, and retentive.

split Also called **stock split**. A division of the existing shares of a corporation's stock into a greater number of shares, so that the value of each share is proportionately reduced (e.g., a 2–1 split doubles the number of shares owned by each shareholder, each worth half of its previous value): often done to attract new shareholders. See also **reverse split**.

split-dollar insurance Insurance on the life of a key executive for which the company pays the amount of premium equal to the annual increase in the policy's cash value and the executive pays the remainder, the company to receive the cash value of the policy and the executive's beneficiaries to receive any additional benefits if the executive should die.

split-off A process of reorganizing a corporate structure whereby the capital stock of a division or subsidiary of a corporation or of a newly affiliated company is transferred to the stockholders of the parent corporation in exchange for part of the stock of the latter.

split shift The standard number of working hours divided into two or more working periods per day.

split-up A process of reorganizing a corporate structure whereby all the capital stock and assets are exchanged for those of two or more newly established companies, resulting in the liquidation of the parent corporation.

sponsor 1. An advertiser who pays for the broadcast of a program as well as for the commercial messages that appear before, during, and after it. **2.** An advertiser whose commercial messages appear along with those of other advertisers during a broadcast program. See also **participation show.**

sponsored film A film created or financed by a company and containing an educational message rather than product information, often made available to any interested audience. See also **business film; training film.**

spot broadcasting Also called **spot buy.** Placement of a commercial by a national advertiser on local rather than network television for the purpose of reaching a selected market.

spot time A time period of 30 to 60 seconds purchased by an advertiser from a television network and its affiliates for the purpose of airing a commercial message before, during, or after a program at a rate that varies in accordance with the size of the viewing audience.

spot trading Buying or selling of a commodity, such as grain or crude oil, usually for cash and for immediate delivery. See also **futures trading.**

spread 1. The difference between bid (offered) and asked prices. **2.** A combined put and call order, used to take advantage of either rising or falling stock prices.

spread-loss plan See **chronological stabilization.**

spreadsheet 1. (*accounting*) A multicolumn worksheet for analyzing several related entries. **2.** (*computers*) A visual display of a simulated worksheet for use in financial planning, records, etc.

staff The aggregate of employees who have no direct responsibility for profit and loss but who provide services for people who do (e.g., market researcher, accountant). See also **line** (def. 1).

staff authority The right to advise or assist those with line authority or other staff personnel.

staffing 1. The hiring of people to run a company, operate a factory, etc. **2.** The aggregate functions of recruitment, training, selection, and evaluation of personnel, determination of compensation, and management of health and safety measures.

stagflation A combination of persistent inflation, stagnant consumer demand, and high unemployment.

Standard & Poor's 500 A group of 500 common stocks considered to be representative of the market, and whose average daily prices form the basis for an index of the day's security prices.

standard cost system An accounting method of production costing by which standard costs, estimated on the basis of a good but not perfect production run, are later compared with actual costs so that any variance can be determined and investigated.

standard cost variance The difference between actual and estimated costs for materials and labor, quantities of materials, labor hours, etc.

standard deduction A certain amount of income that a taxpayer can deduct from gross income to determine taxable income. The amount is adjusted yearly for inflation. See also **itemized deductions.**

standard industrial classification system (*abbr* SIC) A numerical system developed by the Bureau of the Budget to classify business establishments in accordance with the type of activity they perform in order to facilitate the collection and tabulation of business information.

standardization The mass production of uniform or identical goods, the same in weight, color, quality, etc.

standard labor hours The estimated number of hours that will be worked during production.

standard labor rate The estimated hourly labor rate that will be paid during production.

standard material price Also called **standard purchase price.** The estimated cost assigned to one unit of raw material.

standard material quantity Also called **stand-**

ard quantity. The estimated amount of a raw material that will be needed to produce one finished unit.

standard opinion Also called **short-form opinion.** An auditor's statement testifying that financial statements are fairly and consistently presented, that no excessive uncertainties were involved in the audit, and that the auditor adhered to generally accepted auditing standards.

standard price The estimated price of a unit of production.

standard purchase price See **standard material price.**

standard quantity See **standard material quantity.**

standards 1. The criteria by which performance is to be measured. **2.** Standard costs. See also **standard cost system. 3.** Generally accepted auditing standards.

standard time The amount of time an average employee takes to complete a particular task or job under normal work conditions. See also **allowed time.**

standby costs Capacity costs incurred even if operations are shut down, such as property taxes. See also **enabling costs.**

standing order An order for repeated shipment of goods over a specified time period, eliminating the necessity to reorder the items.

star A fast-growing product or company with good potential. See also **cash cow; dog.**

start-up Also called **start-up time.** The time needed to begin production or to reach full capacity after a contract is signed or a project is approved; the time needed for hiring new staff, procuring additional equipment, training staff, etc.

stated capital See **legal capital.**

stated value A value assigned, usually for legal purposes only, to common stock that does not have a par value.

statement of affairs A financial statement showing the immediate liquidation values rather than the historical costs of the assets of a company filing for or approaching bankruptcy.

statement of cash receipts and disburse-

ments Also called **statement of cash flow.** A list of cash receipts and expenditures and the beginning and ending balances of a past or future period.

statement of changes in financial position Also called **funds statement.** A financial statement that shows or explains changes in the working capital (cash) balances during a stated period by showing the sources and uses of the working capital and changes in the working capital accounts.

statement of changes in owners' equity A financial statement that explains any change or changes in owners' equity during a fiscal period, that is the sum represented by paid-in capital plus retained earnings.

statement of financial position See **balance sheet.**

statement of operations See **income statement.**

statement of policy A statement issued by the Securities and Exchange Commission specifying what it has interpreted as misleading information in an open-end investment company's offer of shares.

statement of retained earnings A statement setting forth a company's net profit minus whatever dividends were paid to shareholders during the year.

statement savings account A savings account in which transactions are confirmed periodically by a bank statement. Cf. **passbook savings account.**

state of the art The highest level of current knowledge or development in a particular field, especially those areas associated with modern technologies.

statistical quality control The use of carefully selected samplings during the production process to determine the overall quality of a product and to quickly identify any deterioration in that quality so that corrective action may be taken.

statistics 1. The gathering, analysis, and interpretation of numerical data. **2.** The data itself.

statute of limitations A statute designating a period of time beyond which a legal action may not be brought.

statutory tax rate The tax rate for each type of income, such as ordinary income and capital gains.

stepped cost Also called **semifixed cost.** A cost that rises in steps with increased levels of production.

sticker price 1. The dealer's full asking price of a new automobile as shown on an attached sticker that gives an itemized list of basic and optional equipment and other charges. **2.** Any retailer's asking price or list price.

stock A share in the ownership of a corporation. See also **common stock; preferred stock; stock certificate.**

stock allowance A percentage of production above normal needs that is held in inventory for use in case of unforeseen need.

stock appreciation right The right to receive payment of all or part of the appreciation on a stock option rather than to exercise the option; a nonqualified stock option.

stock average The average price per share of diverse stocks that are considered to be representative of either a given industry or the entire market, calculated by adding the closing prices of the sample stocks and dividing by a Dow Jones divisor that accounts for such factors as dividends and splits. See also **Dow Jones average; New York Stock Exchange Index; Standard & Poor's 500.**

stockbroker See **broker.**

stock certificate A certificate providing evidence of stock ownership, showing the name of the stockholder, the name of the corporation, the number of shares the certificate represents, whether the stock is common or preferred, the par value, and the rate of preferred dividends.

stock dividend A dividend paid in additional shares of stock (up to 25 percent of shares outstanding) rather than in cash.

stock exchange A market where securities are traded, such as the New York Stock Exchange and the American Stock Exchange.

stockholder See **shareholder.**

stock market 1. A particular market where stocks and bonds are traded; stock exchange. **2.** The market for stocks throughout a nation.

stock option See option (def. 1).

stockout An instance of an item normally carried in stock not being available.

stock split See split.

stock table Also called **stock quotation.** A list of (1) all stocks with their high and low prices for the year to date; (2) special information, such as whether the stock is preferred or exdividend; (3) dividends paid per share in the last 12 months; price-earnings ratio; (4) high, low, and closing prices; and (5) the changes in price since the previous day.

stop order A market order to buy a security above the current market price (usually to prevent further loss or reduction of paper profits incurred through a short sell) or to sell below the current price (usually to protect diminishing paper profits or to prevent further loss on securities currently held).

stop payment A bank depositor's request that the bank refuse payment on a check issued by the depositor.

stop price The price at which a stop order is activated.

store brand An item offered for sale under a store's own label. See also **private label.**

straddle A combination of a put option and a call option, primarily used when the investor expects a large change in a stock's price but is unsure which direction the price will move.

straight bill of lading A simple receipt for goods accepted for shipment given by the transportation company to the shipper. See also **order bill of lading.**

straight life insurance. See ordinary life insurance.

straight-line depreciation The simplest method of depreciation, by which the value of a capital asset is reduced at a uniform rate throughout the projected useful life of the asset. See also declining-balance depreciation.

straight time 1. The time or number of hours established as standard for a specific work period in a particular industry, usually computed on the basis of a work week and fixed variously from 35 to

40 hours. **2.** The rate of pay established for the period. See also **overtime**.

strategic plan (*marketing*) A plan spelling out what a company hopes to do in the marketplace and how it proposes to do it, including marketing mix and needed resources.

strategic product-line adjustment Also called **tactical product-line adjustment**. The making of additions to and/or subtractions from the assortment of like products offered by a company, determined in part by the amount of capital available to produce the variations and in part by potential market interest.

street name The broker in whose name stocks purchased are registered, although the investor is entitled to all dividends, corporate reports, and voting rights.

stress interview A simulated interview in which the interviewer is openly hostile and deliberately irritating to the interviewee (used in police, sales, and investigative work).

strict liability Also called **absolute liability**. Liability without fault; the obligation of an insurer to pay damages without assessing blame or proving responsibility.

strike A temporary work stoppage by union members designed to force settlement of a dispute with management or the signing of a contract with the union.

strikebreaker 1. A person employed to replace a striking worker; a scab. **2.** Any person who crosses a picket line to work.

strike fund A special fund collected by a union to provide benefits to members who are on strike.

strike price The price at which an employee's stock option may be exercised, usually the market price at the time the option was granted.

strip mall A retail complex consisting of stores or restaurants in adjacent spaces in one long building, typically having a narrow parking area directly in front of the stores.

stripping The practice of splitting bonds, especially mortgage-backed securities, into two parts, one paying interest and the other paying principal, and selling the parts to different investors. See also **zero-coupon bond**.

structural analysis An analytical approach to understanding the group process that focuses on the interdepartmental and intergroup differences of the members' orientations, interpersonal relations, and goals. See also **group process.**

structural unemployment Unemployment caused by a mismatch between the skills (or location) of job seekers and the requirements (or location) of available jobs.

SUB See **supplemental unemployment benefits.**

subassembly A component of a finished product that is itself assembled from other parts and components.

Subchapter S corporation Also called **tax-option corporation.** A corporation with ten or fewer stockholders, who are permitted by a section of the Internal Revenue Code to report the corporation's profits as though they were partners rather than shareholders, and thus avoid paying taxes twice, once on corporate income and again on dividends.

sublicense A license or contract granted to a third party by a licensee for specified rights or uses of a product.

sublicensee A person, company, etc., to whom a sublicense is granted.

subordinate security See **junior security.**

subscription price (*finance*) A special price offered to shareholders for the purchase of a new issue of stock.

subsequent event (*accounting*) An event that follows the date of a balance sheet but precedes the issuance of a financial statement that is affected by the event.

subsidiary A corporation all or a large part of whose stock is owned by another corporation and whose management is usually chosen by the parent company's chief executive with the approval of the parent's board of directors.

subsidiary account An account that supports or contributes to the balance of a control account (e.g., the accounts receivable account contains the total of the balances of all subsidiary accounts receivable).

subsidiary rights Rights to publish or produce

in different formats works based on the original work under contract, as a paperback edition of a hardcover book or a television series based on a novel.

subsidy 1. A direct financial aid furnished by a government to a private industrial undertaking, a charitable organization, or the like. **2.** A sum paid, often in accordance with a treaty, by one government to another to secure some service in return.

substantial performance The carrying out of all essential terms of a contract, which entitles the contractor to payment. See also **specific performance.**

substitution goods Two products or services so related that an increase in the demand for one is followed by an increase in the price of the other. See also **cross-elasticity of demand.**

successful-efforts method (*gas and oil industries*) An accounting method that capitalizes only the costs of drilling wells that actually produce oil or gas, while costs of unsuccessful efforts are recorded as expenses.

successive scanning An orientation to problem solving characterized by a tendency to start with an overall view of a situation and then to narrow one's focus to those elements that appear to confirm one's theories. See also **scanning.**

suggestion selling A sales strategy by which a person who has bought an item is encouraged to buy complementary items.

suitor An individual or company that expresses interest in acquiring another company.

sum-of-the-years'-digits method A method of depreciating an asset whereby depreciation is accelerated in the early years of the asset's useful life by means of a fraction in which all the years of useful life (n) are added together ($1 + 2 + 3...$ etc.); for an asset with a useful life of six years ($n = 6$), the denominator is 21 and depreciation is $6/21$ the first year, $5/21$ the second year, $4/21$ the third year, and so on.

sunk cost An expenditure or outlay made in the past that cannot be affected by present or future decisions except for income-tax effects (e.g., a decision on whether or not to sell a piece of equipment may depend on the imputed cost of continuing to own it, not on the sunk cost of acquiring it).

sunrise industry A new industry that is gaining in importance, especially in the field of advanced technology (e.g., microcircuitry).

sunset industry An older industry regarded as being in decline because of obsolete technology, decreased demand for products, etc.

superstore A very large store, especially one stocking a wide variety of merchandise.

supervisory management See **first-line management**.

supplemental unemployment benefits (*abbr* SUB) Benefits beyond the legislated unemployment insurance payments made to workers who are laid off, paid by the employer.

supply 1. The quantity of a product, service, or resource available on the open market. See also **law of supply and demand. 2.** The specific quantity of a product that a manufacturer or retailer can supply at a given time.

supply-side economics An approach to the management of the national economy that advocates a reduction in taxes on corporate and personal income, which is believed will stimulate investment in private industry.

support consumables Expense items, such as stationery, typewriter ribbons, and cleaning service, necessary to the day-to-day operation of a business.

suprasystem A system composed of interdependent subsystems (e.g., the suprasystem of which a motor company is a part consists of other motor companies, subsidiaries, and dependent industries).

surety bond A three-way contract by which the first party (the obligor) agrees to be responsible to the second party (the obligee) for the obligations of the third party, the obligee being protected by an insurer (surety) who promises to cover any default on the part of the obligor.

surplus revenue See **appropriated retained earnings**.

surrender value See **cash surrender value**.

survey A questionnaire administered to respondents either in person, by mail, or by telephone to determine their attitudes and opinions.

survey feedback Information acquired from completed questionnaires or from systematic interviews. See also **attitude survey.**

suspense account An account in which accounting items of undetermined destination are temporarily recorded pending a decision as to where they should be posted.

suspense reserve See **appropriated retained earnings.**

suspension A disciplinary action taken against an employee who has violated an established company rule, requiring the employee to absent himor herself from the job without pay for a period of time depending on the severity of the infraction.

sustainable income The portion of distributable income earned in the current period that can be expected to be earned in the next period if operations continue at the same level.

sweat equity Unreimbursed labor that results in the increased value of a property in which one shares or that is invested to establish or expand an enterprise.

sweep account An interest-earning checking account from which money over a certain minimum balance is transferred to another account earning a higher rate of interest.

sweetheart agreement Also called **sweetheart contract.** An agreement between an employer and a union on terms especially favorable to the employer, often arranged through bribery or management's promise not to eliminate jobs and usually put into effect without a vote by the workers.

swing loan See **bridge loan.**

swing shift A work shift, usually from 4 p.m. until midnight.

symbiotic marketing The marketing of a product with the assistance of a company that offers a generally unrelated product for mutual benefit (e.g., the offer of a free airline ticket to anyone who buys a car during a limited time period).

syndicate Also called **venture management.** A temporary association of two or more individuals or companies formed to take part in a joint venture or business undertaking for profit, the members generally sharing in gains or losses in proportion to their individual investments.

syndicated program 1. An independently produced television program sold to individual stations for broadcast. **2.** A successful network program purchased for rerun by local stations.

syndicator A company that provides other companies with fliers and brochures offering products for sale that can be sent to customers with monthly bills.

synectics A brainstorming or creative problem-solving technique that presents problems to group participants in such a generalized way that they are stimulated to achieve highly original solutions through the use of analogies, figurative comparisons, and speculative thought.

synergy The action or interaction of two separate enterprises that when combined produce superior results, as in the case of a corporate merger.

synthetic process A production process by which raw materials or parts are combined to form a finished product that differs from any of its components.

system A group of constituent parts functioning in unison for a common purpose.

system 1 management See **exploitive leadership.**

system 2 management See **benevolent leadership.**

system 3 management See **consultative leadership.**

system 4 management See **democratic leadership.**

systematic risk Risk that cannot be eliminated through diversification. See also **unsystematic risk.**

systems analyst A data-processing specialist whose job (systems analysis) is to identify business problems and to formulate solutions that lead to better ways of organizing, planning, and controlling activities in a company.

systems contract A buyer's agreement to make a blanket order of a product or products from a catalog supplier at a fixed markup in order to minimize administrative costs, all orders being made directly from the buyer's departments to the supplier.

system software See **software**.

systems selling The retail merchandising of a group of items that have a functional relationship in a single package rather than as individual items (e.g., the selling of microcomputers, disk drives, monitors, printers, and some software programs as a complete package).

T

T-account Also called **skeleton account**. (*bookkeeping*) Any account in the standard form of a T, with the title above a horizontal line at the top, the debits listed on the left side of a vertical line below, and the credits on the right side of that line.

tactical planning Planning of the activities of subgroups within an organization to meet short-range objectives.

tactical product-line adjustment See **strategic product-line adjustment**.

Taft-Hartley Act An act of Congress passed in 1947 to amend the National Labor Relations Act by (1) authorizing the president of the United States to obtain an 80-day injunction against a strike that endangers the national health or safety, so that mediators may attempt to bring labor and management to agreement; (2) prohibiting the closed shop; and (3) permitting the union shop in states that have not passed right-to-work laws.

take-home pay The amount of salary remaining after deductions, as of taxes, have been made.

takeover An acquisition or gaining control of a corporation through the purchase or exchange of stock.

taking An action by the federal government, as a regulatory ruling, that imposes a restriction on the use of private property for which the owner must be compensated; an exercise of the power of eminent domain.

tangible asset Any physical asset (e.g., building, piece of equipment, share of stock). See also **intangible asset**.

tangible value The worth of a physical asset to the public.

tare weight The weight of the packing material and container in which an item is shipped.

target marketing Also called **consumer-oriented marketing**. The methods used to (1) identify those consumers most likely to want a product or to benefit from it, (2) create an image for a product that will appeal to such consumers, and (3) inform them of it via the most appropriate media.

tariff Duties or customs imposed by a government on imported or exported products to raise revenue, protect domestic industries, or exert pressure on foreign governments that impose high duties on domestic products.

task cycle The amount of time necessary to complete an assignment, activity, etc., from beginning to end.

task force A committee formed to investigate problem areas and generate workable solutions.

tax-bracket creep See **bracket creep.**

tax credit A reduction of taxes payable, allowed to certain classes of taxpayers for reasons of public policy. See also **tax deduction.**

tax deduction An expenditure or a certain amount that a taxpayer can deduct from taxable income. See also **tax credit.**

tax-deferred annuity (*abbr* TDA) Also called **tax-sheltered annuity.** An annuity to which teachers, college professors, and other employees of nonprofit organizations may contribute to supplement their pension programs, taxes on contributions and income payments being deferred until retirement.

tax-free bond A bond, usually a municipal or pollution-control bond, on which interest is legally exempt from all federal taxes.

tax lien A formal claim by a governmental body against property for taxes due.

tax-option corporation See **Subchapter S corporation.**

tax return A statement, on an officially prescribed form, of income, deductions, exemptions, etc., and taxes due.

tax shelter An investment in certain businesses, activities, or items that legally entitles the investor to avoid, reduce, or defer income taxes.

tax-sheltered annuity See **tax-deferred annuity.**

tax shield An expense that reduces taxable income, either without consuming working capital (e.g., depreciation) or otherwise (e.g., research and development).

T-bill See **Treasury bill.**

TDA See **tax-deferred annuity.**

team building Group learning activities moderated by a trainer for the purpose of identifying and changing patterns of behavior that interfere with group productivity or with relations with superiors.

teaser 1. An advertisement that attempts to stimulate the reader's or viewer's curiosity by withholding certain facts or information of interest. **2.** A short clip shown before the start of a television program for the purpose of gaining audience attention.

technical core The organizational structure that encompasses lower-level subordinates, most often people whose expertise lies in technical rather than managerial or administrative areas.

technical partnership A situation in which one company purchases stock in another company so that the two of them can collaborate as partners on new products and technologies.

technician An individual (e.g., electrician, plumber, computer programmer) with specific knowledge about and skill in the use of a technology.

technobandit A person who steals technological secrets, as from a place of employment, and sells them to agents from competing firms, a foreign government, etc.

technological unemployment Unemployment that results from the introduction of new equipment, methods, or procedures.

technology The aggregate of knowledge and methods used to transform raw materials into a useful product or other improved output.

telecommunications The science and technology dealing with communications at a distance.

telecommuting Working at home using a computer terminal electronically linked to one's place of employment.

teleconference A business meeting, educational session, etc., conducted among participants in different locations via telecommunications equipment.

telemarketing The use of telephoning to make a

sales presentation and attempt to sell a product or service.

teleprinter Also called **teletypewriter**. A machine that operates like a typewriter and is capable of transmitting messages over telephone lines.

telescoping Also called **overlapping**. Splitting a production lot into smaller lots so that one operation can be performed on some of the units while another is being performed on the remainder, thereby reducing the total elapsed time to process the original lot.

Teletypewriter Exchange See **TWX**.

television homes Homes that have television sets. See also **Nielsen rating; share** (def. 2).

telex An electronic system by which written words are transmitted over Western Union lines from one teleprinter to another at a rate of 66 words per minute, used for short messages.

temporary investment An investment in a marketable security expected to be sold within a year and treated as a current asset.

temporary proprietorship account See **nominal account**.

temporary system An organization of formal groups created to investigate and perform specific tasks. See also **ad hoc committee; task force**.

tenancy in common A form of co-ownership of real estate in which the interest of each owner passes at death to his or her heirs rather than to a surviving co-owner. See also **joint tenancy**.

tenant **1.** A person who holds property by any kind of right, temporary or permanent. **2.** A person who has the temporary right to occupy property belonging to another; a lessee.

tender offer An offer by one corporation to the stockholders of another to buy their shares for a specified price above the market value so that the offering corporation can gain quick control of the company.

term bond A bond that has the same maturity date as all other bonds of the same issue. See also **serial bond**.

terminal A hardware device, usually including a keyboard and a video display unit, for entering information into a computer or receiving information from it. A terminal may adjoin a computer, or be located at some distance from it.

term insurance Insurance that gives protection for a stated number of years and has no cash surrender or loan value.

terms of sale Conditions for the payment of an amount due for a sale (e.g., "5/10, n/30" indicates a 5 percent reduction in amount payable if paid within 10 days; net amount is due within 30 days).

test campaign A series of activities focused on an advertisement or promotion that is subject to alterations that may increase its effectiveness.

testimonial Also called **endorsement.** A statement, usually made by a well-known personality, claiming satisfaction with a product, publicized by an advertiser to persuade other consumers to purchase the product: subject to guidelines issued by the Federal Trade Commission for honest use of such endorsements.

test marketing The offering for sale of a new product in one or more preselected markets, for the purpose of assessing customer response before the product is mass-marketed.

test of compliance An audit procedure to determine whether a corporation is adhering to its internal control policies.

test of transactions A detailed audit procedure that determines the accuracy and fairness of account balances by recalculating arithmetic, verifying consistency with supporting documents, and tracing the movements of balances from original transactions to final financial statements.

TF (*abbr for* t*ill* f*orbid*) The indication that an advertisement is to be run until it is canceled.

t-group A training group presided over by a trainer, with the objective of behavior modification within a social context. See also **encounter group; sensitivity training.**

theory X An authoritarian approach to management by which the average worker is regarded as disliking work, having little ambition, and requiring threats and coercion to perform satisfactorily.

theory Y An approach to management by which the average worker is regarded as seeking responsibility and being motivated by rewards.

theory Z An approach to management by which employees at all levels are involved in the decision-making process, employment is guaranteed for life, and jobs are varied to avert boredom.

therblig (*backward spelling—more or less—of* [*Frank B.*] *Gilbreth, founder of time-and-motion study*) A basic indivisible physical movement involved in a manual operation or task.

third-party beneficiary A person who benefits by a legal agreement between two other persons.

thrift institution A savings bank or savings and loan association, which caters primarily to the individual depositor and prospective homebuyer in search of financing.

tickler file A chronological collection of vouchers, memorandums, or bills used to remind someone to make timely payments or perform certain tasks on schedule.

tick mark A symbolic notation (e.g., asterisk, checkmark, number) used by an auditor to indicate a footnote that provides information regarding the amount thus indicated.

tie-in **1.** Designating a sale or advertisement in which the buyer, in order to get the item desired, must also purchase one or more other items. **2.** Relating to two or more products advertised or sold together. **3.** A marketing strategy or campaign in which related products are promoted or sold together. **4.** An item in a tie-in sale or advertisement.

tie-line service A circuit that connects two or more telephone systems.

time-adjusted rate of return See **internal rate of return**.

time-and-motion study The systematic investigation and analysis of the motions and the time required to perform a specific task with a view to devising more efficient methods of production and setting time standards. See also **therblig**.

time deposit Money deposited in an interest-bearing account in a bank that cannot be withdrawn without penalty before the expiration of a specified time period, usually a minimum of three months.

time discount A discount extended to an advertiser who purchases television time in quantity.

time draft A trade draft payable by a specified date.

time management Regulation of tasks and activities according to a specific schedule.

time-series analysis Also called **trend analysis.** Analysis of statistical data collected or recorded at successive intervals over a period of time long enough to permit patterns to be identified that can be used as a basis for business forecasting.

time sharing The sharing of use of a central processing unit by two or more companies or subdivisions of a company, each user being allotted a proportionate amount of operating time.

time study See **time-and-motion study.**

time to maturity The amount of time remaining before a note or other obligation becomes due.

time utility The enhanced value of any product that is available in the marketplace when requested, especially a new product whose availability coincides with the initial barrage of publicity.

tin parachute A guaranteed package of bonuses and benefits for workers in the event of job loss due to a merger or takeover. See also **golden parachute.**

title 1. Legal, registered ownership. **2.** A document certifying such ownership.

title search See **search** (def. 2).

T-note See **Treasury note.**

TOFC (*abbr* for trailer-on-flat car) See **piggyback.**

tombstone advertising Advertising placed by an underwriter, broker, investment banker, etc., usually a boxed ad, very simple in format, with no graphics.

top management Also called **upper management.** The level of professional management at which major policy decisions and long-range plans are made, including such positions as chief executive officer and president.

total advertising The total number of standard lines (or pages) available for advertising in a newspaper (or magazine).

total asset turnover ratio Sales divided by total assets. See also **activity ratio.**

total cost approach An approach to decision making that relies on a formal comparative cost analysis of alternate channels of distribution before commitment to one of them.

total quality management (*abbr* TQM) A philosophy that emphasizes the broad involvement of the entire organization in achieving standards of quality.

total return The percentage gain or loss on an investment over a specific period, including income and price appreciation or depreciation.

total system concept The study of the relationships of all interacting parts of a complex whole and of that of the system and the environment in which it operates.

Toxic Substances Control Act An act of Congress passed in 1976 to empower the Environmental Protection Agency to regulate the production, use, marketing, and disposal of toxic chemicals.

TQM See **total quality management.**

tracer A procedure used to locate a shipment, parcel, or letter that fails to arrive at its proper destination within the normal time period.

trade acceptance A trade draft signed by a customer.

trade association A nonprofit organization of professionals in related businesses and industries, established to serve the common interests of its members.

trade credit Short-term credit issued to a business for the purchase of goods; the most substantial form of short-term liability for most businesses.

trade deficit An imbalance of trade, occurring when a nation buys more goods from abroad than it sells; an excess of imports over exports. Such a deficit is usually expressed in dollars. See also **balance of payments.**

trade discount Also called **trade allowance.** A percentage taken off the selling price for certain dealers who make a large volume of purchases. Discounts often vary, as between wholesalers and retailers or between small and large retailers (functional discount).

trade draft A document drawn up by a supplier to be signed by a customer, who is then obligated to pay the supplier a stated amount in exchange for goods or services within a specified period. See also **sight drafts; time drafts; trade acceptance.**

trade dress In legal parlance, the visual concept and presentation of a product, especially the design of the product itself and its packaging.

trade-in An asset given as full or partial payment for another asset taken in exchange.

trade journal A periodical published for members of a specific profession or trade.

trademark A distinguishing symbol, device, and/or term used in connection with a product or service and whose exclusive use is legally reserved to the owner.

trade name 1. The name used by a manufacturer, merchant, service company, farming business, etc., to identify itself individually as a business. **2.** A word or phrase used in a trade to designate a business, service, or particular class of goods, but that is not technically a trademark, either because it cannot be exclusively appropriated as a trademark or because it is not affixed to goods sold in the market. **3.** The name by which an article or substance is known to the trade.

trade-off A gain in benefits in one area at the expense of a loss in benefits in another area.

trade secret A secret process, technique, method, etc., used to advantage in a trade, business, profession, etc.

trade show An exhibition and demonstration of new products (e.g., automobiles, boats) held to promote sales.

trade union A voluntary affiliation of workers, usually within the same or similar occupational specialties, to further their mutual interests in regard to wages, job security, and working conditions.

trading on equity Investing with borrowed money, on the expectation of a return greater than the cost of the borrowed funds.

traffic manager 1. A person who supervises the transportation of goods for an employer. **2.** An employee responsible for routing items of business within a company for appropriate action by various departments.

trailer-on-flatcar (*abbr* TOFC) See **piggyback.**

trainer An individual who conducts training programs within an organization and selects outside training resources for specialized studies.

training director An individual who establishes and implements training programs for the employees of an organization, generally under the supervision of the personnel officer.

training film A film or videotape created for use in an employee training program.

training manual A printed guide or outline for use in a training program or course of instruction.

trait approach An approach to leadership based on the assumption that effective leaders share a set of personality traits and can be distinguished from other people early on.

transactional analysis (*abbr* TA) A framework for analyzing interpersonal communications that assumes there are three ego states (Parent, Adult, Child) that alternate in each individual.

transaction cost The commission plus tax that an investor must pay for the services of a broker in buying or selling securities.

transaction document An invoice, check, requisition, or purchase order testifying to a transaction.

transaction worksheet A record in which every change in assets (cash, accounts receivable, inventory, real estate, etc.) and equities (accounts payable, salaries payable, capital stock, retained earnings, etc.) is recorded and explained.

transfer 1. The placement of an employee in another position of equal status but often with different tasks to perform. 2. The delivery of a security certificate from the selling broker to the purchasing broker. 3. To record a change in the ownership of a security. 4. Also called **copy; dub.** To duplicate a videotaped program.

transfer agent An agent responsible for recording changes of ownership of securities, canceling obsolete certificates of ownership, and issuing new ones.

transfer line Automated materials-handling equipment with which individual parts are moved from one machine to another where they are properly positioned for processing without the need for manual intervention.

transfer price (*bookkeeping*) A value assigned to an asset transferred from one unit (division, department, subsidiary, etc.) of an organization to another, for purposes of accounting and internal control.

transloading A loading site where incoming goods are repackaged and shipped to other destinations, customers, etc.

transportation in Also called **freight in**. The transportation expense incurred to effect delivery of inventory items purchased.

transportation out Also called **freight out**. The charges paid to transport inventory items sold.

transshipping Also called **transshipment**. **1.** The transfer of goods from one ship, freight car, etc., to another so as to reach a final destination. **2.** The practice of ordering abnormally large amounts of a high-demand product, so as to obtain the most advantageous discount, then reselling the excess to another dealer or dealers who sell it at bargain prices.

treasurer An officer of an organization who is responsible for obtaining and managing corporate capital, cash, and investments.

Treasury bill (*abbr* T-bill) A short-term investment issued weekly by the U.S. Treasury and available from any of the 12 Federal Reserve banks, commercial banks, and brokers, with a face value of $10,000 or more payable upon maturity, usually in 13, 26, or 52 weeks.

Treasury note (*abbr* T-note) A note issued by the U.S. Treasury with a fixed maturity of one to seven years and a fixed interest rate payable semiannually, available from a commercial bank or broker in an amount of $1000 or more.

treasury stock Also called **reacquired stock**. Common stock that the issuing corporation has purchased from its holders as an alternative to paying dividends, such that the earnings per share of outstanding shares are increased, with an expected concomitant rise in the market price of the stock.

trend analysis See **time-series analysis**.

trespass Unlawful or unauthorized entry onto the property of another.

trial-and-error pricing The setting of different

prices for the same item in separate markets in an effort to determine which price will produce the desired sales volume and profit.

trial balance (*bookkeeping*) A listing of account balances in debit and credit columns so that they may be totaled separately and checked for arithmetical accuracy.

trickle-down theory A theory of federal economic policies that providing generous benefits to business and industry will eventually benefit the lower and middle classes.

triple-tax-free (*bonds*) Not subject to federal, state, or local income taxes.

triple witching hour (*stock exchange*) The hour of closing on a particular day when stock index futures, stock index options, and individual stock options simultaneously expire: regarded as a time of extreme volatility in trading.

troubled debt restructuring The granting by a creditor of changes in the terms of a previously contracted debt repayment such that the borrower can repay the debt under easier terms, usually undertaken in the hope that the borrower will not go bankrupt and default on all payments.

troubleshooting The process of locating, diagnosing, and eliminating the source of a problem within a particular activity or operation.

trough The lowest point in an economic cycle.

truck jobber A wholesaler who uses trucks for storage and selling as well as for delivery of goods (generally nationally advertised specialty goods) sold for cash.

trunk show A vendor's display of merchandise offerings to one or more retail buyers.

trust **1.** An illegal combination of companies whose stock is controlled by a central board of trustees, so that prices may be controlled and competition eliminated. **2.** A fiduciary relationship in which one person (the trustee) holds title to property (the trust estate) for the benefit of another (the beneficiary).

trust company An institution whose financial staff manages the financial affairs of trust beneficiaries as fiduciaries or trustees. See also **trust** (def. 2).

trust deed See deed of trust.

trustee 1. A person who holds property in trust for another person (the beneficiary). See also **trust** (def. 2). **2.** An individual or company (often the commercial branch of a bank) appointed to act on behalf of several bondholders in such matters as certifying the validity of the bond issue, observing the legal and financial behavior of the issuing corporation, and taking steps to handle corporate default on payment of interest or principal.

trust estate Property held by one person for the benefit of another. See also **trust** (def. 2).

trust receipt A document signed by a borrower giving a lender a security interest in an inventory (usually of valuable, nonperishable, and easily marketable goods) stored in a warehouse as collateral for a loan.

Truth-in-Lending Act An act of Congress passed in 1968 requiring that before a loan agreement is signed, the borrower must be fully informed of the interest charges, both simple and compound, attached to the loan. See also **Regulation Z.**

turnaround 1. A reversal, especially in business sales, from loss to profit. **2.** The time between the making of an investment and receiving a return.

turnkey operation An operation that is so well supported and self-contained that one need only "turn a key" in the front door to get the operation running, often used to describe equipment whose purchase cost includes everything necessary to make the equipment operational, such as delivery, installation, training, and maintenance.

turnover 1. The aggregate of worker replacements in an organization in a given time period. **2.** The rate at which items are sold in a given period, especially with reference to depletion of stock and replacement of inventory.

two-bin system An inventory control method that physically segregates normal working stock from the reorder-level stock so that the need to replenish is signaled visually whenever normal working stock has been exhausted.

two-tier wage plan A policy or practice of paying new employees on a lower pay scale than that of longtime employees, though all have identical responsibilities. See also **comparable worth.**

TWX (*abbr for* Teletypewriter Exchange) An electronic system by which written words are transmitted over Western Union lines from one teleprinter to another at a rate of 100 words per minute, used when messages uniformly exceed 100 words.

tying contract An agreement by which a purchaser is required to buy goods he or she does not want in order to get goods he or she does want.

U

UGMA See **Uniform Gifts to Minors Act**.

ultimate consumer A person who buys goods or services for his or her own use or for use in the buyer's household.

ultra vires (*Latin*) Beyond the scope of the legal power or authority of a corporation or official (indicating that a contract so designated is not binding).

umbrella policy A type of insurance that provides businesses with more extensive coverage than that provided in a general liability policy.

unconscionable agreement An agreement or contract that a court would refuse to enforce, either in part or in its entirety, because of the inadequacy of the benefits received by one party and unfair advantage to the other.

underdeveloped See **developing**.

underemployment The aggregate of people who are employed at jobs that do not require the full range of their skills or education, or who are working part-time but would take full-time work if it were available.

underlying Referring to a claim, mortgage, etc., that takes precedence over another.

underwater option A situation in which the employee's stock-option price is higher than the market value of the stock.

underwriter 1. An investment firm that acquires new issues of stocks and bonds from a corporation and sells them to individual investors, thus assuming all the risks of ownership unless the arrangement is on a best-effort basis, in which case the underwriter acts merely as a broker. **2.** (*insurance*) An employee who evaluates risks and decides how large a policy is to be granted and at what premiums.

underwriting syndicate A loosely associated group of investment institutions that share the cost and risk of underwriting a new issue of a security.

undirected viewing The viewing of a situation or of data with an open mind rather than with the intention of proving a point.

unearned income Income received from property, as interest, dividends, or the like. Cf. **earned income**.

unemployment 1. The aggregate of people over the age of 16 who are not working. **2.** The aggregate of people over the age of 16 who have no jobs, are available for work, and are actively seeking work. **3.** The number of people in the labor force who do not have jobs divided by the number of those who do. See also **cyclical unemployment; frictional unemployment; seasonal unemployment; structural unemployment.**

unemployment insurance Also called **unemployment compensation.** Insurance that provides monetary benefits to workers who become unemployed for reasons unrelated to job performance, administered by the individual states and financed by payroll taxes levied on employers.

unfair labor practice An illegal activity engaged in by an employer (as set forth in the National Labor Relations Act) or by a union (as set forth in the Taft-Hartley Act).

unfavorable balance of trade An excess in value of imports over exports.

Uniform Commercial Code (*abbr* UCC) The body of laws concerning business transactions adopted by the several states, governing sales, bills of lading, bulk transfers, commercial paper, bank deposits and collections, and letters of credit.

uniform delivery price A price to all buyers for delivered goods, regardless of transportation costs. See also **postage-stamp pricing; zone pricing.**

Uniform Gifts to Minors Act (*abbr* UGMA) A law that provides a means to transfer money or securities to a minor without establishing a formal trust. The assets are managed by a a custodian and turned over to the minor when he or she reaches the age of 18 or 21.

Uniform Transfers to Minors Act (*abbr* UTMA) A law that is similar to the Uniform Gifts to Minors Act, but covers gifts of real estate, works of art, etc., as well as money and securities.

unilateral contract An agreement by which one party (the offeree) performs a certain action in exchange for a promise by another person (the offerer), the offeree being under no obligation to perform the action, and the offerer, once the act is performed, being obliged to keep the promise made. See also **bilateral contract.**

uninsurable risk A risk not usually covered by insurance, such as a decline in economic conditions, a climatic change (e.g., drought), or business losses attributable to poor management or to changes in the law.

union See **trade union.**

union recognition An employer's acceptance, either voluntary or as a result of a representational election, of a particular union as the bargaining agent or representative for the company's employees.

union shop A place of business where by agreement with a union the employer may hire nonunion personnel as well as union members but may not retain such nonunion personnel beyond a specified period, usually 30 days, unless they join the union. See also **closed shop; Taft-Hartley Act.**

union steward See **shop steward.**

unit cost The cost of a single unit of production, calculated by dividing total cost (either actually incurred, predicted, or assigned) by total number of units produced.

United States Employment Service (*abbr* USES) A federal-state system that refers job-seekers to available jobs and provides employment counseling.

United States Trademark Association (*abbr* USTA) A national organization, founded in 1878, that provides information on the use and registration of trademarks in the United States and abroad.

unit pricing 1. The posting of the price per unit (e.g., per ounce or per pound) of goods offered for sale in packages of varying quantities. **2.** The price per item, when several items are offered at one price.

units-of-production method A method of calculating annual depreciation by which an asset's depreciable cost (original cost less salvage value) is divided by its useful life, expressed in hours of use or units of production, the resulting hourly or per-unit depreciation cost then being multiplied by the hours or units actually used or produced in a given year.

unity-of-command principle A management principle that specifies that each employee should be accountable to only one superior.

universal life insurance A type of insurance in which the insured deposits money in a money-market fund, earnings from which pay the premiums on term life insurance, while any remainder continues to earn interest.

Universal Product Code (*abbr* UPC) A type of bar code that indicates number of articles, weight, price, inventory number, etc., and is widely used at supermarket checkout counters.

unlimited liability 1. The legal responsibility of each partner in an unincorporated business for all of the company's liabilities, even if such liabilities exceed the partners' individual or combined investments. **2.** The legal responsibility of a sole proprietor of a business for any money owed by the business or for damages done in the process of conducting the business by the proprietor or any employee. See also **limited liability.**

unsecured loan A loan for which no collateral or other security is demanded from the borrower, usually because of an excellent credit rating.

unsystematic risk A risk that is subject to the influence of predictably random events and that can be minimized by diversification. See also **systematic risk.**

UPC See **Universal Product Code.**

upper management See **top management.**

upscale Also called **upmarket.** Of high or luxurious quality; catering to high-income consumers.

uptick (*stock exchange*) A closing price slightly above that of the previous trading period.

uptime The time during which employees are working or machines are operating or can be operating.

useful life The estimated length of time an asset will be used by its owner, in contrast to its physical life, or the length of time the asset will be of use to anyone at all.

use tax A tax levied by a state on goods purchased outside the state.

USTA See **United States Trademark Association.**

utilitarianism The concept that decision making

must be based on what will benefit the greatest number of people.

utilitarian reward/punishment system A method of increasing employee productivity by the promise of rewards (e.g., raises, bonuses, promotions) for superior performance and the threat of penalties (e.g., docking wages, demotion) for unsatisfactory performance.

utility The capacity of a product or service to satisfy some human want.

UTMA See **Uniform Transfers to Minors Act.**

V

validation The function of a computer program that compares one computer file against another to check the accuracy and program content (raw data, codes, format) of the original file.

validity The degree to which a test, experiment, or survey actually measures what it is intended to measure. See also **reliability**.

value 1. a. The monetary worth or utility of an item, service, claim, product, asset, or right. **b.** To assign such a worth. **2.** The estimated fair-market worth of real estate to a buyer.

value added The additional value that raw materials or components take on as they proceed through the processes of refining, manufacturing, assembly, packaging, etc.

value-added tax (*abbr* VAT) A tax levied on the value of a product at each stage of its manufacturing and distribution processes, each such tax being added to the price of the product as it passes to each successive processor and ultimately to the consumer.

value fund A mutual fund that invests in stocks that are considered to be undervalued by the market and whose share price is expected to rise.

variable annuity A contract that provides lifetime retirement payments to an individual, the amounts of the payments varying with the earnings of the funds that provide the income.

variable base salary A salesperson's salary that rises in regular increments with increases in performance.

variable budget See **flexible budget**.

variable cost An expense that increases or decreases according to the volume of production.

variable life A type of life insurance whose premiums are invested in stocks and whose death benefits depend on the performance of such stocks during the insured's lifetime, though a minimum death benefit is guaranteed.

variable overhead Overhead costs that vary with volume of production.

variable-rate mortgage Also called **flexible-**

rate mortgage. A type of mortgage whose interest rate may fluctuate according to current rates, but may rise no more than 2.5 percent during the life of the mortgage. Changes in interest are usually put into effect annually and, by law, no oftener than every six months. See also **adjustable-rate mortgage, renegotiable-rate mortgage.**

variance (*accounting*) The difference between budgeted and actual amounts, or between standard and actual costs, hours, units, etc.

variety store A retail store that carries a wide selection of household and personal items, most of which are relatively inexpensive.

VAT See **value-added tax.**

VDT See **video display terminal.**

venture capital Also called **risk capital.** Money invested by professional investors (venture capitalists) in a new company with perceived potential for great growth but without a record of proven performance.

venture management See **syndicate.**

venture team A group of specialists assembled from various divisions of a company and guided by a team manager to brainstorm ideas for a highly innovative product designed for a specialized market.

vertical merger Also called **vertical acquisition.** Absorption by a company of one of its suppliers (backward vertical merger) or one of its customers (forward vertical merger). See also **horizontal merger.**

vertical split A division of the formal structure of responsibility of an organization between top management, middle management, and technical staff.

vested benefit A financial benefit that is guaranteed and cannot be canceled.

vestibule training Training in skills in a simulated work environment.

vest-pocket supermarket See **bantam store.**

viatical Of or pertaining to a form of insurance business that pays off on the insurance policies of the terminally ill.

video display terminal (*abbr* VDT) A computer device with a keyboard for input and a screen for the display of images called up from the computer's memory.

videotex A system by which potential customers are linked via computers and telephones with retail merchants, who can display their wares on the home screen and accept on-the-spot orders.

vision insurance See **dental and vision insurance.**

voice mail An electronic communications system that routes voice messages interactively to appropriate recipients, stores the messages in digitized form, and notifies the recipients that the messages are available for playback through the system.

voice-over 1. The voice of an offscreen narrator or announcer, as in a television commercial. **2.** a televised sequence, as in a commercial, narrated by voice-over.

volatile stock Also called **yo-yo stock.** A highly speculative stock whose value tends to fluctuate drastically.

voluntary arbitration Arbitration of unresolved differences by an unbiased third party, agreed to by labor and management.

voluntary bankruptcy Bankruptcy effected by a legal procedure initiated by a debtor. See also **involuntary bankruptcy.**

voluntary chain A confederation of independent retailers who join together in order to obtain such benefits as group purchasing power unavailable to individual businesses.

voluntary deferral plan A plan by which executives (usually at a specified position or earnings level) postpone accepttance of a portion of their income or annual bonus until retirement, after which the deferred amounts plus earnings (at a fixed interest rate) are paid out over 10 to 15 years.

voting rights The rights of shareholders to elect the corporation's board of directors and to vote on certain resolutions at the annual shareholders' meeting.

voting security A stock that entitles the holder to vote on board members, new issues of stock, and other major corporate decisions at the annual shareholders' meeting.

voucher A document that controls and/or separates expenditures by authorizing and/or recording them.

vulture fund See **opportunity fund.**

W

wage Payment for work performed based on the number of hours or days worked or the number of items produced.

Wage and Hour Law See **Fair Labor Standards Act**.

wage and price control Also called **wage and price stabilization**. A legislative measure that freezes wages and prices at existing levels in an effort to combat inflation.

wage and salary administration The function of human resource management to establish wages and salaries that conform to the overall policies of the organization.

wage incentive plan A method of remuneration by which employees' wages, individually or as a group, are at least partly based on the number of units produced.

wage-push inflation An inflationary trend caused by wage increases that trigger a rise in production costs and prices.

Wagner Act See **National Labor Relations Act**.

waiting-line theory See **queuing theory**.

waiver The relinquishing of a right or presumed right to a piece of property or other asset that is owned or controlled by another.

walkout See **strike**.

Wall Street 1. A street in New York City, in downtown Manhattan: the major financial center of the United States. 2. The money market or the financiers of the United States.

WAN See **wide-area network**.

want ad See **classified ad**.

want-slip system A system by which retail stores record out-of-stock or unstocked items requested by customers.

warehouse 1. A facility where goods are stored until they are distributed to retailers or consumers. See also **bonded warehouse; public warehouse**. 2. To keep apartments in a building vacant in order to receive additional tax benefits for depreciation on unrented units or, when a building is going co-op, to sell such apartments to nonresidents at inflated prices.

warehouse receipt A written record of items stored in a particular warehouse, often used to prove ownership of goods that the owner wishes to use as collateral for a loan.

warrant A certificate entitling its holder to buy a specified security at a specified price within a specified period.

warrantor A person or firm that gives a warranty.

warranty See **express warranty; full warranty; limited warranty.**

warranty deed A legal instrument transferring title to real property and certifying that the property is free of all liens and encumbrances and that the warrantor will defend the buyer against all claims in regard to it.

watered stock Capital stock that is intentionally assigned a par value greater than the market value of the assets of the issuing company.

waybill A document prepared by a carrier of cargo that describes the shipment, states the charges, names the consignee and consignor, and specifies the origin, route, and destination. See also **bill of lading.**

Web site A connected group of pages on the World Wide Web regarded as a single entity, usually maintained by one person or organization and devoted to one topic or several related topics.

wedding A slang term for a business merger.

weighted average 1. Also called **weighted average cost.** The average cost of a unit of inventory, calculated by dividing the total cost of all items (even if they were bought at various costs) by the total number of units. See also **FIFO; LIFO. 2.** The average value for a group of items, where one or more of the individual items are assigned an extra degree of importance.

Wheeler-Lea Act An act of Congress passed in 1938 to amend the Federal Trade Commission Act by extending the power of the Federal Trade Commission to move against firms that engage in practices harmful to the public (e.g., deceptive advertising of foods, drugs, and cosmetics) as well as those that injure competitors.

wheel of retailing A business cycle in which a store featuring low-priced merchandise gradually upgrades or is forced by economic conditions to raise its prices until it is no longer competitive with other stores in its original price range.

when-issued Relating to a transaction involving securities expected to be issued and for which payment is not required until the securities are actually registered and issued.

where-used The identification of those products or customer orders for which a specific batch of parts will ultimately be used.

whiplash effect The effect of unusual and unexpected changes in the demand for a product, resulting in either excessive or inadequate inventory at various points in the channel of distribution.

whisper stock The stock of a company rumored to be the target of a takeover attempt.

white-collar Belonging or relating to the ranks of office and professional workers whose jobs generally do not involve manual labor or the wearing of a uniform or work clothes.

white-collar crime Any of various crimes, as embezzlement, fraud, or stealing office equipment, committed by business or professional people while working at their occupations.

white knight A friendly company that attempts to forestall a hostile takeover by outbidding the raider for the fellow company's stock.

whole life insurance See **ordinary life insurance**.

wholesale price index Also called **producer price index**. An index that measures the average change in prices paid by wholesalers and manufacturers for 2000 selected goods.

wholesaler A seller of merchandise and/or services to commercial, industrial, and institutional users for use in their operations or for resale.

wide-area network Also called **WAN**. A computer network that spans a relatively large geographical area.

wildcat strike A work stoppage that is not authorized by the union representing the striking workers and that is in violation of the labor contract.

will-call Also called **layaway plan.** A method of purchasing by which the customer reserves an article with a down payment and takes possession of the article when payments have been completed.

Wilshire 5000 An index of U.S. stocks traded on the New York Stock Exchange and American Stock Exchange, as well as actively traded OTC stocks. The index is actually comprised of over 6000 stocks, each weighted according to its market capitalization.

Windows (*trademark*) Any of several microcomputer operating systems or environments featuring a graphical user interface.

wire transfer An order transmitted by telephone, telegraph, or electronically from one bank to another to pay or credit money to a payee designated by a payer.

withdrawal plan A system allowing periodic withdrawal of specified amounts of interest and/or principal from a mutual fund, or of a fluctuating amount determined by the periodic redemption of a fixed number of shares.

withholding tax That part of an employee's tax liability withheld by the employer from wages or salary and paid directly to the government.

word processing Writing, editing, production, and storage of documents, as letters, reports, and books, through the use of a computer program or a complete computer system designed to facilitate rapid and efficient manipulation of text.

word processor A computer program or computer system designed for word processing.

work design A scientific approach to effective performance by which some work is divided into small task segments and other work is subjected to job enlargement and enrichment in order to meet the individual needs of employees with different attitudes, abilities, and goals.

worker buyout A method of reducing a company's payroll by offering older employees bonuses (e.g., one or two years' salary) and other incentives to resign or take early retirement.

workers' compensation Insurance benefits that cover lost wages and medical costs of employees who become ill or are injured in the course of their work, such benefits not being dependent on a showing of negligence on the part of the employer.

workfare A government plan requiring welfare recipients to accept public-service jobs or enroll in vocational training.

work-flow integration A sequencing of technological activities to be carried out by employees in a work environment, with much thought given to the order of events in terms of ease or difficulty, degree of automation, and interdependence of tasks.

work force 1. The total number of people in a country who are employed or are looking for work and are considered employable. **2.** The number of people employed by a company or in a particular industry or occupation.

working asset Invested capital that is comparatively liquid.

working capital Also called **net current assets.** The excess of current assets over current liabilities.

working control Control of voting at a shareholders' meeting achieved by ownership of more than 50 percent of the corporation's voting securities or by acquisition of a greater number of proxies than any other group or individual has secured.

work-in-process inventory Also called **work-in-progress inventory.** (*abbr* WIP) The aggregate of products entered into the manufacturing process (i.e., all those started but not yet finished); a current asset account with a normal debit balance.

work measurement The evaluation of employee performance based on predetermined standards for effective work output.

work papers Also called **working papers.** An auditor's schedules and analysis of work done and conclusions drawn before the issuance of an opinion on a financial statement.

work rules Policies and regulations regarding the work required of employees and the working conditions that management will provide, usually arrived at by collective bargaining between unions and management.

work sharing A reduction in the number of hours worked per week by each employee, with a concomitant reduction in wages, instituted to avoid the necessity of laying off some workers.

workshop A course of instruction or a seminar in which management skills are developed through group practice in such skills as planning, decision making, and report writing.

work station also **workstation 1.** A work or office area assigned to one person, often one accommodating a computer terminal or other electronic equipment. **2.** A computer terminal or microcomputer connected to a mainframe, minicomputer, or data-processing network. **3.** A powerful microcomputer, often with a high-resolution display, used for computer-aided design, electronic publishing, or other graphics-intensive processing.

work stoppage The collective stoppage of work by employees in a business or an industry to protest working conditions.

World Wide Web (*abbr* WWW) A system of extensively interlinked electronic documents: a branch of the Internet.

worst-case scenario The worst possible outcome of a situation.

wraparound mortgage (*abbr* WAM) A second mortgage that includes payments on the first mortgage, usually assumable at a considerably lower rate of interest.

write-off 1. A reduction of an amount in an account as required by abnormal or unfavorable circumstances (e.g., uncollectible receivables, unsalable assets or inventory). **2.** Reduction of book value; depreciation.

written-down value The value of an asset reduced by the depreciation already taken.

W-2 A standard tax form showing the total wages paid to an employee and the taxes withheld during the calendar year: prepared by an employer for each employee.

WWW See **World Wide Web.**

WYSIWYG (*acronym for* What *you* see *is* what *you* get) The capacity of a computer to print out what is shown on the display screen.

X

XD See **ex dividend**.

Y

yardstick See **benchmark**.

yearly order See **blanket order**.

yellow-dog contract A contract between a worker and an employer whereby the worker promises, if hired, not to join or remain in a union (a practice prohibited by the National Labor Relations Act).

yield Also called **return**. The dividends or interest paid to shareholders and bondholders, expressed as a percentage of the current price of the security in question.

yield management A management concept that attempts to respond realistically to a variety of market factors (e.g., demand, season, competition) that constantly fluctuate. One such response is to maintain flexible price structures based on one or more of these factors.

yield to maturity Also called **maturity yield**. (*bonds*) The return on an investment expressed as a percentage of its cost, if held until it can or must be redeemed by its issuer.

yo-yo stock See **volatile stock**.

YTD (*accounting*) year to date.

YTM See **yield to maturity**.

Z

zero-balance account An accommodation by a bank allowing a commercial customer to write checks on a subsidiary account in which no funds are maintained. Checks are paid when presented, after which funds are transferred from the master account to bring the subsidiary account back to zero.

zero-based budgeting (*abbr* ZBB) The practice, followed only by governmental and some nonprofit organizations, of assuming that budgets for all programs, activities, and projects are zero at the beginning of each financial period and basing their budgets on an analysis of past performance and probable future costs and benefits, for the purpose of trimming or shedding projects that are marginally profitable or no longer useful. See also **incremental budgeting**.

zero-coupon bond A type of bond having no coupons. It is sold at a discount and redeemed after a specified period at face value, the profit being the difference between purchase price and selling price.

zero-salvage value A salvage value of a depreciable asset that is less than 10 percent of the asset's cost and that is assumed to be zero for purposes of tax and financial reporting.

zero-sum Denoting an economy or other system or situation in which gains equal losses.

zone of acceptance The area within which subordinates accept and comply with the majority of orders and requests received from superiors without considering other options.

zone of indifference The area within which subordinates follow orders and are indifferent to a superior's right to exert authority over them.

zone pricing The practice of pricing goods to be distributed on the basis of a customer's location in relation to the distribution point, each customer being charged a base price plus a standard rate for the zone in which he or she is located. See also **base-point pricing; phantom freight**.